Earthly Delights from The Garden of France

WINES OF THE LOIRE

VOLUME ONE

THE KINGDOM OF SAUVIGNON BLANC
SANCERRE ❧ POUILLY FUMÉ
AND THE SAUVIGNON SATELLITES

JACQUELINE FRIEDRICH

An American wine, food and travel journalist, Jacqueline splits her time between Paris and the Loire Valley. The author of *A Wine & Food Guide to the Loire* (Henry Holt 1996; Mitchell Beazley 1997) and *The Wines of France: the Essential Guide for Savvy Shoppers* (Ten Speed Press, 2006), she has also written regularly for publications such as *The New York Times*, *The Wall Street Journal*, and *The Los Angeles Times*, as well as all of the usual suspects in the wine, travel and leisure category.

Also by Jacqueline Friedrich

A Wine & Food Guide to the Loire
The Wines of France: the Essential Guide for Savvy Shoppers

JACQUELINE FRIEDRICH

Earthly Delights from The Garden of France

WINES OF THE LOIRE

VOLUME ONE

THE KINGDOM OF SAUVIGNON BLANC
SANCERRE & POUILLY FUMÉ
AND THE SAUVIGNON SATELLITES

PUBLISHED BY THE AUTHOR

2011

This edition published by Jacqueline Friedrich
Copyright © Jacqueline Friedrich 2011
57 Rue Condorcet, Paris 75009, France
Email jacqueline.friedrich@wanadoo.fr
www.jacqulinefriedrich.com

ISBN: 978-1-4477-7745-8
Ed: 10893659

Designed in Kingfisher type by Geoff Green Book Design, Cambridge CB24 4RA

Order this book from
www.lulu.com

Acknowledgements

Starting at the source, I shall be eternally grateful for the admirable competence and kind assistance of Benoît Roumet and the rest of the staff at the *Bureau Interprofessional des Vins du Centre,* and of Marie Gaudel, Jeanne Perron and all the terrific *filles* at Clair de Lune. Heartfelt thanks – and, I hope, many shared bottles — to the numerous friends and colleagues who gave me invaluable feedback and *morale* support, in particular miracle worker Françoise Villenga and two people I know only via email: David Schildknecht, the White Knight of Wine journalism, for many constructive and thought-provoking discussions; and Monty Waldin, for generously guiding me over and around the hurdles of self-publishing. And to my Dream Team: the super-duper, soon-to-have-a-corner-office Arrie Brown at Lulu, my wonderful typographical and design wizard, Geoff Green, and my eagle-eyed indexer, Christopher Phipps, bless you all!

Contents

Preface

Once upon a time the world of French wine was a binary world – from whichever angle you looked at it. There were the Blue Chip wines – the Cru Classés of Bordeaux, the Grand Crus and Premier Crus of Chablis, the Côte d'Or and Champagne and the occasional break out star from other regions like Hermitage or Alsace. Everything else was an Unassuming Country Wine. The latter category came in two styles: surprisingly good, and predictably not good but capable of overachieving in a great vintage.

Radical changes within the past twenty or so years have resulted in near total diversification and/or segmentation in the world of Unassuming Country Wines throughout France. (Some of these changes have even trickled up to the Blue Chip wines but that's another story.)

Exciting, riveting wines began to emerge from obscure regions and overlooked appellations. And in significant numbers — not just the anecdotal cuvée or the lone-genius vintner. It became nearly impossible to keep up with the stunning wines that were surfacing at tastings, on wine lists and shop shelves. Maybe these wines weren't of Grand Cru status but they were characterful, specific, far from anonymous, and mighty delicious. They demanded to be taken seriously.

Further diversification could be observed among the people who made these wines. Simplistic stereotypes no longer applied. Now winemakers were as diverse as the wines they made : there were the unreconstructed types who made wine as their fathers did (if these wines turned out well, it wasn't their fault); there were the unreconstructed types who made wine as their great grandfathers had done (these had always had a cult following; now they have a greater cult following); there were those who went to local winemaking schools and made competent wines by the book; there were those whose wines were fashioned by consulting enologists who might have brought in soil analysts; there were those who had apprenticed at wineries in the New World and who brought new-fangled ideas back to Old Europe; there were bankers turned vintner; gastroenterologists turned vigneron; there were those who practiced sustainable farming, or organic farming, or biodynamic farming, or hypernatural, noninterventionist winemaking, and those who pampered their vines like a weekend gardener tending his or her patch of tomatoes, basil and green beans, and who camped out next to the fermenting must. And there were as many variations on these themes as can be imagined. No surprise that the wines, themselves, were as varied as were the people, the philosophies and the methods that created them.

Also segmented and/or pixel-ated (sorry!) was the world of the wine consumer. There were the wine geeks, the wine snobs, the Trophy wine suckers, the Commanderie de Bordeaux effetists, wine bloggers, wine clubbers, wine wannabes, and a helluva lot of oft overlooked wine *likers.*

In this heady, complex environment, when faced with updating "A Wine & Food Guide to the Loire," I experienced analysis paralysis. I had been living and breathing Ligerian air for over twenty years and every single element of the Loire's winemaking evolution, from the elemental to the anecdotal, lobbied to be expressed immediately.

After much agonizing, self-flagellating, and obsessing, I began to see a clear path and a coherent solution: I would write four Loire books – one on each of the major subregions for geeks like me and then an abridged edition for wine likers.

I cannot deny that self-indulgence played a role in this. Having begun to blog was at least partly to blame. To say all I wanted to say about Loire wines and about the changes I've seen (and tasted) over the past twenty-plus years and to have incorporated all of that in one single book would have resulted in a doorstop of a tome.

By separating the Loire into three basic blocks or subregions – les Vins du Centre (Sancerre, Pouilly and company), Touraine, and the Pays de la Loire (Anjou, Saumur and the Nantais) – I could write a manageable volume on each.

I also happen to believe that the quality of the wines of the Loire has improved so much that each of these regions deserves its own book.

I have decided to start with Les Vins du Centre. Among all the subregions of the Loire, this is the one that separates itself the most from the rest of the pack. Geography and geology combine to situate it half in the Loire and half in Burgundy. It is also the least volatile of the three subregions and, as the Kingdom of Sauvignon Blanc, its wines are among the most popular of those made, not only in the Loire, but in France.

*

I anticipate that Volume II will be Touraine (and will include the orphaned Orléanais).

Updates of Volume I can be found on my website – www.jacqueline-friedrich.com or www.thewinehumanist.com — and will be keyed to the pages in the book.

Rigny-Ussé, June 2011

Chapter One
Introduction to the Region

"In the past we were considered Burgundy; now we're in the Loire."

Edmond Vatan, vigneron in Chavignol,

part of the Sancerre appellation.

The eight appellations forming an arc from Gien to George Sand-country at the foothills of the Massif Central are known as the Vignobles du Centre. They lie halfway between the vineyards of Touraine and those of Burgundy and cover roughly 5,400 hectares.

Vines have been cultivated in the region for over 2000 years. Latin agronomists such as Pliny wrote of specific grapes such as Bituricus that could be found here. In 582, Gregoire de Tours, in his ecclesiastical history of France, mentioned the wines of Berry. In 1180, Guillaume le Breton, poet-in-residence to Philippe-Auguste, talked of the "generous wines" of the Comte de Sancerre. Various sixteenth century documents refer to specific wine villages – Reuilly, for example, and Chavignol, and Menetou.

Many of the vineyard areas were cultivated by religious orders. They planted vines, cleared forests and, thanks to donations, had extensive land holdings and large, well-equipped cellars. Wine was needed for the celebration of the mass as well as for entertaining nobles passing through the parish. In the eleventh century, monks of the Abbey of Cluny are said to have introduced plants from Burgundy into the Tannay area. In the 12th century, Augustinian monks from the Abbey of Saint-Satur played a key role in extending the vineyards of Sancerre.

There was commerce in wine as well. In the Middle Ages wines from the Centre traveled to Orléans and from there to the capital – as well as to England, Normandy and Flanders. In 1642 the opening of the Canal de Briare linked the Loire and the Loing, giving more direct access to Paris. Wines from Menetou-Salon, and those from Quincy, traveled to Bourges.

Historians surmise that during the Middle Ages the region's wines were white. In the beginning of the fifteenth century Pinot Noir (called Noirien or Morillon) appeared; by the seventeenth century it covered Sancerre's vineyards, while numerous white varieties continued to flourish in Pouilly and Quincy. Those cited include Pinot Gris, Chardonnay, Melon, and "Muscat Gennetin" (one of many names believed to correspond to Sauvignon).

Degradation of the region's vineyards started in 1577 after the Paris Parliament issued a law forbidding wine merchants, *bistrotiers,* and tavernkeepers from buying wine within eighty-eight kilometers of the city. Growers from Orléans and eastern stretches of what today constitutes Touraine – Montrichard and Blois, for example – as well as Sologne responded by replacing Pinot Noir, Chardonnay and the like with higher yielding grapes such as Pinot Meunier, Gamay Noir *à jus blanc,* Gamay Teinturier and Gouais. After the Revolution and through the nineteenth century, properties continued to change hands, vineyard plantings were extended, and yields continued to rise. The vineyards of Pouilly, which at the end of the nineteenth century included at least a dozen varieties, were largely given over to Chasselas. The grape existed in the area and was much sought after by Paris fruit merchants who came to the region looking for table grapes, for which they were willing to pay higher prices than they paid for wine.

At about the time that Paris fruiterers were buying up the Chasselas crop in Pouilly, the vine louse phylloxera was eating its way through the French vineyards, entering the Centre in the 1880s. Hybrid vines replaced them, including Noah and Othello. Two world wars followed and there occurred a great exodus of the young from the countryside.

The reconstitution of the vineyards began in earnest in the 1930s with the nascent appellation system which was instituted in 1936 and resumed its work in the 1950s. Specialized farming replaced polyculture and, throughout France, cooperative cellars were founded, schools of viticulture and enology were created, and nearly every aspect of viticulture was mechanized. These upheavals revolutionized the production of wine in France.

Before considering some of these developments, which are, in essence, man-made, I'd like to examine Mother Nature's contribution to the region's viticulture by looking at its climate, its soils and its choice of grapes.

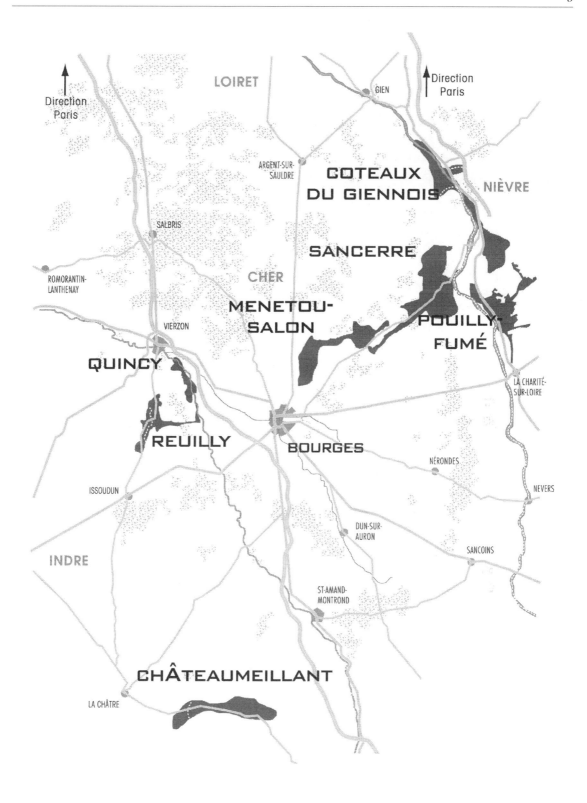

LOIRET

Direction
Paris

Direction
Paris

GIEN

ARGENT-SUR-
SAULDRE

COTEAUX
DU GIENNOIS

NIÈVRE

SALBRIS

SANCERRE

ROMORANTIN-
LANTHENAY

CHER

MENETOU-
SALON

POUILLY-
FUMÉ

VIERZON

QUINCY

LA CHARITÉ-
SUR-LOIRE

REUILLY

BOURGES

NÉRONDES

NEVERS

ISSOUDUN

DUN-SUR-
AURON

SANCOINS

INDRE

ST-AMAND-
MONTROND

CHÂTEAUMEILLANT

LA CHÂTRE

Climate

Weather forecasters in France use the Loire to demarcate climatic regions, describing tendencies for all areas north of the river, then those to the south. The river, too, marks the limit of viticulture, which is generally described as running along the right bank of the Loir, approaching the Loire downstream of Angers. Balmy ocean air, sucked up the corridor of the Loire and its tributaries, brings a tempering maritime influence far into the continent.

As we move east, however, the ocean's influence becomes attenuated, the climate more continental. And by the time we arrive in the Sancerrois, the climate is as much "continental" as it is "oceanic." The Butte of Humbligny, the highest point in the Paris Basin, traps rainfall before it reaches Sancerre and Pouilly, which are, as a result, relatively dry. Spring frosts and hail, however, are constant threats, seriously diminishing, even annihilating, entire crops. (In Quincy and in Reuilly — and to a lesser extent in Pouilly and Sancerre – anti-frost towers with heat generators, and wind turbines have been erected as a way of mitigating frost damage.) The best vineyards are on hillsides and ancient alluvial terraces.

Average rainfall is between 600 and 800 millimeters; temperatures range from –1 degree C in winter to over 26 degrees C in summer.

Climate change is, of course, an issue, as a look at the dates at which harvest began from 1965 to 2010 indicates. From 1965 to 1987 only seven vintages began in Sancerre earlier than the first of October. From 1988 to 2010 harvest in Sancerre generally started between the 22nd and the 25th of September, the earliest being in 2003 when harvest started on the 7th of September in Sancerre and on the 19th of August in Reuilly. If 2011's growing season continues as it has started, Sancerre's harvest may begin in August.

Bertrand Daulny, a technician with SICOVAC (the Service Interprofessionel de Conseil Agronomique de Vinification et d'Analyses du Centre), explains that 80% of this change is due to the climate and 20% to yield reduction by the growers (debudding, green harvesting, and so forth).

Soils

The Sancerrois is part of the Paris Basin, a large, geological bowl formed by thousands of years of sea immersion and erosion which left marine deposits – shells, fossils – embedded in the varied geological strata that make up its complex composition.

As described by James E. Wilson in *Terroir: The Role of Geology, Climate, and Culture in the Making of French Wines,* the Cretaceous and the Jurassic strata had been deposited in widespread seas. Eons later, during the late Tertiary and Quarternary periods, the basin sagged. As the beds of the region's key rivers– the Loire, the Seine, the Aube and the Yonne – had already been established, the sagging of the Central Paris Basin allowed erosion gradually to fashion bands of chalky marl called Kimmeridgian capped by hard Portlandian limestone in the southeastern section of the basin which, over time, would become an archipelago of wine areas — the Aube (the easternmost Champagne zone), Chablis and the Sancerrois.

And here I must quote Wilson directly because the point he makes leaves me shaking my head in wonder every time I think of it: indeed, it seems nothing less than Cosmic Design.

"For 200 miles (320 kilometers), this classic cap rock slope supports one area after another...The wine areas are 'islands' that are separated from the major regions with which they are traditionally associated: the Aube, 75 miles (120 kilometers) southeast of the Marne; Chablis, the same distance north of the Côte d'Or; Pouilly-sur-Loire and Sancerre, 80 miles (130 kilometers) from Touraine-Anjou..."[1]

Given the fundamental importance of *terroir* in the character of any wine, one wonders why the kinship of these three regions has never been recognized officially and made into one appellation: the Kimmeridgian Chain.

Be that as it may, a couple of words on the three major soil types: Kimmeridgian marl or *terres blanches*, *caillottes*, and silex.

Terres Blanches soils are composed of varying amounts of limestone and clay embedded with fossilized oyster shells. They are found mostly in the western part of the zone, perhaps most famously on Les Monts Damnés. This chain peters out as it goes further south and west, until it finally ends in the Reuilly appellation. Well-structured and characterful, wines from these soils "take longer to express themselves" and are long-lived.

Stone-and pebble-covered soils of pure, fine-grained limestone embedded with seashells also date from the Jurassic period. These soils are called *caillottes* in the region and there are several subvarities, including Portlandian (after a type of limestone found in Dorset), and Oxfordian. These soils may be found in Sancerre on low hills or the bottom of steep slopes as well as in Bué (Le Chêne Marchand), Verdigny, and Sury-en-Vaux. In Pouilly they are found in the eastern part of the appellation, at the southern

1   Wilson, James E., *Terroir: The Role of Geology, Climate, and Culture in the Making of French Wines*, Mitchell-Beazley, 1998.

and eastern limits of le Bouchot, as well as in the hamlet of Les Loges and
the zones of Boisfleury and Boisgibault. Wines from these soils tend to
express themselves quickly. Lively and aromatic, they are the first wines to
be bottled and the first to be drunk.

The third most important soil type of the region is Silex – or flinty clay
– which can be found in Pouilly, for example, on the Butte of St. Andelain,
in St. Laurent l'Abbaye, on the slopes of Tracy, and at the northern limits
of the appellation, approaching Cosne-sur-Loire; in Sancerre, along the
town's fault line, in Ménétréol (Les Romains and Les Belles Dames) and
Saint-Satur. Wines coming from these soils are usually age-worthy, vivid,
potent and decisive.

Beyond the three major types of soils – found mostly in Sancerre, Pouilly
and Menetou-Salon – are a myriad of other variations, principally sandy
or gravelly terraces of ancient alluvial deposits on the banks of the Loire,
the Cher and the Arnon. These make floral, spicy, early-drinking wines.

Grapes

This is the kingdom of Sauvignon Blanc, the sole grape permitted in
Pouilly-Fumé, in white Sancerre, Menetou-Salon, Reuilly and Quincy and
the Coteaux du Giennois. Of the 5,394 hectares (13,323 acres) of vines in
production in the Centre in 2010, 4,306 hectares (10, 635 acres) are planted
to the grape. It is here that Sauvignon created a style of wine – a full, fresh,
instantly recognizable white – that has been imitated the world over, from
Napa to New Zealand to Chile.

This much was true in the mid-1990s when I wrote about Sauvignon
Blanc in "*A Wine & Food Guide to the Loire*", as was the conventional wisdom
that Sauvignon Blanc was a good, useful grape but not a noble one, a grape
that made wines that were easy to recognize, easy to like and easy to understand, but not a varietal that could express pedigree, raciness or majesty.
Sauvignon so blithely lent itself to making tangy quaffers that we never
thought it capable of producing profound wines.

Often raw and nervy, the aromas and flavors that made the Sancerrois
Sauvignon so easily identifiable include grass, grapefruit, green bean,
asparagus, crushed cassis leaves and cat's pee. (French tasters use the somehow more polite and less revolting sounding "*pipi de chat*.") And it must be
said, that through the 1980s, the bulk of the wines being produced in the
region confirmed this low level of expectation.

Over the years my understanding of and feelings about Sauvignon Blanc
have undergone a sea change – much as have the wines themselves, though

here I am limiting the discussion to the evolution of the Sauvignons of this special region of France.

It is an evolution that has occurred in several stages, beginning in the 1990s, and surely with the now mythic winemaker Didier Dagueneau. Growers began to lower yields, to wait to harvest, to pick riper grapes. Some fermented and/or aged the wines in new or newish oak barrels. This style of Sauvignon was riper, less aggressive, ampler (occasionally blowsy), with aromas and flavors recalling fig, nectarine, peach and melon as well as floral and muscat notes reminiscent of Pinot Gris and other varietals from Alsace. This development was not universally well-received: many were the sentimental wine lovers who, recalling their first love affair with a feisty and green Sauvignon, lamented "Where are the Sancerres of yesteryear?"

As we entered the 21st century, Sauvignon evolved even further. The quality of Sancerrois wines has improved exponentially. Frankly, my mind has been blown by the elegance, the beauty, the gravitas of more than a few I've tasted.

I'd put a Sancerre from Stephane Riffault or Thomas-Labaille, or a Pouilly from Benjamin Dagueneau or Jonathan Pabiot – to cite just four examples – next to Premier Crus and Grand Crus of Chablis. In a real way, that's as it should be: speaking geologically, they are practically kissing cousins. The only difference is the grape. And what I find breathtaking about fine Chablis and fine Sancerre is that the grape fades into the background. Those simple, pungent varietal flavors that make Sauvignon Blanc the first grape debutant tasters can recognize blind is replaced by a ripe, mellow, yet fresh vinosity, a resilient support for achingly exquisite minerality, for flavors of stone, of tisane and citrus zests. These are indeed wines that have their place alongside the best Chablis.

There were yet other surprises in store for me. I had never much liked the way Sauvignon aged. Given that most of the grapes were picked before achieving aromatic ripeness, that's not surprising: an aged Sauvignon tasted like stewed, recooked vegetables rather that fresh ones. The wines from the Cotat brothers were notable exceptions, largely, I think, because the grapes, when picked, had reached aromatic ripeness. Suddenly, circa 2005, I began finding an increasing number of Sancerrois Sauvignons reminding me of the Sancerres of the Cotats. Not only that, they also made me think of Loire Chenin blanc – a top-notch Montlouis or a Vouvray *sec* or *tendre*, with heightened flavors of *tisane*, stone and minerals.

I also learned that Sauvignon and Chenin were related. Back in the last century it was thought that Sauvignon originated either in the Loire or in the Bordelais. Another hypothesis is that it was part of the Carmenet family. It is now believed that Sauvignon, like Chenin, is a descendant of the Traminer (aka Savagnin) of the Jura. (Some theorists posit that Sauvignon is the child of Traminer and Chenin but the more widely held view is that they are both descendants of Savagnin – Sauvignon is described as being a "seedling of Savagnin" — and that the other parent remains unknown.)[2]

In the section of this chapter devoted to *Les Vignerons*, I will describe the changes that have revealed Sauvignon's heretofore unsuspected nobliity and virtuosity.

Pinot noir, the region's second most important grape, was first planted in Sancerre in the 15th century. And it was Sancerre's sole grape from the 17th century until the end of the 19th when phylloxera struck. Pinot noir now accounts for about 20% of the vineyard plantings in the Centre. It is also the sole red grape in Menetou-Salon and Reuilly and is used in the reds and the rosés of the Giennois, and Châteaumeillant, as well as in the Vins de Pays Coteaux Charitois and Coteaux de Tannay. Progress here, while not as far-reaching as with Sauvignon Blanc, is nonetheless considerable. Many of the wines can be compared favorably to top-notch Pinot Noirs from Irancy in Northern Burgundy and Mercurey or Montagny in the Chalonnais.

Ancillary grapes are Gamay, Pinot Gris (vinified as a rosé or *vin gris)*, Chardonnay, and Chasselas. Melon is also cultivated in the Vin de Pays des Coteaux de Tannay.

Les Vignerons

We now return to man, the fourth and most variable factor in winemaking. And since World War II, man has done nothing if not vary in his role as vigneron.

The first stage was the evolution from polyculture – a hectare of vines plus cereal crops, a horse, poultry, perhaps goats and goat cheese – to specialized farming. Concurrently schools specializing in viticulture and enology were created. Cellar hygiene began to improve, local enologists, either government sponsored or private consultants, came on the scene. Growers continued to sell part of their crop in bulk to négociants and local cafés as well as to customers who drove up to the cellar door with a trunkful of cubitainers ready to be filled. Increasingly, however, they bottled their pro-

---

2   *Les Origines du Sauvignon*, Jean Bisson, Docteur en Oenologie Ampelogie, December 2010

duction themselves. This more or less brings us up to the 1980s.

In many ways I think of the region's approach to winemaking in the late 1980s-early 1990s as emerging from the dark ages of cultivating grapes as one would any other agricultural crop and of 'come-what-may winemaking,' into a brave new world of technology – of new oak, aromatic yeasts, temperature-controlled tanks, reverse osmosis experiments – as well as continued reliance on chemicals in the vineyards and sugar in the cellar.

A few enlightened souls – first and foremost, Didier Dagueneau – had begun to rethink every aspect of winemaking, starting in the vineyards. And that is the revolution in quality – one that is ongoing – that we are witnessing – and tasting – today, in part due to a change of generations: when I arrived in the Sancerrois in 1990, one generation was in the process of taking over from its predecessor; twenty years later, a new generation – including many who have traveled and worked in New World wine regions – is taking over from their parents. And the most critical of these changes are occurring in the vineyards.

Until very recently, most viticulture in the Sancerrois could be described as "conventional," which meant reliance on weed killers, fertilizers and insecticides; indifferent pruning methods, high yields (over 100 hl/ha) and early harvesting, before the grapes were fully ripe.

There has been an enormous change of attitude about viticulture. Of the several hundred producers who are represented in this book, few continue to practice "conventional" viticulture. Most now practice some kind of sustainable farming, referred to in France as "*lutte raisonnée.*" While this method works essentially on the honor system, it does acknowledge and promote an eco-friendly approach, asking the grower to reflect before resorting to the use of chemicals in the vineyards. Often this leads the grower to convert to fully organic viticulture or to its more extreme form, biodynamics. The reason for this? The painstaking methods produce riper, better fruit. It's that simple. But the devil's in the details.

Starting in the vineyards, the INAO requires minimum vine density of about 5,700 plants per hectare. Many growers have increased vine density well above 7000 plants per hectare, with quite a few at or near 10,000 plants and some experimenting with well above that. Instead of spreading weed killers and indiscriminately plowing, many – really most – sow cover grass between the vine rows and hoe between the vine plants. They prune hard and then, if necessary, debud; if needed, they cluster thin once or more during the growing season and may deleaf as well. Natural compost and infusions made of plants such as nettles have, for many, replaced fertilizers and vine treatments. And yields are considerably lower.

The INAO sets a limit of 65 hl/ha for whites, 63 for rosés, and 59 for reds. There's some wiggle room here, permitting, for example, yields of 75 hl/ha for whites. The pre-wiggle room limits aren't bad. You can make very good dry white wine at 65 hl/ha. Yields for most of the producers in my top classifications are between 35 and 45 hl/ha, on average.

Then comes a question of prime importance: when to harvest. Pre-1990, the conscientious grower would wait – weather permitting – until the grape's sugars had reached a potential of, say, 9.5 to 12 alcohol and send in the harvesters. Then concepts of aromatic ripeness and phenolic maturity began to enter the language. (The first time I ever heard of this was in 1990, from the mouth of none other than Didier Dagueneau.) Aromatic ripeness and phenolic ripeness – which involve the development of "ripe" aromas and flavors – do not necessarily coincide with the grape's production of sugar. Growers began to look for other indicators, such as tasting the grape skins and seeds for ripeness before bringing in the harvest, which an increasing number do by successive *tris* or passes through the vineyard, followed by a hand sorting of the grapes at the winery.

Machine harvesting still predominates in the Sancerrois. Personally, I don't have a problem with this. Though reflexively I prefer hand harvesting, I believe that excellent dry wines can be made with machine-harvested grapes.

The major changes in the cellar are vineyard- related as well, particularly in the Sancerre, Pouilly-Fumé and Menetou-Salon appellations. Increasingly, producers vinify by *terroir* – either from single vineyards or a selection of grapes from various parcels all sharing the same soil composition. This results in an ever- expanding number of cuvées at individual properties. Indeed, it's difficult keeping up with the yearly changes in portfolios.

Partly thanks to the weather but even more significantly thanks to a change in philosophy, chaptalization seems no longer to be an issue. Some producers have abandoned the practice entirely, others may rely on it in "off" years but only in remedial doses. The days of artificial sunshine appear to be over, resulting in much purer, less attenuated tasting wines. Additionally, most use less sulfur than they did fifteen or twenty years ago but all but a few do use some. (And, in most cases, should.)

Which brings up the subject of hypernatural, noninterventionist winemaking. There are a couple of members of that band in the Sancerrois but nowhere near as many as there are in appellations further west which has been and continues to be a veritable hotbed of Extreme Winemaking. (An issue that will be addressed much more fully in Volume Two.)

How to use this book

The heart of this book is devoted to the eight appellations and two Vins de Pays that make up *les vins du Centre*. Each chapter starts with an overview of the appellation and, where relevant, a classification of its producers. Individual reviews follow.

There are three Appendices: the Gastronomy of the Sancerrois; a general glossary, and Wining, Dining, and Touring – recommendations on where to eat, where to stay and what to visit while you're in this charmed area of the world.

How the tastings were done

When I was researching "*A Wine and Food Guide to the Loire*", I spent two years traveling the length and breadth of the Loire basin. I rented gîtes, installed phone lines (this was before the age of cell phones), and visited over six hundred producers.

Since 1991 I have been living in France, at first only in Touraine, and, since 1997, splitting my time between Touraine and Paris.

I have attended every Salon des Vins du Loire since 1991 as well as innumerable other tastings – ginormous, large, small, minuscule – and served on wine juries. I regularly visit producers throughout the Loire and, needless to say, drink Loire wines in sufficient quantity to skew the consumption curve of a small city.

For this book, I decided to ask that samples be sent to me. I worked with the BIVC (Bureau Interprofessionel des Vins du Centre) and contacted USA importers and distributors as well as individual producers, asking for whatever samples and documentation they could give me. I often followed up with in-person or phone interviews and/or emailed lists of questions.

The beauty of this method was that I could taste slowly. Below I have defined what I came to call "Slow Tasting". Briefly, it's me alone with the wine. No distractions. Not even the radio. I taste at 11AM and again at 6PM. And repeat this process until I feel I have fully appreciated and understood the wine, which I often pair with food.

The wines described in this book, unless otherwise stated, were tasted between 2008 and the spring of 2011. As you'll see, many of the tasting notes are very long, some of them tracking the "slow tasting" evolution of a given wine or wines for two days or more.

My hope is that, taken together, these chatty, bloggy tasting notes will not only give you a sense of the wine and how it evolves, but what foods it might go with, as well as how a given producer works. Taken globally, I hope they will give you a greater sense of the appellations in question, how my palate corresponds to yours, and, most important, that they will invite you into the world of wine rather than make you feel as if you had to have been born into it to gain admission.

All the wines submitted for my evaluation are included here in some way as are the wines of people who did not send samples but who regularly "show" their wines at tastings such as the Salon des Vins de Loire, the Renaissance des Appellations, Les Gens de Metier and scores of other groups. If a producer is missing, it's because he or she declined to send samples and does not participate in public tastings.

A related point: No matter what you ask to taste or how often, producers will open or send the wines they want. It's just a fact of life, and over the years you stop pulling your hair out because that's just the way it is.

Producer classifications

I have rated the producers within each appellation. My classifications are as follows:

Outstanding: These producers are among France's "artist-vintners." They make the best and most exciting wines in their respective appellations, and in the Loire. Every year. Often the conscience, the benchmark of their appellations, they are the ones who, because of their rigor and/or creativity, have pushed – and continue to push — the region further in the direction of quality. They are exigent in the vineyards and in the cellar. Yields are low, many practise either organic or biodynamic viticulture (although this was not a criteria), vinification is painstaking, based on reflection and sometimes on divine madness. There is often a touch of genius in the wines. (To be in this category, a producer's entire line must be of extremely high quality, even if not every bottling attains the level of the best cuvées.)

Excellent: These producers are first rate. Their wines are classic. Often very close qualitatively to those in Outstanding, they sometimes — in certain years and with certain cuvées — outshine them. On the other hand, certain cuvées may disappoint – which is why I heartily recommend reading the entire commentary.

But the overall quality of a particular producer's wines must be Excellent. There are artist-vintners here, too, as well as innovators. Why don't they qualify for Outstanding? It varies from winery to winery. Some will surely move up. In other cases, it may be a question of cutbacks due to financial hardship; or of young vines; or of too great a discrepancy between the top cuvées and the generic bottlings. Some producers are ever-so slightly less exigent; still others simply lack that spark of genius. The wines — and the winemakers — are usually more "rational" than their confrères in Outstanding. But they are true ambassadors for their respective appellations, year after year. The majority of their wines are, in a word, Excellent.

To Follow: Newcomers — or new-ish, serious vintners who haven't yet found their voice — who I expect to evolve into Outstanding or Excellent.

Hypernatural: This is a word I coined to cover producers whose philosophy of winemaking is to intervene as little as possible in the winemaking process. Resolute practioners of one of the various forms of organic viticulture (although they may thumb their noses at anything as bureaucratic as accreditation), they vinify their wines with indigenous yeasts, they eschew sulfur, added enzymes, added sugar (chaptalization), tannins, fining, filtration and so forth. When I felt a hypernatural producer belonged in a more general category, such as Highly Recommended, I listed him or her there; those whose wines, to me, are *sui generis* and/or very much works in progress only a member of the club could love, are listed here.

Highly Recommended: Reliably good producers, who make very good wines, these domaines, generally, are the best representatives of a"typical" winery within an appellation. Some, however, are very close to qualifying for an "Excellent" classification. So do read my commentary. The wines are, on the whole, very good. Sometimes more.

Recommended: In most years, pleasant drinking, and fairly accurate representatives of the good middle ground of their appellations.

Other: It either means I have a strong, specific opinion which precludes a recommendation or that I don't much care for the wine but think others might like it.

By the Glass: producers whose wines would be interesting to taste in a wine bar — though you might not want to commit yourself to a whole bottle.

No matter the classification, all of the wines in this book can be considered "Recommended." Context is key. In my tasting notes, I often say that a particular wine would be a great find in a wine bar; another wine I place on the table of a 3-Michelin-star restaurant.

You'd expect the latter to be an excellent to an exceptional wine. It should be, and it will probably have a price tag to match. (Although most Loire wines are relative bargains.) And it might even be considered a *vin de méditation.*

The former wine, the one that shines in the wine bar, may be idiosyncratic or simple or simply an underachiever. That doesn't mean won't be the perfect wine within a given context. You may also find you enjoy the wine a lot more than you thought you would, particularly if you are sharing it with good pals who aren't wine geeks like us. (The price should match here, too.)

Note: The listings always start with the name of a producer or a domaine. Where producers make wine in a number of appellations, contact specifics appear in his or her principal appellation, eg Domaine Henri Bourgeois's contact information appears in the Sancerre listing.

Note, too, that the listings are organized alphabetically, using the first defining noun or adjective and not "Domaine" or "Château." Thus, Domaine Henri Bourgeois would be listed under Bourgeois. It is also worth noting that producers often use different names for the same wine in different markets. Domaine Henri Bourgeoís' Sancere "Les Baronnes" may, in other markets, be labeled "Grande Réserve", Les Bonnes Bouches" or La Vigne Blanche".

Winespeak: on aromas and flavors

The aromas and flavors of wine fall into nine or ten recognized groups. These have been classified by enologists, for example Emile Peynaud in his *Goût du Vin*. The groups include fairly easy associative leaps into categories like flowers (violets and roses); fruits (berries, apples, lemon, and figs); vegetables (bell peppers and green beans); and spices (cinnamon, clove, and pepper). There are also less familiar comparative categories such as animal (visceral aromas and tastes like musk, and game); balsam (pine, cedar, eucalyptus, and, mint); wood (vanilla and coconut); roasted scents (toast, coffee, *crème brulée*, and leather); chemical/fermentation (yeasts, hard candy); and off odors (rotten egg, garlic, and onion).

Some words or associations will be more meaningful than others to a given taster. Here are several descriptions I often use, some of which may seem strange or off-putting.

Goût du terroir: The concept of terroir unites the specifics of a vineyard site — its soils, subsoils, exposition, the opening of the countryside. When a wine expresses this specificity, this uniqueness, it has a *goût de terroir*. This is a stamp of identity and an aspect of complexity. It is something I look for in a wine.

Herbs, quinine and herbal tea (or tisane): I adore the nuances of quinine and herbal tea (tisane in French) and such medicinal herbs as chamomile, linden blossom (tilleul), and verbena (verveine) in wine (and in other beverages, like Schweppes Bitter Lemon and Campari). They are slightly bitter and extremely appetizing.

Lacy: the French often use the word "*dentelles*"—lace—to describe a delicate, ethereal, very fine wine.

Pits: Many fruity red wines have a flavor reminiscent of cherry pits. While you may never have tasted cherry pits, this flavor is quite focused and succulent—mixing the flavor of the cherry with that of bitter almond. You may recognize the taste from cherry eaux-de-vie or liqueurs, since cherry pits are often macerated with the pulp in the production of fruit brandies.

Pee (Cat)/Pipi de Chat Ever since I began tasting wine seriously I have felt that many Sauvignon Blancs had an aroma of cat's pee. As revolting as this sounds, it is not necessarily a disagreeable scent in a wine, particularly in very small doses. It's a pungent vegetal aroma with a bit of something feral in it. If you've ever had a close relationship to a cat, you'll probably agree that the image is apt.

A very personal lexicon

Frequently used words and terms that don't fall into technical glossary explained here. (There is a mainstream glossary in Appendix II.)

First, my apologies for using so many of same words, eg lemon and lime, zests, stone, mineral, herbal tea, cherry etc over and over and over again. These are key flavors I find in the wines and, as much as I dislike the constant repetition of words, accuracy is more important than originality in this case.

Eco-friendly: I have generally used eco-friendly to indicate that the wine-maker tries to respect nature and avoid using chemical treatments. Related terms are *lutte raisonnée* (in the main glossary) and sustainable farming.

Gourmand: this is a French term that, in this context, does not refer to a person. It's a quality of wine, a wine that is lipsmacking, that seduces the taste buds and makes you dream of dinner.

Hypernatural: This is a word I coined in order to describe a growing trend in viticulture and winemaking that seems to regard with suspicion any procedure that came after the industrial revolution. Practitioners are often among those whose winemaking is "noninterventionist."

Marrowy: I often use this term in association with wines that have aged on their lees, a practice which can impart a thrilling textural quality to a wine. Ever so slightly *perlant* – or not – the wines have a fullness that you feel you can wrap your tongue around. Think of the texture of marrow in roasted beef bones.

Quiet Red: My own designation for red wines that tend to be light in color and saturation, relatively low in alcohol, with little to no oak age. The polar opposite of trophy wines, these Quiet Reds are not flashy, eye-catching, nos-tril-permeating, or tooth-staining. They will impress no one but other lovers of Quiet Reds. You need to pay attention to them or they'll slip by unobserved. And that would be a real pity for they are gems with tons of character packed into a light, lean, gentle, unassuming package.

Some grapes, by their very nature, typify, for me, Quiet Reds: Pineau d'Aunis, for example, or Trousseau and Poulsard. Pinot Noir can enter the Quiet Red category, particularly when grown in areas like Irancy in northern Burgundy or in Sancerre, Reuilly, Châteaumeillant, Menetou-Salon and the Giennois.

PMG: or *Pour ma gueule* literally translates as "for my own mouth/trap/kisser." It refers, in this context, to a wine I like so much I want to keep it and drink it myself — either alone or with a small circle of friends.

Slow Tasting: A luxurious necessity or a necessary luxury, what I mean by Slow Tasting is a) tasting alone, just me and the wine; and b) taking whatever time the wine seems to need for me take with it in order to assess it as accurately as possible.

This can mean a single tasting but more usually it means tasting at least twice: at 11am and 6pm and frequently it means retastings that last over several days or even recorking bottles, leaving a little empty space in the neck, and coming back to the wine weeks or months later. I'm trying, without being too sanctimonious, to get to the truth of a wine.

When I feel it may be useful for fellow wine lovers, I have included the entire record of tasting notes that lasted over several days. This may indicate how a specific wine will age – or taste, once it has had a chance to breathe –and, taken together, the various "Slow Tasting" notes may provide further insight into the appellation's wines – what they taste like, how they age and, since I often pair them with food, what dishes go well with them.

Specificity: This is a term I often use when a wine seems clearly to come from a particular place. Specificity is related to, but not entirely synonymous with, terroir. For example, a tasty, light red from Châteaumeillant might not have the kind of *terroir* that makes a Grand Cru statement but it may very well speak of a certain time and place. If it does, it's specific. I mean this as a compliment.

Wacko Wines: Usually made by hypernatural, non-interventionists, in other words the wing-nuts of what has come to be called the "natural wine" movement, "wacko" wines are wines that are the results of "what if" ruminations. They push the envelope. Sometimes they are delicious as well as intriguing. Sometimes they represent ideas that should never have been put into practice. They are always interesting. Try them by the glass.

Frequently used abbreviations

g/l =s grams per liter
hl/ha =s hectoliters per hectare
PMG =s *Pour ma gueule.*
C =s Celsius.

Price indications

$ indicates that the wine costs up to $10
$$ indicates that the wine costs from $11 to $24
$$$ indicates that the wine costs from $25 to $55
$$$$ indicates that the wine costs over $55

Vintages of the Centre

As time goes on, I put less and less stock in vintages. Excluding the cata-strophic – eg frost or hail wiping out an entire crop – most good winemak-ers make good wine in most years, whether the weather is poor, fair to middling or sublime. True, there are differences from vintage to vintage but each vintage has its unique character. And what's that the French say? *Vive la différence!*

Think about it: Increasingly we decry standardized wines. Yet if we're serious about this, why not rejoice in the variations created by differences in growing seasons? Sure, some years may produce wines with structures that demand cellaring and others that cry out to be consumed immediately. Where's the problem?

In the first case, you'll cellar that age-worthy wine and bring it out cere-moniously for your as-yet-unborn daughter's marriage; in the second, you'll keep the bottles close to hand to enjoy when good friends come for dinner – taking care to carafe those young reds at least an hour beforehand. And often there are very pleasant surprises that reveal themselves as the wine ages, as I hope to make clear below.

The wines that you are most likely to find in shops and restaurants are 2010, 2009 and 2008. You may occasionally come across 2005, 2006 and 2007, particularly with the more ambitious cuvées. My vintage observations end with 2002, the first really fine *millésime* of the 21st century.

Before discussing the last three vintages, I would like to note here that I have refrained from judging wines not yet in bottle. At the time of this writing, May 2011, more than a few of the 2009s, especially the reds, were not available for tasting – either because they had not yet been bottled or because the producers were not yet ready to present them. Addition-ally, I think that in order to appreciate the unique character of each vin-tage, a good percentage of its wines must already have spent six months in bottle. That's one person's point of view and, as I taste the 2009s, and the 2010s I'll update my notes on my website, as always, keyed to the page or pages in the book. That said, I'll throw out some generalizations and report on weather conditions.

2010: A Great Classic? Living through the 2010 growing season in Touraine, my sense was that the wines of the broad and long expanse of the Loire would be heterogeneous, varying in quality from one zone to another, but that the overall quality would be good, even very good. And I still feel that way. On the other hand, many growers in the Sancerrois were thrilled that 2010 was not 2009. The wines are much livelier, much fresher, they said. This is surely true.

The growing season was fairly dry, with considerable ups and downs of temperature, which, among other things, led to a flowering season that stretched out over three weeks. Véraison was similarly heterogeneous. Châteaumeillant was hit by hail, there were minor cases of mildew but more virulent cases of oidium and esca or black dead arm, a worrisome vine malady that spread its symptoms through more than 15% of the vineyard area. The rhythm of light showers interspersed with extremely hot temperatures ripened the grapes beyond what had been expected. Cool nights and warm, sunny days allowed the grapes to reach maturity. Harvest began in late September and lasted until mid-October – largely due to the extended period of flowering. The harvest has been deemed a classic and time may well prove it to be just that.

As I write this, at the beginning of June 2011, I've had the opportunity to taste some of the early bottlings, for the most part whites and for the most part entry-level cuvées. Based on this small sampling, the 2010 vintage seems to be every bit as "classic" as predicted. It may even be the second *millésime du siècle.* I weigh my words. The whites are unusually pale, indeed, translucent, but what they lack in color they make up for in flavor, balance, really, everything that matters. As aromatically ripe as 2009, they are livelier, punchier, more exuberant. They are excitingly fresh. In other words, I'm becoming very "Bullish" on the 2010 vintage in the Sancerrois.

2009: Chill. When you want to uncork a wine from this vintage, chill it first. And chill the whites a couple of degrees cooler than you normally would. The whites from this hot vintage can be bombastic and that extra bit of chilling gives them the lift they need. Some are downright off-dry, some lack acidity, some are well-balanced, fresh, rich miracles based on superb vineyard management and intelligent vinification.

April and May were warmer than usual but June and July were normal for the region. Flash hail storms in May and July, however, decimated vineyards in parts of Menetou-Salon, Sancerre, Pouilly and the Giennois, and mildew remained a menace throughout the season. In mid-August the temperatures shot up and a period of heavy rains prevailed over drought conditions. September was fine and the harvest stretched from mid-September to mid-October.

Growers compare the quality of the 2009 harvest to that of 1947. In general, the grapes reached aromatic maturity but, as noted, some lack acid and freshness, some are heavy, some come across as not quite dry. None lack character. I have found much fewer over-blown disasters than I feared and many, many more lovely wines that I'd drink anytime, and with pleasure. (I would like to note here, as I did above, that I have refrained from judging wines not yet in bottle. At the time of this writing, June 2011, more than a few of the 2009s, especially the reds, were not available for tasting – either because they had not yet been bottled or because the producers were not yet ready to present them.)

2008: Fat and Sassy. The 2008 vintage was remarkable to me in two ways. First, there was a significant lack of sunlight during the growing season. Indeed, the weather was so dreary that when *la rentrée* – the back to school, back to work time – approached, I predicted that there would be more than the usual number of suicides because people hadn't gotten the remedial dose of Vitamin D that summer weather usually brings. (Haven't fact checked that.) In addition to the cool, gray weather, spring frost killed off a fair percentage of the potential harvest, as did *coulure* and mildew. There was a fine Indian summer and harvest took place under generally good conditions, beginning slowly on September 22, and then in earnest between the 6th and the 15th of October. In general, those who waited to harvest did best. It was one of the smallest harvests on record.

Second, the wines of 2008 – particularly the whites – are unique. The acidity is as clamorous as a wake-up call. But the wines are hefty. The alcohols are relatively high. Sugar accumulation was not a problem. But it's the rare Sauvignon that reached phenolic maturity. So we have this shrill, piercing acidity. Luckily, it's cushioned by the plumpness of the wines. This is a profile I've never experienced before in Loire wines. And it's fascinating to compare the acidity of 2008 – which is rather raw – to the finely etched acidity of the 2007 vintage.

2007: To paraphrase: it ain't over until the wine's in the bottle and has had a chance, if not to sing, at least to find its voice. 2007. What a disaster, we all thought, as we lived through this bizarre growing season that started off with an April that seemed like August only to be succeeded by miserable weather during the cold, wet months that followed. Winemakers had to be extra vigilant, removing grapes affected by rot and mildew, thus losing much of their potential harvest not to mention the three-week advance that April had given. In August, growers began to worry if such grapes as remained on the vine would ripen. And naysayers laughed at growers who persisted in farming organically. Then, hallelujah! As of August 24th a cold, dry north wind swept the vineyards clean. The temperatures rose and the days were warm, the nights cool. This was just the weather that was needed for the grapes to produce sugar; the length of the growing season took care of phenolic maturity.

Now I was one of those who, called upon to make a rush to judgement, wrote off 2007. But, as the years pass, as I taste hundreds of 2007s for the update of the Loire book, I have an increasing admiration for the dry whites from 2007 – across the long Loire Valley, from Muscadet to Pouilly. And what I most admire is the quality of the acidity. That's something I don't think I ever paid much attention to in the past. But 2007 has brought home a wine truth: not all acidities are created equal. And the Loire's 2007s, particularly its whites, are characterized by very, very fine, downright elegant acidity. I think the whites are terrific; the reds tend to be light but there are some real gems. And yes, some of the best wines were those made from organically grown grapes.

2006: I beg to differ. Many top vintners of dry Loire whites dismiss their 2006s as being too heavy, blatant and lacking in acidity. All I can say is that I enjoy them immensely and that, at least through spring 2011, the wines had evolved well and were drinking beautifully. That said, the growing season presented some challenges. The reserves of water, thanks to rains in March and May, benefited the vines in the hot, dry months of June and July that followed. Only young vines on poor soils suffered. September was dramatic, starting off uncommonly hot, punctuated by violent storms, then settling into a period of showers. Growers had to be vigilant and, above all, to harvest quickly – taking advantage of that small window during which the grapes had attained the desired ripeness and before they started to deteriorate. Again, Know Your Vintner.

2005: Does a great vintage raise all boats? The near perfect growing season of 2005 produced ripe, full-flavored, generally well-balanced – if sometimes high in alcohol-wines. It is considered a great vintage and, to a large extent, it is. A surprising number of the Pouillys and Sancerres I sampled, however, tasted green and unripe. They were still good wines but somewhat disappointing. One explanation for the lack of phenolic maturity in quite a few of the whites is that ripening was blocked due to drought conditions. It's also possible that growers picked early to keep alcohol levels within a tolerable range but drought is the more likely culprit. That said, there are many truly superb wines here – to drink now or to cellar. (The harvest was early, beginning on September 7th in Sancerre, a sure indication that this was not a typical vintage.)

2004: Know your winemaker. The vines responded to the extreme heat and relatively small harvest of 2003 by rebounding with an abundance of grapes. Good winemakers responded by diligent cluster thinning. Those who did not, made dilute wines. The growing season started about a week late but was calm and cool throughout June. It turned rainy and occasionally stormy in mid-July. Warm weather in the beginning of September accelerated ripening. Harvest began on September 23 in Reuilly – with the early ripening Pinot Gris – but got underway in force the beginning of October. Both Quincy and Sancerre lost a percentage of their crop to hail. Rain during harvest in some of the appellations necessitated painstaking work by the growers to sort out grapes that were unripe or that had been affected by rot. Overall, however, it was a "Loire" vintage with good fruit-to-alcohol-to acid balance.

2003: Some like it hot. The first of the heat waves to end all heat waves. It is unlikely that anyone of this generation will forget the 2003 vintage. The hottest year on record and the heat of the day didn't let up until near dawn of the following day. The average temperature was 2.5 degrees Celsius above normal and there were long periods – the entire month of June, the first two weeks of August, for example – when the temperatures ranged from 4 to 10 degrees above normal. Young vines suffered, their grapes and their leaves burned, but the vines – because of a reserve of water in the soils and just enough rain at the right moments – did not suffer stress. Harvest began 3 weeks in advance – in August. Fortunately, the weather at the end of August resembled that of the end of September – cool nights, mild afternoons. Ripeness slowed to a normal pace, sugars rose but acidity, which had been dropping, stabilized. In all, it was a smaller than usual harvest and the wines were, by no means, the usual. Fat, high in alcohol, with extremely ripe fruit and relatively high pH, the wines often lacked sufficient acidity to balance the richness. Though some may have been worth cellaring, most were better drunk early.

2002: Classic "Loire" in the best sense, 2002 was the first "great" vintage of the 21st century and a vintage that vignerons continue to love. Bud break was early, roughly ten days in advance of 20th century norms. A heat wave in mid-June resulted in a significant percentage of shot berries and *coulure* and a reduction – less significant – in the potential volume of the harvest. A second heatwave, around August 15th, led to rapid and homogeneous *véraison*. There were no major maladies or weather catastrophes. Harvest took place between September 16th and October 15th in mild, dry weather. The grapes were healthy, and an increasing number of growers harvested by *tri* to get riper fruit. The wines are concentrated and structured, with good, ripe flavours.

Best of the recent past: '97, '96, ('93), '90, '89.

Chapter Two
Sancerre

Status: AOC: 1936 for whites; 1959 for reds and rosés.

Types of Wine: Dry white, reds and rosés.

Grapes: Sauvignon Blanc for whites; Pinot Noir for reds and rosés.

Zone: Situated within 14 villages in the département of the Cher, on the left bank of the Loire, east of Bourges, the Sancerre appellation extends over 2,926 hectares (out of a potential of 3600 hectares), or 7,227 acres. Over 2200 hectares are planted to Sauvignon Blanc, the rest to Pinot Noir. The villages are Bannay, Bué, Crézancy, Menetou-Ratel, Ménétréol, Montigny, Sainte-Gemme, Sancerre, Sury-en-Vaux, Thauvenay, Veaugues, Verdigny and Vinon. The most famous "village" — Chavignol – is a hamlet, as are Amigny and Maimbray.

Production: In 2010, the appellation produced 175,108 hectolitres of wine; 140,160 of white; 22,478 of red; and 12,470 of rosé.

Soils: The region has three basic soil types: 40% "*terres blanches*", the so-called "white soils" composed of clay and limestone (*argilo-calcaire*), also known as Kimmeridgian marl, on the westernmost hillsides of the zone; 40% "*les caillottes*," pebbly compact limestone, on the slopes and low hills; and, on the hills at the eastern limits of the appellation, 20% flinty clay, or Silex.

When to drink: Most should be drunk before their seventh birthday. The whites will age better than the reds.

Price: $$ to $$$$

The first view of Sancerre is stunning. A steep hill appears out of nowhere, a shock after the flat fields of Sologne to the west. When you drive down from its summit, you feel as if you're in an airplane doing a nose dive. Vine-covered slopes spin around you. In the distance, along the leftbank of the

Loire, are the hills and valleys of Chavignol, Bué, St. Satur and the other hamlets and villages composing the Sancerre appellation. You sense you're in an important wine region.

Sancerre sits on the high summit of a fault line. Its panoramic views in every direction have made it a strategically important town since Roman times. And many are the legends suggesting that vines have been cultivated here since antiquity. Gregory of Tours speaks of vineyards in documents dating from 582. In the 12th century the vineyards flourished, thanks to the monks of St. Satur and the Counts of Sancerre. Jean, the Duc de Berry, considered the region's wines the best in the kingdom, as did Henry IV and, indeed, they were often served at the royal table.

Perhaps before, but certainly by the 15th century, Pinot Noir (called Noirien or Morillon) had become the grape of choice, and by the 17th century, it covered Sancerre's vineyards. It is said that the Champenois came here in search of raw material. The reign of Pinot Noir lasted until phylloxera devastated the vines, after which all manner of grapes, many of them hybrids, replaced Pinot, enjoying brief popularity. Sauvignon Blanc, among the various grapes planted, was the one that proved perfectly adapted to the climate and the soils of Sancerre. Sauvignon-based Sancerres received appellation status in 1936.

"Phylloxera had a silver lining," an elderly vigneron said to me, pointing out that Sancerre was the only region in France to replant white grapes in a vineyard previously planted to red and that half its young people moved to Paris "where they became police or bureaucrats — and the major ambassadors for our wines."

In 1946 Edmond Alphonse Mellot opened a wine bar — Le Sancerre – on Avenue Rapp. Artists, writers and gastronomes — from Jean Cocteau to Jean Marais to Curnonsky — regarded Sancerre as the little white they drank with shellfish platters. Then Chablis prices skyrocketed after a killer frost in 1956, converting even more wine buffs to the charms of the edgy Sauvignon Blancs made an hour to its west. Later, autoroutes took Parisians past Sancerre on their way to the ocean. Its success has not yet peaked.

Quality, however, has changed dramatically, as I have described in Chapter One. Further promoting quality are the growers *syndicats* in each of Sancerre's 14 villages. They sustain a kind of participatory democracy in which decisions are made collectively, and internal, quality-oriented, regulations promulgated.

Some producers tell me, shaking their heads in dismay, "We still have a long way to go." To which this implicated outsider replies, "You can't see how far you've already come."

Back in what seems like the distant 1980s most vignerons made more than one style of Sancerre. With parcels scattered over various slopes and hillsides, each grower had a mix of the appellation's soil types. More often than not, they blended wines from the various soils to make more balanced wines, offering an early-drinking cuvée, from, say, *caillottes* soils and young vines, and then, perhaps, something along the lines of a Vielles Vignes bottling or a barrel-aged wine named after a newborn child or an ancestor.

A handful had started bottling by parcel to highlight the character of the vineyard. In today's Sancerre, rare is the vintner who doesn't vinify and bottle at least some of his or her wines by soil type. And here I must elaborate a bit on the special soils and dramatic landscape of Sancerre.

The town, itself, sits on a fault that brought into contact sedimentary layers from the Cretaceous, the Kimmeridgian and the Eocene periods. Erosion resulted in over fifteen types of soils and sub-soils, the three most common being *terres blanches, caillottes* and silex which form Sancerre's slopes. The appellation's steepest hillsides rise up to nearly 400 meters high, with inclines of over 50%. The best of these are well known and much coveted *lieux-dits*.

Pierre Bréjoux, in his book *Les Vins de Loire*, organized some of the most celebrated according to soil type. Those on Kimmeridgian marl or "*terres blanches*" include part of La Poussie in Bué, the Côte de Champtin and the Clos du Roy in Champtin, les Monts Damnés and les Culs de Beaujeu (or, as it is sometimes written, le Cul de Beaujeu) in Chavignol. Lieux-dits with "*caillottes*" soils include Chêne Marchand, Chemarin and the other half of la Poussie in Bué, les Bouffants in Chavignol, le Paradis in Sancerre and la Perrière in Verdigny.

By all rights, these lieux-dits should be granted cru status. While I believe that France has created too many appellations – and continues to do so – I feel that the hillsides cited here are every bit as special as the crus of Chablis, the Côte d'Or or Alsace. But, like most everything in France, any endeavor to establish a cru system would be insanely complicated and lead to internal warfare.

I recently asked Benoît Roumet of the BIVC about this. His response was that he didn't think we'd see grand crus or premier crus in Sancerre or Pouilly or in the other appellations in the near future. Although some growers had asked for them, a study showed that it wasn't a great idea. "AOC is the blend between climate, parcel, grape and human," he said. "To give a parcel special standing is to undercut the importance of the human hand. And producers can put the name of the parcel on the label which seems to be the best solution."

Maybe. At least it keeps the peace. But, from me to you, treat yourself to the Monts Damnés bottling from one of my top-rated producers. Bréjoux, for his part, declared that, when drinking the Sancerres of Bué, he would like to have a neck as long as a swan's, the better to appreciate them. Amen.

Sancerre *rouge* and rosé became AOCs in 1959, more than thirty years after Sancerre *blanc*. In the '70s, Parisian sommeliers began proposing the red with fish. The '82 vintage (good quality and large quantity) put the wine on the map; Sancerre *rouge* replaced Bouzy *rouge* (from Champagne) as the chic light red of *nouvelle cuisine*. This trend, not surprisingly, engendered a backlash: Sancerre *rouge* was denounced as a sommelier invented fad. How quickly we forget that it was Pinot Noir that once covered these hillsides!

Much of the best comes from the *terres blanches* hillsides in two communes — Crézancy (particularly the Côte de Champtins and the Clos du Roy) and Verdigny. Silex-rich soils are also appreciated, making some of the region's most deeply colored, powerful reds.

Rosés may be made by direct press or by bleeding the vats of the red grapes. They are then vinified like whites. Few vignerons take them seriously. That's regrettable. When they do, the results are extremely pretty tea-rose colored wines, floral, vinous and mouthfilling. Totally seductive wines, they can accompany anything from melon with prosciutto to Moroccan bstillas and tagines.

Producers often make two styles of red, an early-drinking cuvée and a more serious version. Depending on the style, the reds ferment for from six days to three weeks or longer. The first cuvée may not age in barrel but most of the rest do, either in new (or newish) barriques or old demi-muids, for several months or longer.

For the most part these are seductive, light to medium-bodied Pinots. The simpler version is – or should be — a succulent red with vibrant flavors of cherries, plums and strawberries. Depending on the vintage and the vintner, it may be cool and lean or warm and plump. The more serious cuvée is weightier, more structured, with hints of sweet spices, black tea and orange zests. They definitely *pinotte*. And though most don't plumb the depths of that grape's possibilities, they can be supremely satisfying, absolute charmers.

That said, I believe Sancerre can go further with its reds. Its vintners really only began to take the wines seriously within the past 15 years. Producers like Vacheron have always put as much emphasis on the quality of their reds as they did (and do) on the quality of their whites. From my vantage point, what really signaled a new commitment to quality reds was when Alphonse Mellot #19 joined Alphonse Mellot #18. Alphonse *père,* typical of his generation, seemed to treat Sancerre *rouge* as an after-thought. With Alphonse *fils*, it moved front and center. Other members of his generation – from Stephane Riffault, to the Morin brothers, among many – show every sign of being committed to making great Sancerre *rouge*. As a die-hard lover of red Burgundy, I, for one, am not only optimistic but cautiously ecstatic and ferociously thirsty.

Producers

There are 350 winemakers, 25 grower-négociants and one cooperative. About a fourth of Sancerre wine is distributed by the grower-négociants. Sixty percent is sold by the vigneron. It is important to pay attention to first names here. In the commune of Verdigny, for example, there are 33 vignerons whose family name is Reverdy.

Outstanding

Domaine Didier Dagueneau Girard & Pierre Morin
Domaine Claude & Stéphane Riffault Domaine Vacheron

Excellent

Domaine Gérard Boulay Domaine Henri Bourgeois
Domaine du Carrou/ Dominique Roger Clos la Néore
François Cotat Pascal Cotat Domaine Lucien Crochet
Domaine François Crochet Domaine Vincent Delaporte
Vincent Gaudry Domaine Pascal Jolivet Serge Laloue
Domaine Laporte Domaine Alphonse Mellot
Domaine Vincent Pinard Pascal & Nicolas Reverdy
Domaine Claude & Florence Thomas-Labaille

Hypernatural

Sebastien Riffault

To follow

Domaine Michel Vattan/Pascal Joulin

Highly recommended

Domaine Bailly Reverdy Domaine Emile Balland
Domaine Hubert Brochard
André Dezat & Fils/Les Celliers Saint-Romble
Domaine Merlin-Cherrier Domaine Henry Natter
Domaine Henry Pellé Domaine Paul Prieur
Roger & Didier Raimbault Domaine Bernard Reverdy & Fils

Domaine Hippolyte Reverdy 🐌   Domaine Reverdy-Ducroux 🐌
Domaine Matthias and Emile Roblin 🐌   Jean-Max Roger 🐌
Domaine de la Rossignole/Pierre Cherrier 🐌
Domaine de Saint Pierre/Pierre Prieur & Fils 🐌
Domaine Michel Thomas 🐌   Domaine Tinel-Blondelet/La Croix Canat

🐌 Recommended

Ackerman-Remy Pannier 🐌   Domaine des Brosses/Alain Girard 🐌
Domaine Jean-Claude Chatelain 🐌   Domaine Daniel Chotard 🐌
Domaine Fleuriet & Fils 🐌   Domaine Masson-Blondelet 🐌
Domaine la Gemière/Daniel Millet & Fils 🐌
Domaine Fernand Girard & Fils 🐌   Gitton Pere & Fils 🐌
Vincent Grall 🐌   Château de Maimbray/George Roblin 🐌
Joseph Mellot 🐌   Domaine Jean-Paul Picard 🐌
Domaine David Sautereau Domaine Michel Thomas 🐌
Domaine Roland Tissier 🐌   Domaine André Vatan 🐌
Domaine des Vieux Pruniers/ Christian Thirot-Fournier

🐌 By the glass

Domaine Balland-Chapuis/Guy Saget 🐌
Domaine Roger Champault 🐌   Eric Louis/Celliers de Pauline 🐌
Domaine de la Perriere/Guy Saget 🐌   Château de Sancerre 🐌
Domaine des Grandes Perrières/Jérôme Gueneau 🐌

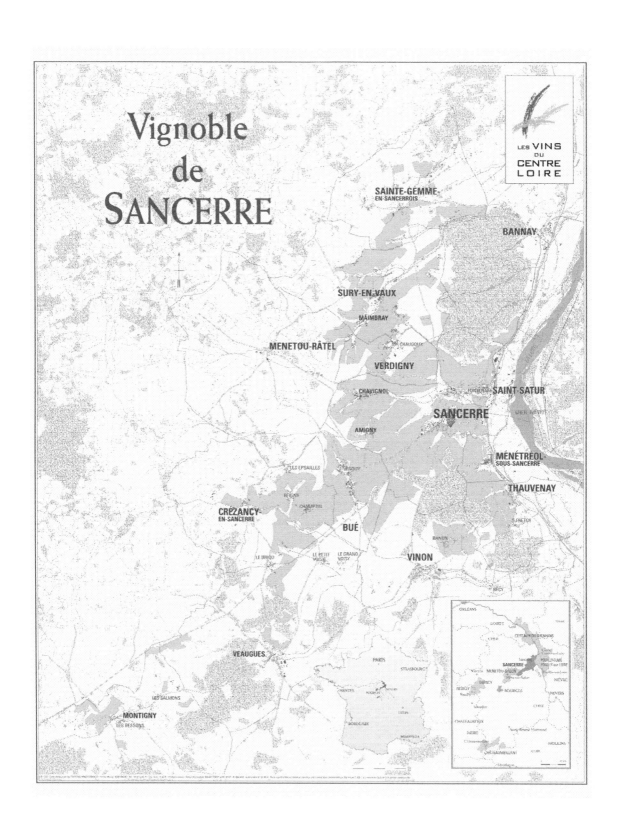

Vignoble
de
SANCERRE

SAINTE-GEMME-
EN-SANCERROIS

BANNAY

SURY-EN-VAUX

MAIMBRAY

CHAUDOUX

MENETOU-RÂTEL

VERDIGNY

CHAVIGNOL

SAINT-SATUR

SANCERRE

AMIGNY

MÉNÉTRÉOL-
SOUS-SANCERRE

THAUVENAY

LES EPSAILLES

REIGNY

CRÉZANCY-
EN-SANCERRE

CHAMPTIN

BUÉ

BANON

LE PETIT VOISY

LE GRAND VOISY

LE BROU

VINON

VEAUGUES

PARIS

STRASBOURG

NANTES

LYON

LES SALMONS

BORDEAUX

MARSEILLE

MONTIGNY
LES BESSONS

LES VINS
DU
CENTRE
LOIRE

SANCERRE

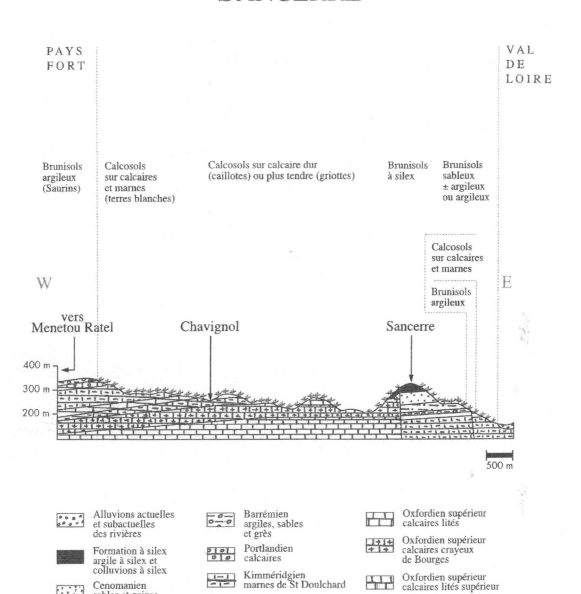

PAYS FORT

VAL DE LOIRE

Brunisols
argileux
(Saurins)

Calcosols
sur calcaires
et marnes
(terres blanches)

Calcosols sur calcaire dur
(caillotes) ou plus tendre (griottes)

Brunisols
à silex

Brunisols
sableux
± argileux
ou argileux

Calcosols
sur calcaires
et marnes

Brunisols
argileux

W

E

vers
Menetou Ratel

Chavignol

Sancerre

400 m
300 m
200 m

500 m

Alluvions actuelles et subactuelles des rivières	Barrémien argiles, sables et grès	Oxfordien supérieur calcaires lités
Formation à silex argile à silex et colluvions à silex	Portlandien calcaires	Oxfordien supérieur calcaires crayeux de Bourges
Cenomanien sables et gaizes	Kimméridgien marnes de St Doulchard	Oxfordien supérieur calcaires lités supérieur
Albien argiles sables et argiles	Kimméridgien calcaires de Buzançais	

🐚 Recommended

🐚 Ackerman-Remy Pannier

49400 St. Hilaire- Saint Florent, Saumur; 02.41.79.80.03;
www.ackerman.fr

This mega-company sources its Sancerre from Hubert Brochard who practices sustainable farming on his 40 hectares of vines in the commune of Chavignol. Grapes are machine harvested and ferment in temperature controlled stainless steel tanks. The wines are estate bottled. The 2006 Domaine Moulin Granger was grapy, somewhat foxy, but correct. Not a bad choice for a chain hotel like Mercure.

🐚 Highly Recommended

🐚 Domaine Bailly-Reverdy

18300 Bué, 02.485418.38; bailly-reverdy@wanadoo.fr

This domaine incarnates, in the best sense, the evolution that has taken place in Sancerre over the past twenty years. When I first visited the property in 1990, the wines were hit-or-miss, with the Chavignol bottling the clear stand out. Now, every single wine is heartily recommended and, frankly, I'm tempted to classify the domaine as "Excellent."

Before Bernard Bailly took over domaine in 50s, its wines were sold to négociants or to local cafés where they were delivered in barrel. Bernard began bottling all of his production. He had married Marie-Thérese Bailly in 1952 and added her name to the label – an effective way of distinguishing their family the many other Baillys in the neighborhood. He also adapted his vineyards to produce quality wines – selecting the best rootstock for each soil type. Of the Bailly's five sons, two joined Bernard on the domaine – Jean-François, who died in 2006, and Franck, the baby of the bunch, who studied viticulture and enology in Bordeaux.

Bernard retired in 1996. The next generation is represented by Aurelien, Jean-François' son, who studied viticulture and enology in Montpellier and worked at Fromm in New Zealand and Domaine Drouhin in Oregon before returning home and joining his uncle in 2010.

Franck currently works 22 hectares, mostly in the commune of Bué, in addition to five hectares in Chavignol. He subscribes to the principles of sustainable farming and has installed weather monitors in key spots to follow his vines as closely as possible. Grapes are hand harvested, sorted and pressed slowly. Most are then transferred to small, temperature-controlled, stainless steel tanks for fermentation. Only natural yeasts are used.

The domaine's generic Sancerre *blanc* is called La Mercy-Dieu. A blend of grapes from different soils, it is bottled by the spring following the harvest.

The 2010 exudes aromas of ripe peach. It's also salty and steely, making for nice contrasts and a delightful quaff. The 2009, fresh, focused and tense, seemed ever so slightly off-dry, with definite flavors of pineapple mingled with minerals, citrus and steel. A satisfying, adaptable, upscale meal wine.

The "Chavignol" bottling is made from grapes on four hectares within that commune. Soils are predominantly *terres blanches* with about one-third *caillottes.* Harmonious and nicely balanced – the acidity lightens the perception of 15% alcohol –, the 2009 was full and even more tense than La Mercy-Dieu, adding distinct aromas of pear to floral, lime, peach and chalk notes. Very nice. The 2010, not quite as tart as 2008, had strong gooseberry and mineral flavors and a steely backbone. A vivacious bistro white.

Grapes from the domaine's single hectare of vines on Monts Damnés ferment in a mix of new barriques and barriques used for the previous year's wine. With 13% alcohol, the 2009 was mouthfilling, with flavors of grape-fruit, tropical fruit and mild notes of vanilla. Minerality and a chalky quality, however, upstaged the fruit flavors, resulting in a very fine, pedigreed and savory Sancerre.

Made by a direct press of the grapes, the 2010 rosé was full and dry. It could have used a bit more backbone but I loved the fleeting aromas of *fraises des bois* (wild strawberries). The domaine's red is made from old vines growing on *terres blanches* soils. The extent of destemming depends on the ripeness of tannins in the stems. The grapes ferment in tank, with regular punching down and pumping over until the end of fermentation when the wine is transferred to barrels – some of which are new – for malolactic. It ages in barrel for a year before bottling. The 2008 was a cool stream of black cherry and black tea, with the lively acidity of the vintage.

&. Domaine Emile Balland   &. Highly Recommended

B.P.9 Route Nationale 7, 45420 Bonny-sur-Loire; 03.86.39.26.51; emile.balland@orange.fr (See Coteaux du Giennois)

Up until the late 1990s the name Balland-Chapuis was one to be reckoned with in Sancerre and the Coteaux du Giennois. The family had important enough property holdings in each appellation to make it what the French call a "locomotive." Joseph Balland, Emile's father, sold the ensemble of vineyards to Guy Saget sometime in the late '90s – another victim of France's laws of inheritance.

In 1999, when Emile finished his studies in Angers (agricultural engi-neer) and Toulouse (enology) and wanted to set about making wine, he essentially started from scratch. Today he has managed to put together a five-hectare domaine, consisting of 4 hectares in the Coteaux du Giennois and one hectare in Sancerre.

Most of his Sancerre vineyards – 88% — are located in the communes of Bué and Amigny, on a south-facing slope so steep it wasn't replanted after phylloxera until 2003. He makes three Sancerres, an old vines red from a .12 hectare parcel in Bué previously owned by his family and planted by his grandfather, and two whites, from *caillottes* soils. The 2006 Sancerre Blanc "Champ de Scandals" was full and fresh, dense and tight, with an exuberance of grapefruit, mineral and flint flavors. Very good. A domaine to watch.

By the glass

Domaine Joseph Balland-Chapuis/ Guy Saget
La Croix Saint-Laurent – BP 24 – 18300 Bué; 02 48 54 06 67 – 02 48 54 09 01; balland-chapuis@wanadoo.fr; www.balland-chapuis.com (See Guy Saget/Pouilly)

The sprawling, 36 hectare Balland-Chapuis domaine began its existence in the 17th century and remained in the Balland family until 1998 when it was taken over by Guy Saget.

In addition to the wines made under the Balland-Chapuis name in the Giennois, the Sagets make at least five cuvées of Sancerre, including the red "Comte Thibault," "Le Chêne Marchand," the sweet, late-harvest "Cuvée Pierre", Le Vallon and Le Chatillet. The two last, each fermented in temperature-controlled, stainless steel tanks, are the only Balland-Chapuis Sancerres I've tasted since the domaine was taken over by Guy Saget. The 2008 "Le Chatillet" blanc, was meaty and fresh, with flavors of creamed corn, lemon zests and minerals. It seemed a bit shallow but was tasty. A good Sancerre for a noisy brasserie. The "Le Vallon" bottling, which comes from a parcel of the same name, is made from 30 year old grapes growing on *caillottes* soils. The 2003, tasted in 2005, was ripe and floral, almost chewy, with tangy flavors of grapefruit and a satisfying mineral presence.

Excellent

Gérard Boulay
Chavignol 18300 Sancerre; 02.48.54.36.37; boulayg-vigneron@wanadoo.fr

The Boulay domaine was created in 1380. Today, it is run by Gérard Boulay who took over in 1972, and consists of 11.5 hectares of vines, two of which are located in Bué and Crézancy and planted to Pinot Noir.

Fans of the Sancerres of the Cotat family would do well to get to know the wines of Gérard Boulay. Not only is he their neighbor and not only do they ply many of he same slopes – the privileged, 60% inclines of the Monts Damnés with its Kimmeridgian marl soils – but they work in much the same manner. Grapes are harvested very ripe – the wines often have more than a kiss of residual sugar – and viticulture is basically organic. The Boulays use only natural yeasts, ferment all but their basic Sancerre *blanc* in barrel and use minimal amounts of sulfur. Harvest is by hand with the exception of the grapes for the basic Sancerre bottling, "Tradition," which accounts for two-thirds of the domaine's production. It comes from various parcels in Chavignol and Crézancy, from both *terres blanches* and *caillottes* soils, as well as the young vines from Monts Damnés and Cul de Beaujeu.

A note with regard to the commentary below: I tasted all the 2006s at home, alone, in 2008; all the other wines were tasted at the winery in 2009.

At the winery, we started with a tour of tank and barrel samples of the 2008s – an incredibly apple-y "Tradition;" a lemon zest, mineral, and qui-nine rich "Tradition;" a textured Monts Damnés; and a creamy, oak and mint scented Clos du Beaujeu. Then on to bottled wines.

The domaine bottling, or "Tradition," ferments in tank and is aged on its fine lees. The 2007, tender as a caress, added a zing of grapefruit to mel-low flavors of ripe exotic fruit and minerals. The 2006, slightly richer and a bit rustic, was a characterful Chavignol with appetizing flavors of lime, herbal tea, minerals and lemon zests.

Boulay ferments his other whites in used barrels which he purchases from larger Sancerre houses like Henri Bourgeois and Alphonse Mellot. First among equals in this triad of beautiful cuvées is Boulay's Monts Damnés, from a 1.5 hectare parcel of forty year old vines.

A fine example of Chablis in Chavignol, the 2006 Monts Damnés was profoundly mineral, crystalline and graceful, yet rich and dense. Perfectly ripe, with steel girding and a long citrus zest finish, it exemplified the term "*cru*" and the thrilling way in which *terroir* trumps *cépage*. The 2005, after a bit of aeration, was creamy and anise-scented, as intriguing as the 2006. I found the 2007 a bit hot and raw when tasted in 2009 but would love to revisit it.

We're once again in Chablis-in-Chavignol with the Clos de Beaujeu bot-tling. Made from a .75 hectare parcel on the privileged slopes of Cul de Beaujeu, it is bottled without filtration. (In the 14th century wines from the Clos du Beaujeu supplied the vinous needs of the Cathedral of Bourges.) Minerals, stone, and citrus zests characterized the 2007 which had lively acidity – as well as some residual sugar – and a long, savory, salty finish. The racy 2006 was equally long, a big, cult, Rhone-style white with Loire freshness. (Chavignol, Chablis, Hermitage. Yes.) Greatly mineral, the wine was meaty and unctuous, with notes of mint and preserved lemon, stone and herbal tea. Super.

The 2002 was a dulcet weave of lemon, lime and minerals. The '96, with a patina of age, was a mix of truffled asparagus, lime, minerals tea, honey and hay. The '95, even more honeyed, added caramel to the mix and, still fresh, slipped across the tongue like liquid silk.

The Boulays were surprised that I preferred the two previous cuvées to "Comtesse" as that bottling comes from the heart of Monts Damnés, the very center of the slope. True, I find the Monts Damnés and the Clos de Beaujeu bottlings more riveting but I'm hardly kicking Comtesse out of bed. The 2008, tasted from barrel, was high strung yet full and mineral. Very promising. Even more marked by minerality was the racy 2007 with its juicy lime, lemon tang. White flowers, creamed corn and slate were added to the weave of flavors in the 2006. And the 2005, with 4 to 5 grams of residual sugar, was mellow, nuanced, honey-tinged and lightly oaky. Very special.

The Boulays also make a small amount of rosé and red. I've not tasted the former and sampled only one vintage of the latter, the 2000, which was slightly gamy and a bit rustic, but had attractive cherry notes. I'd love to taste more.

🐚 Excellent

🐚 Domaine Henri Bourgeois
18300 Chavignol, Sancerre: 02.48.78.53.20;
www.henribourgeois.com

Domaine Henri Bourgeois was born in 1950 with two hectares of vines in the Sancerre appellation. Reputedly the sixth largest house in the Loire – though Jean-Marie Bourgeois demurs, saying it's just a family property – the domaine currently has 75 hectares of vines in Sancerre and in Pouilly Fumé, most of it planted to Sauvignon Blanc. Additionally, the firm's roster covers every appellation in the Sancerrois – from the Giennois to Châteaumeillant – and produces zippy, easy slurping rosé (Pinot Noir), red (Cabernet Franc) and white (Sauvignon Blanc) as Vin de Pays. And the latest adjunct is Le Clos Henri, a vineyard in New Zealand where Bourgeois produces convincingly "French" Sauvignon Blanc and Pinot Noir.

Run today by Jean-Marie Bourgeois, his son Arnaud, and his nephew Jean-Christophe, the firm is a solid and an excellent ambassador for the region. Bourgeois practices sustainable farming. Yields for the top cuvées – of which there are more than a half dozen — are between 39 and 50 hl/ha. Fifty-five percent of harvesting is done by hand – again, for the top cuvées

– and the rest by machine. Bourgeois' cellars sprawl under the steep hills of Chavignol, a warren of gleaming, high-tech equipment, where gravity is used at each step in the vinification process.

Bourgeois' two simplest white Sancerres come from both domaine and purchased grapes, about half and half, and are harvested both by hand and by machine. Les Baronnes, which may be labeled Grande Réserve, Les Bonnes Bouches and/or La Vigne Blanche depending on the market, comes from the hillsides separating the village of Chavignol from the town of Sancerre. Its soils are a mix of clay (65%) and chalk (35%). The wine ferments at low temperatures in thermoregulated tanks and ages on its fine lees, for five months before bottling. The 2008, tasted at the end of 2010 and in the spring of 2009, was well structured, vigorous, with a definite sense of place. The fruit seemed to have been picked just at the verge of phenolic ripeness, producing light notes of gooseberry and grass, and 2008's strident acidity was tamed to a mere wake-up-call. A fine choice for an upscale bistro. The 2002, tasted in 2003, was mineral and fresh, with firm flavors of lemon, a hint of petrol and a long finish.

"La Chapelle des Augustins" is also a mix of purchased and domaine-owned grapes. (The domaine's grapes are a *tri* of 35+ year-old vines on silex soils above limestone subsoils.) Like most of Bourgeois' top whites, it ferments in thermoregulated stainless steel tanks at low temperatures and ages on its lees, in this case, for five months. The 2002, which debuted at the 2003 Salon des Vins de Loire, was full, appetizing, lightly salty, decidedly mineral, and an impressive expression of its terroir.

Next: a slew of special cuvées, all from domaine's vines, all hand harvested.

"Le M.D." comes from a steep south and southeast facing slope in Chavignol with Kimmeridgian marl soils over a a composite of fossilized seashells and clay. (Reading between the lines, it comes chiefly from land very close to les Monts Damnés.) Harvested by *tri*, the ripest grapes are selected, pressed slowly and transferred to thermoregulated stainless steel tanks for fermentation at 15 to 18 degrees. The wine ages on its lees until bottling. The 2002, tasted in 2003, flaunted its pedigree. Rich and characterful, it was a lipsmacking mix of mineral and citrus flavors. The 2003, tasted in 2005, was a rich, potent wine, all stone and steel.

"La Côte des Monts Damnés, which replaces "Les Monts Damnés," comes from the low-yielding 35 to 48+ year old vines on the Kimmeridgian marl soils of the famous slope. The grapes ferment slowly in temperature controlled stainless steel tanks. The 2008, tasted in 2009, was tight and crystalline, with exotic notes of ginger and lime. The 2005, tasted in 2007, was rich and complex, a cross between Sancerre and Chablis. A tank sample of the 2006, tasted in early 2007, was both highstrung and deep, with vivacious flavors of grapefruit and a long finish. Very promising. The 2003, tasted in 2005, was rich and ample – with, perhaps, a degree or two of residual sugar – and enough acidity to balance the sumptuous fruit.

"La Bourgeoise" white is made from 50+ year-old vines on the silex soils of a southwest facing slope in the commune of St. Satur. The grapes ferment in barrels of Tronçais forest oak and the wine ages on its lees — which are regularly stirred up — for roughly eight months. The wine spends an additional year in barrel before bottling and another year in Bourgeois' cellar before being sold. The 2005, tasted in 2007, was closed up tight; the excellent 2002, tasted in 2003 and in 2004, was vibrant, vivacious, ample, mineral, and enormously tasty.

Now come my two very favorite bottlings, Sancerre d'Antan and Jadis. Sancerre d'Antan, which translates as "yesteryear's Sancerre," debuted at Vinexpo 1995. Made from vines planted in 1936 on a silex-rich/clay-poor hillside in St. Satur, it ferments with indigenous yeasts in barrels ranging from one to ten years old, ages on its fine lees, and is bottled without having been fined or filtered. The 2006, tasted in the spring of 2009, was marrowy, its flavors, all flint and minerals. The 2003, tasted in 2007, was thrilling – rich, tense, deep and textured; the 2001, tasted in 2004, was a fine blend of minerals and lemon; tasted again in 2009, it had evolved into a weave of hay, honey and roasted vegetables, particularly asparagus – no surprise, then, that it paired beautifully with a dish of asparagus; the '99, tasted in 2003, was pungent, slightly oaky and extremely characterful. A lot going on here.

The name "Jadis" also evokes olden days. It comes from 50+ year-old vines on Kimmeridgian marl soils at the heart of les Monts Damnés. The grapes are pressed and the juice is left to decant for two days before being transferred to cement tanks or barrel for fermentation (without the addition of yeast). It is bottled without having been fined or filtered. The 2006, tasted in 2009, was racy and tense as a highwire, the whole mellowed by mild oak accents. Tasted in 2007, the 2003 was concentrated, complex, rich, mellow and long. Excellent. PMG. The 2002, tasted in 2005, thrilled the palate with its tingly, fleshy, sur lie marrow. Fabulous. The 2000, tasted in 2003, was elegant, limpid and lacy, with etched flavors of ripe, exotic fruit.

The "Etienne Henri" cuvée was inspired by and named after an ancestor who was the first in the region to make wine in new oak barrels. For this bottling, Bourgeois uses 50 to 60 year old vines on a slope characterized by silex-rich soils – essentially the same raw material as is used for the La

Bourgeoise bottling. The grapes ferment in new oak barrels and age for 12 months on their fine lees before being bottled unfiltered. Big, creamy and oaky, the 2003 verged on the ripeness and richness of a late harvest wine. It was very stylish though less marked by its terroir than I would have liked, which I took to be a function of the extreme nature of the 2003 vintage paired with the use of new oak. As it was so lush and nearly sweet, I served it as an aperitif at a dinner party in 2007. A year later, the near-overripeness of the fruit was even more pronounced, all but swallowing the oak. I suspect that this is a 2003 that has now aged to a fine mellowness. The 2000, tasted in 2004, was pungent but mellow, its oak well integrated; the '99, tasted in 2003, was ample, nicely harmonious and satisfying; the '95, tasted at the same time, was a succulent marriage of oak and ripe fruit.

Rosés and reds are harvested by hand. The reds undergo a brief cold-soaking before fermentation. None of the reds are filtered. Bourgeois' basic Sancerre rouge, Les Baronnes, is made from 25 to 40 year old vines on clay-limestone soils, with about a third coming from purchased grapes. Fermentation lasts for about 12 days at moderate temperatures, with a punching down of the cap and pumping over of the must twice daily. After malolactic fermentation, the wine ages in Tronçais oak barrels (a third of which are replaced yearly), for six to eight months. The 2003, tasted in 2005, was a charmer. Plumper than usual, vintage *oblige*, but captivating.

"La Bourgeoise" rouge comes from 50 to 70+ year old vines on a south-west facing slope with flint-and-clay soils. Fermentation lasts for ten to 14 days at temperatures between 26 and 32 degrees, during which time the cap is punched down and the must pumped over twice daily. Malolactic fermentation takes place in 228 litre Tronçais oak barrels after which the wine ages in barrel for ten to twelve months, and for an additional eight to twenty-four months before being released for sale. Though a touch jammy, the 2003, tasted in 2007, was rich yet "light," cool, specific, and *gourmand*. Pure pleasure to drink, a bottle would disappear very quickly. Despite a bit of heat in the finish, the 2001, tasted in 2005, was a red you could really cozy up to. The 2000, tasted in 2003, was well-balanced and appealing, an engaging expression of Pinot Noir nicely mingled with oak.

In addition to the very good wine Bourgeois makes on their own property, Clos Henri, in New Zealand, Bourgeois also offers some one-off specials. In exceptional years, for example, Bourgeois produces a sweet, late harvest Sancerre. Frankly, this isn't a style of Sancerre I love – with its sweet, often roasted vegetable flavors — but it's definitely worth tasting. This was the case with the last tasted (in 2007), the 1997 Vendange de St. Charles.

More mainstream but unique in its own way is the "Le Chêne St. Etienne" bottling. There are only three vintages of the wine in each color. What makes this wine so rare is that the oak used in the making of the barrels in which the wines ferment and/or age came from a tree planted in 1560 outside the town of Bourges. The tree was struck by thunder in 1993 and then felled in 1995. At the time, it measured 37 meters in height (roughly as tall as a ten-storey building); it had a circumference of 6 meters and weighed 35 tons. Master coopers went to work on the tree, drying the staves for four years, and then fashioning them into 40 barrels of either 228 litre or 600 litre capacity.

The white, made in 2000, 2001 and 2002, comes from a selection of very old vines on the Kimmeridgian marl soils of Monts Damnés. The wine ferments slowly in barriques made from the St. Etienne oak which are equipped with serpentines to control the temperature. While aging, the wine's lees are stirred twice weekly.

The 2000, tasted in 2003, 2004 and 2007, was a creamy, mellow wine that seemed a blend of Old World and New. By 2007 it was drinking beautifully. I'd have paired it with roast ham. Round, mellow and still fresh, the 2002, tasted in 2009, was rich and nuanced, with flavors of hay, honey and herbal tea.

The red, made in 2000, 2002 and 2003, came from from very old vines on the *terres blanches* soils of a slope in Chavignol. The alcoholic fermentation follows the recipe for the other reds after which the wine is transferred into the mythic barrels for malolactic. Here it will age for 18 months. The 2000, tasted in both 2004 and 2003, was smooth, well balanced, a definitive wine that was all too easy to drink.

As a tribute to this ancient tree, which was named after Bourges' Cathedral St. Etienne, Bourgeois collected the sprouts born of its acorns and planted 1000 trees near the spot where it stood in the hope that, by 2200, the St. Etienne oak tree will live again.

&❧ Highly Recommended

❧ Hubert Brochard

Le Bourg 18300 Chavignol; 02 48 78 20 10;
www.hubert-brochard.fr

The Brochard family's viticultural roots extend back to the 16th century, most recently passing from Aimée and Hubert to Thérèse and Henri, and, currently to Jean-François, Daniel and Benôit.

The family has 55 vineyards spread throughout Sancerre's many communes and in part of AOC Pouilly-Fumé as well. Given the domaine's many parcels, the basic Sancerres are a mix of the region's soils. The white, for example, comes from soils that are 40% pure limestone, 30% silex and 30% clay, on slopes with a south/south-west orientation. Yields average 68 hl/ha. Harvest is conducted both by hand and by machine. The grapes ferment in temperature controlled tanks – either stainless steel or enamel.

The 2008, tasted in December 2010, was crystalline yet ample, with floral scents and a trace of honey. The vivid acidity of the vintage was extremely well cushioned and the wine was rather elegant, with a long mineral and citrus finish. Very good indeed. Note: this bottling has different names in different markets: "Classique," "Tradition," and/ or "Les Collines Blanches."

"Côte des Monts Damnés" comes from the famous slope. The 2006, tasted in spring 2011, was textured and statuesque, its flavors lightly evolving toward those resembling aging Chenin Blanc – herbal tea, quinine, wax – as well as preserved lemon, licorice, lime and tilleul. An appetizing bitterness is a constant thread, leading to a fresh and vigourous finish.

"Aujourd'hui comme Autrefois" is Brochard's hand-harvested, unfiltered Sancerre made, as the name suggests, as was done in bygone days. As with Bourgeois' Jadis bottling, this may be my favorite cuvée *chez* Brochard. I drank the scrumptious, lipsmacking 2008 in the spring of 2011. Pure and crystalline, it opened with light pear and mineral scents. After several hours, the pear facet metamorphosed into a fleshier, compote-like aroma, and added notes of lemon juice and zests of both lemon and lime. The sur lie marrow was thrilling and the wine was simultaneously subtle and decisive, and rather elegant.

Under the Henry Brochard label, the domaine offers a Sauvignon Blanc Vin de Pays. The 2008, dominated by flavors of gooseberry and green pea, had forceful acidity and good mineral undertones. Also under the Henry Brochard label is "Les Carisannes," another Vin de Pays. The 2008 had appealing aromas of blossoms and white-fleshed peach, well cushioned acidity, and bright lemon zest flavors.

The Pinot Noir grapes grow on a slightly different mix of soils – 20% limestone, 30% silex and 50% clay – on slopes with south-south-east exposures. Yields average 62 hl/ha, grapes are hand harvested, destemmed and ferment in temperature controlled stainless steel tanks. The wines age in 225 litre oak barrels. The 2007, tasted in December 2010, was smooth and tender, its flavors dominated by black tea and cherries. The tannins were light and discreet. As Elizabeth David said, an omelet and a glass of wine.

∾ Recommended

∾ Domaine des Brosses/Alain Girard

Route de Sancerre, 18300 Veaugues: 02.48.79.24.88;
m.alaingirard@wanadoo.fr

In a way, this fairly traditional, 11 hectare family domaine illustrates how far the Sancerre appellation has come. Their pungent 2006 Sancerre *blanc*, with loud cat pee odors, was zingy but relatively full and smooth. In the '90s it would have been considered stellar; in 2010, it qualifies as a goodish, lively bistro white.

∾ Excellent

∾ Domaine du Carrou/ Dominique Roger

7 place du Carrou, 18300 Bué; 02.48.54.10.65;
www.dominique-roger.fr

Dominique Roger, whose family has been making Sancerre wine since the 17th century, represents the sixth generation to work the vineyards of Bué. Roger has 21.4 hectares of vineyard land though only half of that is in production. Roger practices sustainable farming, ploughs the soil, seeds the earth between the vines and debuds every plant. Roger has also installed weather monitors in key parcels in order to follow precisely the health of the vines and the need for treatment against maladies. Harvest is by hand and yields range between 37 hl/ha to 42 hl/ha.

Once known primarily for their red wines, the Domaine du Carrou now produces excellent whites as well. There are three cuvées, starting with the domaine bottling which comes from a classic Sancerre mix of soils: shallow, stony, *caillottes*, Kimmeridgian marl, and flinty silex. Harvested by hand, fermented in temperature-controlled tanks, and aged on its fine lees, the pungent 2008 had depth, texture and saliva-inducing, juicy acidity. Its strong *pipi de chat* aromas indicated a lack of phenolic ripeness, not uncommon in 2008 whites. The crystalline 2006, fresh, mellow and mouth-filling, mixed flavors of grapefruit zest and citronelle as well as chalk and slate. With its marvelous texture, it was what the French so rightly call *gourmand*.

Carrou has .37 hectares on the *caillottes* soils of the famous lieu-dit Chêne-Marchand. The 2006, both creamy and salty, tasted of grapefruit zests and stone, with an appetizingly bitter core and a long, long finish of all of the above.

Forty-five year old vines on principally *caillottes* soils produce the La Jouline Vieilles Vignes bottling, thirty percent of which ferments and ages in one-year old barrels. The 2006 was downright Burgundian – *with* the freshness of the Loire. Textured and layered, it was creamy, full, ripe and elegant, with flavors of citrus and minerals. PMG!

The domaine's reds come from vines planted on a mix of *caillottes* and *terres blanches* soils. They grapes are cold soaked for a week before fermentation, which lasts two weeks. The grapes macerate for another week after fermentation. The wines go through malolactic and age for a year in oak barrels (3 year rotation) before bottling without having been fined or filtered. There are two cuvées.

The 2006 "domaine" bottling, tasted in 2010, was a suave, smooth weave of plum, cherry and black tea flavors with an appetizingly tangy finish. Cuvée La Jouline is made from slightly older vines —35 as compared to 25 years old – and ages for 15 months in slightly newer oak. The 2005, also tasted in 2010, was brighter and fuller than the 2006 domaine, but equally smooth, suave and well-balanced. A pleasure.

🎻 By the Glass

🎻 Roger Champault et Fils

5, route de Foulot, Champtin,18300 Crézancy;02 48 79 00 03; www.rogerchampaultetfils.fr

This family domaine traces its origins to the 11th century. Today it consists of 20 hectares and is run by Claude and Laurent, the sons of Roger. Viticulture seems vaguely eco-friendly — the soils are aerated as gently as possible in the spring, for example. Grapes are machine harvested. There are numerous bottlings, including a Menetou-Salon and a Pinot-Noir based eccentricity called Perpétuelle which is aged by the solera system used in the making of sherry.

The best wines I've tasted from this domaine are two whites from the 2002 vintage, which I sampled at the Salon des Vins de Loire in early 2003. The first was their basic Sancerre *blanc* "Les Pierris" which comes from predominantly *terres blanches* soils (70%) and the rest from *caillottes* soils. The wine was herbaceous, grassy and mineral, with a light petrol note. It had character. The second was the 2002 Sancerre *blanc* from the well-known lieu-dit "Clos du Roy". Broader and higher pitched than the previous wine, it was grassy, grapefruity and herbaceous, and revealed a strong mineral core. The 2001 Sancerre blanc "Clos du Roy" was mineral, lightly gas-y, adequately ripe and balanced. Tasty. A 1999 Sancerre blanc "Côte de Champtin" was quite oaky but also creamy and relatively ripe with pleasant lemon flavors.

A barrel-aged 2000 Sancerre rouge made from 60 year old vines on the lieu-dit "Côte de Champtin" was relatively light (the vintage played some role here) but appealing and rather accurate. Not a bad bistro wine. The '99 red "Champtin" was lightly gamy and quite drying. My least favorite.

I haven't been as fortunate with recent vintages. Tasted in January 2011, the 2008 Sancerre *blanc* "Les Pierris" was tart but not shrill (normal for 2008), it had some depth and was mellow, chewy and mineral, but I was put off by funky notes as well as unidentifiable vegetal flavors – which I'd also found in the 2003 bottling tasted in early 2004. The 2008 rosé was simply bland, flat and, curiously, watery but not dilute. Similarly watery but not dilute was the 2007 Pierris *rouge*. This wine comes from red and sandy soils, the grapes are cold soaked for 48 to 72 hours, and the wine is aged half in tank and half in demi-muids. The wine's siena-like color surprised me, particularly given the cold-soaking, and the only taste sensation was one of unripe tannins.

I dislike being so severe about the work of sincere vignerons. There is obviously an audience for these wines – including people whose taste I respect – but I don't understand why.

By the Glass

Château de Sancerre/Marnier-Lapostelle
18300 Sancerre; 02.48.78.51.52; www.grand-marnier.com

This 46 hectare domaine has been owned by the Marnier-Lapostelle family – better known for Grand Marnier — since 1919. Their entry level Sancerre *blanc* is made from grapes grown on a mix of Sancerre's three classic soil types. Harvest is both by machine (70%) and hand (30%), and the grapes ferment in temperature controlled stainless steel tanks. The 2006 was just fine – if you weren't paying attention. Aromas typical of the appellation mixed with hints of mint and chlorophyll. The wine seemed somewhat stretched, a bit confected and lacking definition.

The Cuvée du Connétable, in a heavy bottle, is their top-of-the-line Sancerre. It comes from their best parcels, which include parts of the Clos du Roy. Entirely hand harvested, it ferments and ages in oak barrels (20% new) for a year, and spends six months in tank after *assemblage* and before bottling. The 2005, tasted in 2009, was extremely oaky, allowing only brief glimpses of attractive grapefruit flavors. The finish was somewhat astringent and hot, and the wine was surprisingly sour and acid for such a fine vintage.

🐌 Domaine Jean-Claude Chatelain
(See Pouilly)

The firm produces Sancerre from purchased grapes. The 2008 Sancerre *blanc* "Sélection Jean-Claude Chatelain," tasted in December 2010, was a wake-up call of acidity with undertones of ivy and citrus zests.

🐌 Domaine Daniel Chotard
18300 Crézancy-en-Sancerre; 02.48.79.08.12;
daniel.chotard@wanadoo.fr; www.chotard-sancerre.com

Melomane Daniel Chotard is the most recent head of this family domaine that was created more than two centuries ago. Today, the domaine has 11.75 hectares of vines, chiefly on Kimmeridgian marl soils. The Chotards practice sustainable farming. White grapes are harvested by hand and machine, reds by hand, and rosés by machine.

The grapes for domaine bottlings in white, rosé, and red all ferment in temperature- controlled stainless steel tanks. The white ages on its fine lees until bottling. The 2006, tasted in 2008, was grippy and focused, very fresh with mineral, flint and floral notes. The 2008 was as revivifying as the vintage and quite nice, with flavors of lime, verbena and mineral. The 2008 rosé had attractive light strawberry fruit but was tart verging on sour. Much better was a 2006 rosé — dry, appetizing and quite mineral with strawberry-ginger-and-stone accents. The 2006 red was firm and medium-bodied, with good cherry fruit. A 2007 red, tasted in 2010, was also firm but light (not surprising for the vintage).

🐌 Clos la Néore
Le bourg 18300 Chavignol; 02 48 54 12 50

You never know whom you're going to bump into in a good wine village. When walking to a winery in Chavignol two years ago, who did I spy but Nady Foucault from Saumur-Champigny. Natural. As he was married to Anne Vatan, a gracious, lovely young woman, who was out working on the one hectare of vines that had remained in the family after her father Edmond retired. The spiritual father of many of today's vignerons, Vatan worked much like his neighbor, Francis Cotat, and made rough, quirky, green apple, Muscat and petrol-scented Sancerres which he sold to Taillevent. One suspects that the marriage of Anne and Nady was, indeed, made in heaven. But I digress.

Nady, never out of character, corralled me and my friends and brought us to the Vatan home – in front of which he had installed handsome (and historic) gates retrieved from Fontevraud Abbey near Saumur.

Soon Anne, in pink overalls and flipflops, joined us and brought out the 2008 which had been bottled the week before. With a potential of 14º, the finished wine was 13.8º. It was dense and creamy. The oak was evident but seemed to have melted into the whole. There was a sense of chalkiness, vibrant mint accents and an overall sense of a fast flowing stream.

I had tasted the 2007 about 8 months earlier when my notes read, "crystalline, mineral, light oak, tart but racy." Now the wine, with 13.5º alcohol, was full and textured, dry but tender, and scented with anise. It had lots of character but demanded attention. Not a wine to glug in a noisy brasserie. As so many fine Chavignols do, it made me think of Chablis. And we talked about the similarity of the two appellations, separated only, when you come right down to it, by a grape variety.

Ample and pungent was the lightly hot 2005, a toothsome weave of menthol, grapefruit and gooseberry. And although this wine did have a whiff of the varietal characteristics of Sauvignon Blanc, it still recalled Chablis.

Then, a '96. It was a delectably appetizing blend of creamed corn, cream of asparagus, verbena and honey. Next, an '83. With its bouquet of hay and wax and herbal tea, it could have been an aged Chenin. On the palate, however, it once again made us say "Chablis." A beautifully aged Chablis. Anne disappeared and came back with a grimy bottle. "This is very anecdotal," she said, pouring the burnished gold wine into our glasses. There was the scent of honeyed hay again, and verbena, and the furniture wax of a fine antique shop. Very much in the style of the '83 and the '96 except that they had a tiny bit more vigor and bounce. So what was it?

"It's called ChaChaCha," said Anne, pronouncing the words ShaShaSha (as a French person would). It was a wine made from Chardonnay vines, from Chablis, planted on Monts Damnés, and therefore in Chavignol. Edmond Vatan long ago realized the kinship uniting good grapes grown on Kimmeridgian marl hillsides.

Excellent

François Cotat
18300 Chavignol; 02.48.54.21.27

François Cotat officially took over the family domaine in 1998, a succession that had to be a double-edged sword: on the one hand, he was assuming the mantle of legend-in-his-own-time vigneron Paul Cotat; on the other hand, he was stepping into the shoes of legend-in-his-own time vigneron,

Paul Cotat, with whom he had worked for many years in preparation for this eventuality.

The transition appears to be seamless. After working in the ramshackle grange shared by his father and uncle, François recently built new cellars. Today he has roughly 4 hectares of which a bit over one hectare is on Monts Damnés, .9 ha on Les Culs de Beaujeu; and .9 on La Grande Côte. The latest acquisition was a small parcel of young Sauvignon Blanc vines on the rocky, chalky soils of Les Caillottes.

François continues to work much the way his forebears did: harvest late, no added yeasts, no *débourbage*, fermentation in small tanks or barrels of 600, 500 or 300 litre size in six or seven year rotation. Rack the wine at Christmas; rack again in March. First bottling in May; second in June. In fact, the only thing that appears to have changed is the world *around* the Cotats: a significant percentage of the local vignerons have begun working in the same way and making wines that taste as if they could have been made by the family. Herewith, a sampling of François Cotat's line-up.

The first three wines to be described were tasted in April 2011, starting with the 2006 Les Monts Damnés, which immediately recalled Chenin, with aromas of herbal tea and quinine. A big, generous, textured wine, it drank like a Vouvray from the Domaine Huet, with flavors of stone and quinine, lemon zest, a nuance of oxidation, lime, and tilleul. It weighed in at 13.5% alcohol, the heat of which remained in the distant background, like an echo. It was one of those wines you just keep on tasting and tasting, discovering now a note of papaya or maybe mango, now and accent of ginger. And, lo, you've finished the bottle.

The 2007 Les Culs de Beaujeu, similarly, opened with slightly sweet Chenin-like aromas and traces of lime and tilleul. Dryer on the palate than the nose suggested, it came across as a true *sec-tendre*. (My guess would be 2 to 3 grams residual sugar.) On the palate it was long and strong, with a distinct mineral core and notes of lime zests, lemon curd, quinine, pea pods, and salt. It was smooth and suave, mouthwatering and, as the French say, *bien dans sa peau* – which I translate as 'at home with itself.'

Now my experience with the 2008 Les Caillottes was what might be called a "teachable" moment. It's certainly something I haven't lived before and don't know how to explain.

Initial nose, basic enough: creamed corn; attack: tight, steely, but wait, a hint of corkiness. I put the bottle back in the fridge to try later. The next day the wine reeked and, without tasting, I assumed, This was sulfur speaking. I returned the wine to the fridge. I knew that a couple of vignerons with fine palates were coming to see me in a couple of days and thought I'd taste it again with them.

The day arrives. I pull the wine from the fridge, pour it into the first glass and sniff. It smells just fine. Typical Cotat Sancerre — oxymoron watch— loaded with aromas of lime and verbena. The creamed corn is still there and so is that corky note. I'm stumped because a corked wine, to me, if it's really and truly corked, always seems broken or aborted or disembodied on the palate. And this wine was very much alive. It was forceful, patrician, commanding, transforming that 2008 acidity into a statement of authority. Two days later, the wine was even better – steely, aerodynamic, a quinine rapier. Yet there was still that corky note that came and went like so many of the fleeting sensations in wine that come and go and come back again – though it completely disappeared when the wine was paired with food. And by now, I've finished the bottle.

A handful of earlier tasting notes: I tasted the 2006 Culs de Beaujeu in spring 2010 at Jacky Dallais, one of the best restaurants in the Loire. Lightly off-dry, it was a bit hot and rustic, with notes of mint. One of my companions, a winemaker in Bourgueil, thought it was corked. I didn't and neither did the sommelier. But it was surprisingly dull. I tasted the 2001 Cuvée Paul demi-sec, named for François' son, in June of 2010 at La Pomme d'Or, a good restaurant in Sancerre. It was well-balanced, with flavors of creamed corn, celery seed and minerals. Had I known then what I know now, I'd have taken each of these bottles home and watched them evolve over time.

Peter Vezan, Cotat's exporter, was kind enough to round up three bottles for me in 2005 when I was working on my Wines of France book. Each was fascinating, starting with the 2002 Les Monts Damnés which was a vin de table: it had been denied the Sancerre label because it had too much residual sugar. It did have a fair amount of residual sugar but so what? It was also rather oaky. But it was greatly nuanced and I liked that a lot. The 2004 La Grand Côte, also off-dry but less sweet than the 2002, mingled flavors of lime, tilleul, and minerals. And the 2004 Monts Damnés wowed me with its complexity. Indeed, its nose, alone, gave me the chills. Its tartness was typical of 2004. There were notes of iodine, lime and tilleul, an edge of sweetness and an abundance of character.

&• Excellent

&• Pascal Cotat
Chemin des Groux 18300 Sancerre; 02 48 54 14 00;
f: 02 48 54 14 00

In late fall of 1990 I made my first pilgrimage to the cellars of the Cotat brothers, Francis and Paul. My appointment was with Francis, and my friend, the brilliant and hilarious *caviste* Jean-François Dubreuil, on his way back to his native Vendée from Beaujolais where he had been selecting his *primeurs*, accompanied me.

A grey day. We parked the car somewhere level and climbed a narrow dirt path to the barn that served as the winemaking facility. It was filled with aging demi-muids and a press circa 1880. We were met by Francis, a thin man of a certain age, with thinning reddish hair and a tentative smile. At first blush, he seemed self-effacing but, like an old diesel engine, once contact had been made, he purred on cheerily for hours.

A born *raconteur*, he explained the unofficial motto of the domaine: "On n'a pas le droit mais on le prend" (we don't have the right but we take it). He explained: Sancerre sometimes gets distinctly smaller billing than Chavignol on the Cotat label because, INAO be damned, the Cotats believe that, as Chavignol had been more famous than Sancerre, they were cheated out of their rightful appellation. These wines should be called Chavignol.

Anyone who has spent any time drinking a wide sampling of Sancerres will be tempted to agree. The Cotats don't have much land but what they do have is, as Spencer Tracy might have said, *cherss*. The two branches of the family share four hectares of hillside vines, all on Kimmeridgian marl, on the region's most celebrated slopes. Francis and Pascal, Francis's son, make, among other wines, a Les Monts Damnés bottling and a La Grande Côte bottling.

Cotat could extend the application of his aforementioned dictum much further. For example, by law, Sancerre is supposed to be dry but taste a Cotat wine: is it dry or is it sweet? Mostly the wines are dry, albeit with a bit of residual sugar, but you never really know until you taste. And then you don't care because these are, for the most part, very special, cult Sancerres. Big, mouthwatering, Rhone-like Sancerres. The Cotat family has been making Sancerre that might or might not be *"moelleux"* for more than fifty years — long before the trendy cuvées of '89 and '90. (And the Cotats have always made Sancerre to age. Restaurants lucky enough to carry their wines often list a half-dozen or more vintages.)

His wines, Cotat told us, are made as they have always been made. Hand harvest, of course — given the pitch of the Cotat's steep vineyards, they can't even use a tractor. Organic fertilizers. No destemming. The merest decanting to keep most of the "nourishing yeasts." Barrel fermentation. No temperature control. No fining. No filtering. The wines are racked at the end of January — the week before the new moon — and again, two months later, when the phase of the moon favorably affects atmospheric pressure and tides.

We taste the '89 la Grande Côte. It's rich and textured, an opulent flow of licorice, peach, apricot, blossoms and almonds. Completely original. Jean-François and I were in wine orbit while Francis was telling us how they'd judge the ripeness of the harvest. Not ripe enough? No problem. He and his dozen or so harvesters, all friends, went fishing.

On to the '89 Grand Côte *moelleux*, really more of a *demi-sec*, which reprised the flavors of the *sec*, adding hints of oak, pineapple and orange zests. An '88 Monts Damnés was another stunner, simultaneously incisive and luxuriant.

Then the '93 la Grand Côte and the lightly off-dry '94 les Monts Damnés. Surprisingly they each recalled Champagne (without the bubbles) as well as Chenin. (Maybe not so surprising, given the soil similarities with Champagne and the linked DNA lineage with Chenin.) Each wine was creamy, lime-tinged and mineral, with mellow fruit flavors and a hint of old wood. A bit rustic for some tastes, but I adored them.

In a state of euphoria we went for lunch in Sancerre. Jean-François, another born *raconteur*, explained the concept of the Screwpull to Francis, who'd never heard of the gadget. (Jean-François later sent him one.) And on to the Clos Néore to visit Francis's good friend, Edmond Vatan, a fellow unreconstructed *artiste-vigneron*. More tasting, more stories, and back to the Cotat cellar where we sat on improvised benches and pulled corks, tasted wine, and told stories late into the night.

In 1997, when Pascal, officially, at least, succeeded Francis, they built spanking clean cellars in Sancerre. Pascal has a garage just beyond the town's centre and they extended this to accommodate a pneumatic press that feeds the juice of the crushed grapes, by gravity, into tanks – and later into old demi-muids. To one side, there's a small, rustically cute tasting room which is where I had my most recent tasting with Francis and Pascal in May 2009.

Between the two visits, I never missed an opportunity to drink Cotat. For example, in the fall of 2005 I tasted the 2004 rosé and the 2004 La Grande Côte. Meaty and high strung, the first was a rosé that drank like a white. Very mineral, vibrant with citrus zests, it was both a delight and a discovery as well as a serious rosé. In fact, it recalled Rosé de Ricey, the drop-dead rosés from the Champagne region. (Alas, the Cotats are phasing out the rosé!) The Grande Côte was rich and lively, with a gram or two of residual sugar. With its deep mineral and quinine flavors, it was absolutely riveting, a *vin d'exception*.

Our May 2009 tasting opened with the lightly off-dry 2008 Monts Damnés that had been bottled barely a month earlier. Minerals, lime, stone, great freshness and a remarkable amount of personality, particularly for a wine so recently bottled. Then an unfined, unfiltered rosé that was labeled Vin de Table. Why wasn't it Sancerre? I asked. Because the local politicians had declassified the land from appellation status because they wanted to use it for a parking lot. All politics is local. And often, as in this case, moronic. The wine was a pure jewel — firm, mineral, simultaneously dry and tender, with scents of rose petals.

Far from lost in the midst of a four-vintage vertical of La Grande Côte was a dulcet but definitive tisane of a 2005 Monts Damnés but first, the 2008 Grande Côte that provoked my "eureka" moment. Like the first Monts Damnés, this wine, too, had just been bottled. It seemed to contain the breeze itself, so expressive was it of the great ventilation of its site. It was tender, too, and had a resilient core of minerals, quinine, and herbal tea which mixed with salt in the long, long finish. And, Eureka!, it reminded me of Vouvray! I dare anyone to have guessed the grape variety. And I started thinking that maybe the reason we all love Cotat wines so much – or one of the reasons – is that they recall great Vouvrays – or at least meet them in wine paradise.

The 2007, very much in the family style, had beguiling notes of lime and lime zest but showed better later that year. (See below.) The 2006 had delicate peach notes and a creamy, mellow texture. The wine flowed like a fast stream, spreading flavors of peach and herbal tea over the palate. The plump, slightly hot 2005, perhaps the richest of them all, seemed closed, coming across as less expressive than the others at that moment.

Next we tasted Pascal's first vintage of La Grande Côte, the 1997. Lightly oxidized – the neck level was low –, it was nearly viscous, with light scents of pineapple, creamed corn, preserved lemon, lemon zest, and a long, herbal tea finish. Then the off-dry '96, which added notes of licorice to the above palette.

The Cotats make a Cuvée Speciale when, in a given year, a specific "lot" seems to merit its own bottling. And so Francis uncorked two. The first was a '90 La Grande Côte Cuvée Spéciale. Francis explained that hail had removed all the leaves on the vines and the grapes had burned. On the nose, the wine seemed oxidized – which Francis thought came about when he changed the corks – but on the palate, the wine was fresh. Hot but fresh, potent and creamy, with flavors of butterscotch, stone, chamomile, tilleul and minerals. The last wine tasted was the 2003 La Grande Côte Cuvée Spéciale, harvested with a potential alcohol of 18%. The wine spent two years in oak and had about 25 grams residual sugar. A pure delight, a nuanced *moelleux*, a cream mixed with honey and herbal tea. Then on to lunch at

Cheu l'Zib where we brought all the opened bottles and supplemented them with good reds from Menetou-Salon.

One last tasting note: I spent New Year's Eve 2009 with one of my favorite winemaking couples, Guy and Annie Bossard, in the heart of Muscadet country. One of the bottles I brought was Cotat's 2007 La Grande Côte, which I insisted Guy taste blind. While he applied himself to the challenge at hand, I wrote, the wine, 13% alcohol, has evolved beautifully since tasted in May. It is supple, off-dry and tangy, with flavors of verbena, lime, grapefruit, mineral and stone. It's creamy, with grassy accents and mouthwatering minerality. Very real. Unique. A wine to savor, a presence. Guy's first comments: "finesse, elegance and power; harmonious, good progression, powerful." He guesses it's a Chenin Blanc and is stunned when I say it's Sauvignon Blanc. Well, he says, it must be a grand terroir to so dominate the varietal and he asks if it's from Benjamin Dagueneau, as it's in the refined, harmonious style of François Chidaine, with whom Benjamin had worked. So where do you put all that on a point scale? Pretty high up, I'd say.

🐚 Excellent

🐚 Domaine François Crochet (formerly Robert Crochet)
Marcigoué, 18300 Bué-en-Sancerre; 02.48.58.21.77;
françoiscrochet@wanadoo.fr

In 1998 François Crochet joined his father Robert in working the family vines. Prior to taking the reins, he studied at the Lycée Viticole de Beaune and worked at wineries the world over, at Château Angélus in Bordeaux, with Bruno Clair in Burgundy, and in New Zealand. His first vintage was 2000. And he quickly emerged as one of Sancerre's rising stars.

Today François and wife Corinne own 10.5 hectares of vines. These are spread out over some thirty parcels within four communes – Bué, Sancerre, Crézancy and Thauvenay. Viticulture lies somewhere between sustainable and organic farming. Crochet likes to keep yields between 35 and 45 hl/ha. All grapes are harvested by hand. (As Crochet's parcels tend to be dispersed around the countryside, he transports the grapes in vibrating bins to keep them from being crushed *en route.*) Crochet makes four cuvées of white Sancerre, two of red and a rosé.

The 2006s were all tasted in December 2010; the 2005s and 2004s were tasted at the Salon des Vins de Loire in February 2006.

The entry level white, or the *cuvée classique,* assembles grapes from all of Crochet's soils, to wit: 80% *caillottes,* 10% each of silex and *terres blanches.* Crochet aims for yields between 50 and 60 hl/ha, presses the grapes slowly, ferments the wine in tank, and ages the wine on its lees for six months. The 2006 was beginning to develop mellow, Chenin-like flavors. While it didn't have the depth of the Chêne Marchand bottling, it was lighter on its feet. Clean, clear cut and straightforward. A 2005, tasted in February 2006 — three weeks after the wine had been bottled – was full, ripe and very promising.

Les Amoureuses comes from 30 year old vines on *terres blanches* soils. The name "les Amoureuses" reflects the soil type: in wet weather, when mud stuck to the soles of shoes, Berrichons (people from the Berry) said that "la terre est amoureuse" (the earth is in love). Yields for this bottling are kept between 40 and 50 hl/ha. Eighty-percent of the grapes ferment in tank and twenty percent in 500 litre new oak barrels. The wine ages on its lees for over ten months and is fined but not filtered for bottling.

The 2006 Amoureuses, smooth and creamy, was also evolving in the Chenin direction. A white with character, it had a clear sense of place. A 2005, *brut de cuve*, was mineral and textured. Truly promising. The 2004, limpid, structured and fragrant, was very pure with an appetizing mineral undertow.

The Chêne Marchand bottling comes from Crochet's one hectare of 40 year-old vines on that famous hillside's calcareous soils. Vinification is similar to that for Les Amoureuses and the wine is bottled without having been filtered. As with the other 2006s, by December 2010, it was mellow and reminiscent of Chenin. Ample and textured, with perhaps a gram of residual sugar, it was also saline. More importantly, it had a real sense of *terroir*. It wasn't majestic but definitely in the peerage. A Sancerre with flavor and vigor, as was the deep, textured 2005. Very impressive. The 2004 was a waterfall of purity, minerality and character. Majestic and site specific.

Crochet's most recent issue is his cuvée "Exils." Given the name, it's no surprise the grapes grow on silex soils, in this case, on a recently purchased parcel in Thauvenay. The vines are eight years old; the wine ferments in tank (though up to 20% may ferment in new oak) and spends six months on its lees before being lightly fined (but not filtered) for bottling. The results are excellent. Both the 2009 and the 2010 reveal ambition and mastery. The 2009 is so supple as to be almost tender. Lime-tinged, mineral and chalky, it is quite fine; the 2010, highstrung and pellucid, is crystalline and as fresh as a mountain stream. When these vines get older, watch out!

Crochet's basic red comes 25+ year old vines from parcels with either pure limestone or clay-limestone soils. Yields are generally between 45 and 50 hl/ha. After harvest, the grapes are cold soaked and then vat for 15 to 25 days. Half of the wine ages in tank, half in 228 litre barrels. After 18 months, the wine is bottled without having been fined or filtered. The 2004 was mellow, with fine fruit and admirable structure. It is a mark of Crochet's mastery of his craft that neither this cuvée nor the more "serious" red bottling were marked by oak.

That 'serious' bottling is called Réserve de Marcigoué. Its grapes are, on an average, 35 to 40 years old and come several celebrated *lieux-dits*, among them, Petit Chemarin and Grand Chemarin. After destemming, the wines vat for 20 to 30 days and age for a year in 500 litre barrels, of which half are new oak. The 2004 had fine balance and structure. It had been bottled for only one month when I tasted it and was extremely promising.

🍇 Excellent

🍇 Domaine Lucien Crochet
Place de l'Eglise, 18300 Bué; 02.48.54.08.10;
www.lucien-crochet.fr//

Domaine Lucien Crochet was one of Sancerre's best winemakers and finest ambassadors back in the fall of 1990 when I went to the region to visit producers for the first edition of my Loire book. I'd started researching the book in the westernmost regions of the Loire, in Muscadet and Anjou, each of which was undergoing a thrilling revolution in quality. Sancerre – the complacency of most of its producers, the mediocrity of most of its wines – came as a real disappointment. Lucien Crochet's wines, however, showed me what Sancerre *could* be. It wasn't simply a case of being the best of a bad lot. Crochet's concentrated, elegant Sancerres had nothing in common with the high-yield, under-ripe, over-chaptalized Sancerres I was tasting. Serious and fine-tuned, these were – and still are — Sancerres for *haute cuisine* and contemplative sipping.

At the time, Lucien's son Gilles, an articulate, thoughtful Dijon-trained enologist, had taken over the running of the domaine and that is still the case.

The property consists of 38 hectares, mostly in and around the village of Bué, including some of its most famous lieux-dits, as well as parcels in neighboring Sancerre, Crézancy and Vinon. Additionally, Crochet augments volume by 15% by purchasing the entire harvest of a neighboring grower. (Crochet manages the vines.) Crochet's offices, with vast meeting rooms and modern underground cellars seem to cover half of the village.

Back in 1990, I doubt that I spent much time discussing viticulture other than, say, pruning and yields, with Crochet. Mostly we talked about vinification. A sign of the times. Given his perspicacity, it's no surprise that Crochet has adopted rigorous vineyard practices – increasing vine density to

8,700 plants per hectare, growing cover plants between vine rows, using organic vine treatments, and so forth. Harvest is by hand.

Crochet has 29 hectares of Sauvignon Blanc, most of it planted on *caillottes* soils, mid-slope, between 240 and 260 meters, with south, south-east, and south-western exposures.

For the domaine's basic white, Le Chêne, whole bunches of grapes are pressed in order to avoid bruising the skins. Fermentation occurs in thermo-regulated stainless steel tanks and lasts for about 35 days, with frequent stirring up of the lees. The wine is racked in July and bottled in September. Both the 2006, tasted in 2009, and the 2007, tasted in 2011, had the same nearly transparent, platinum tinged pallor. Rather serious, deliciously tingling, the 2006 had an inviting mineral, stone, and lime nose. It was crystalline, focused and bordered on elegant. The 2007, with rich sur lie marrow, came on strong in the pungency department. With aeration, it calmed down, settling into flavors of gooseberry, grapefruit, lemon zest, and a note of licorice. Simultaneously full and streamlined, it all but demanded to be paired with shellfish.

Grapes from his oldest vines, in the best vintages, make Crochet's Cuvée Prestige. The grapes ferment for thirty days in temperature-controlled tanks, with a regular stirring up of the lees. The pale gold 2005, tasted in 2009, was envigoratingly fresh, so light on its feet you didn't feel the 14.5% alcohol – although *that* may explain the note of rock crystal sugar on the palate. A Sancerre for *hautest cuisine*. The 2006, tasted in spring 2011, came across like a big-boned Montlouis, with rich tisane, stone, quinine and apple compote flavors.

Crochet has recently expanded his line, adding a bottling from Le Cul de Beaujeu and another from Le Chêne Marchand. The 2009 Cul de Beaujeu, tasted in spring 2011, was graceful, textured, and harmonious from beginning to end, sheer pleasure, with its fresh flavors of mineral, stone and lemon zest. The 2008 Chêne Marchand, tasted at the same time, was a veritable cascade of purity and freshness. Nervy, racy, tense, it made 2008s characteristic acidity downright exciting, and there were intimations of plushness beneath its tight surface.

Crochet follows essentially the same procedures for his rosé as he does for most of his white bottlings. He presses whole clusters of grapes, then transfers the must to tanks where it will ferment for around twenty days. The 2007, tasted in 2011, was the color of pale, watered silk. Vinous, tart and a bit green, it drank like a white, with a clean, dry finish.

The Pinot Noir for Crochet's reds grow on the *caillottes* and Kimmeridgian marl soils of east and southeast facing slopes. Grapes for the La Croix du Roy bottling ferment for 28 days, with a daily punching down of the cap and pumping over of the must. Half of the wine ages in barrel, half in stainless steel tanks for a period of 16 months. The 2005, tasted in 2009, was smooth and balanced, appetizingly tart, with flavors of ripe cherries and sweet spices. A charming wine, it benefits from being slightly chilled. The 2006, tasted in the spring of 2011, was a mouthwatering blend of black cherry, black tea and strawberry with light oak flavors. I managed to down quite a bit of it with well-aged cheddar.

Like the white version, Crochet's Cuvée Prestige *rouge* is made from the domaine's oldest Pinot Noir vines, (50+, on average), and is produced only in the best vintages. After harvest, the grapes undergo a six-day cold pre-fermentation followed by a temperature controlled fermentation for seven days and vatting for three day post-fermentation. The cap is regularly punched down and the fermenting must pumped over. The wine ages in barrels – of either 228 or 600 litre capacity — on a three year rotation.

The substantial 2005, tasted in 2009 had juicy, focused flavors of morello cherries and sweet spices. Oak made the finish slightly drying but food helped. In all, a fleshy, fresh, succulent wine, downright mouthwatering. The 2005 was the vintage Crochet was selling in the spring of 2011 and it was about to be replaced by the 2006 — a vivacious, delicate but definite Sancerre *rouge* with rose petal accents, emerging flavors of oak and an appetizing bitter note in the finish.

At D'Antan Sancerrois, a wine-serious restaurant in Bourges, I drank a lovely 2006 red, a lower-priced bottling sold only to restaurants. In June 2010, the wine was smooth, well balanced, flavorful, just right for a good dinner.

The heatwave of 1989 inspired a number of Sancerre and Pouilly producers to make a sweet, late-harvest wine from shriveled and/or botrytized grapes. Frankly, this is not my favorite expression but the best – and Crochet's are always among the best – are impressive, thought-and-conversation provoking, and could inspire some interesting food and wine pairings. The wine also makes a good aperitif which is how I served Crochet's 2002 Sancerre Blanc Vendange du 19 Octobre on Christmas day, 2010. I think the wine was closer to 15 degrees alcohol rather than the stated 14 and tasted over-ripe but not *moelleux*. The grapes had been picked twenty days after the normal harvest when the berries were very ripe, golden, and slightly dessicated. Two-thirds fermented in tank, one-third in barrel. Nicely balanced, fresh, with attractive minerality and very fine acidity, it was long and balanced, and proved very popular, even with initial naysayers.

🍇 Domaine Didier Dagueneau

(See Pouilly)

The Dagueneaus have 60 *ares* on the Kimmeridgian marl and *caillottes* soils of Les Monts Damnés, a slope pitched at a 40 to 60 degree incline. From their very first vintage there, 2005, this cuvée has been stunning: Sancerre doesn't get better than this. The grape variety disappears. The wine is simply a grandiose expression of its terroir. And a vivid reminder that Sancerre shares the sames soils as Chablis. This is, indeed, a Grand Cru. My notes from vintage to vintage vary little but here goes: the 2009, tasted from barrel in 2010, was long, textured, and layered with flavors of peach and mandarin oranges. Incredible raciness. A diamond. The 2008 mixed flavors of creamed corn with those of citrus, melon, peach and salt. Simply magnificent. The oak is there but is merely a light support. The wine flows over the palate like satin over bare skin. Chiseled, racy, fresh. A joy. The 2007 was crystalline, broad, racy and pellucid with devastating purity and exquisite freshness. A *vin de méditation.*

🍇 Domaine Vincent & Jean-Yves Delaporte

Chavignol 18300 Sancerre; 02.48.78.03.32;
www.domaine-vincent-delaporte.com

I vaguely recall tasting with Vincent Delaporte in the fall of 1990, in his gleaming cellars, sipping his firm, sleek Sancerres, and talking about his son, Jean-Yves Delaporte, a student at the Lycée Viticole de Beaune, who would soon be joining him on the domaine.

Today, the two oversee the 24 hectare domaine, 75% of which is planted to Sauvignon Blanc, spread out over some twenty parcels, most of which are exposed to the south. Silex characterizes 50% of the domaine's soils, the remainder is an even mix of *caillottes* and *terres blanches,* with a rather high vine density of 8800 plants a hectare.

The Delaportes practice sustainable farming. Gilles Magnin, their viticulturist, surveys each and every plant, thins clusters, and keeps yields between 48 to 65 hl/ha. Grapes for the basic white are harvested by machine, the rest by hand. And the basic white, assembled from 28 different plots from vines with an average age of 35 years old, ferments in thermoregulated stainless steel tanks at around 18 degrees Celsius. The wine ages on its lees until it is prepared for bottling in March.

Are we in Alsace? Are we on that noble Grand Cru Rangen de Thann? That's what I marveled at while tasting Delaporte's 2006 Sancerre *blanc*.

This was in December 2009. A pellucid wine, full and flavorful, somehow snowy (!), with scents of peach and apricot against a backdrop of quinine, tea and slate. Definitely PMG. Discreet and elegant, the 2010, was an ethereal blend of lemon, lime, verbena and thyme.

The Cuvée Maxime Vieilles Vignes is even more deliciously intriguing. The bottling thus named comes from 50+ year old vines on *terres blanches*. Harvest (by hand) takes place sometime in October when the grapes are fully and completely ripe. The grapes are then hand sorted, lightly pressed and placed in 228 litre Tronçais barrels of one to three wines. Production is limited to 12 barrels. The wine stays in barrel for seven months with a regular stirring up of the fine lees. It is lightly filtered at bottling in spring.

The 2006, tasted in January 2011, was sensual and mellow. With its light grapefruit flavors mixed with those of tropical fruit, minerals, and mild vanilla from the oak, it made be think of a grand Pinot Gris from Alsace. Or maybe a Châteauneuf-du-Pape *blanc*. In any event, it was a sumptuous wine and fit for *un poisson noble*. The statuesque 2009, tasted in June 2011, was a waterfall of freshness and purity, with fine flavors of minerals and lemon zests. I'm a bit worried about the oak which, for now, seems to stand apart. But there's so much to admire about this wine that I'm hopeful the oak will blend into the whole in a year or two.

Delaporte makes two cuvées of red, a basic Sancerre *rouge* and a Cuvée Maxime. In one of those bizarre quirks of communication, whenever I have requested samples of their red wines, the Delaportes have most kindly sent me their whites. I will persevere. When I do get to taste those reds, the notes will be on my website.

Recommended

⚘ Domaine Bernard Fleuriet et Fils
La Vauvise 18300 Menetou-Ratel; 02 48 79 34 09;
fleuriet.vauvise@wanadoo.fr

I prefer the whites from this 19 hectare family domaine over the reds. The Sancerre *blanc* "Tradition" comes from Sancerre's classic soils – half *terres blanches*, half *caillottes*. Wines ferment in thermoregulated concrete tanks in a cellar that was renovated in 2008. Tasted in December 2010, the nicely ripe 2006 wasn't majestic but it was a lovely Loire Sauvignon Blanc, with flavors of apple, lemon, even a suggestion of quince, and lovely balance. "La Baronne," the deluxe bottling, comes from the best slopes with *terres blanches* soils. The grapes are hand harvested, hand sorted, fermented at low temperatures in barriques, and are bottled without filtration. Fresh and structured, the 2006 was ripe, with notes of pineapple and gooseberry as well as oak, and as the wine aerated, it seemed to become creamier.

I followed the wine for three days and, on the last, found it solid, substantial, with steel girding and tangy citrus zest flavors. The wine goes the distance.

My reservation about the domaine's reds is that they taste like Cabernet Franc. There are two cuvées – "Tradition" and "Anthocyane" — and both see a certain amount of oak. The latter is by far the more interesting bottling. Handharvested, destemmed, put through a long maceration, and aged in barriques, it is bottled unfiltered. The 2005, tasted in January 2011, was smooth and lightly tannic, with flavors of crushed berries. Very cablike to my palate, but still tasty. The domaine also makes wine in Menetou-Salon.

☙ Domaine Vincent Gaudry

☙ Excellent

18300 Sury-en-Vaux; 02.48.79.49.25; vincent.gaudry@wanadoo.fr; www.vincent-gaudry.com

Another domaine to watch. Forewarned: many of Gaudry's wines are *sui generis*... and downright fascinating.

Vincent Gaudry, 36, took over his family's 9 hectares of vines in 1993 and began the conversion to organic farming, followed, in turn, by a conversion to biodynamic farming. He has received Demeter's certification. And he has gone further. If there's a name for his system, I don't know it. Let's call it spiritual viticulture. Gaudry says he works with his energy and his emotions. In this, he's guided by an old vigneron who "speaks the language of energy." He recently installed three menhirs on his land. Actually, "installed" is not the right word. He tried to place these multi-ton blocks of stone in a triangular formation on his silex soils where he thought they would most benefit his vines only to find that they had, on their own initiative, moved to where *they* thought they should be. No joke.

Now, I know other idealistic, talented young vintners who've adopted a similar philosophy. They abandoned traditional viticulture and felt it sufficient to go into the vineyards and give off good vibes. Their land quickly reverted to a jungle-like state of nature. Still others rely on energy and emotions but rarely speak about it or take it as far as Gaudry has – and still make good wine.

As you might suspect, yields are kept low, between 35 to 40 hl/ha. Harvest is by hand. Only wild yeasts are used.

Most of Gaudry's production is Sancerre *blanc*, of which he seems to make a new cuvée year after year.

"Le Tournebride" is a bottling that comes from 30 year old vines on a mix of the three major soils – *terres blanches, caillottes* and silex. Tank fermented, it spends eight months on its fine lees before bottling. I tasted the 2010 a week after it had been bottled. It was very young and tight, with good balance, a satisfying thread of sur lie marrow, and flavors of mineral and slate. The 2006, 12.5 alcohol, tasted in 2009, was a quick trip to Chablis-land. Perfectly ripe, the wine was structured and fresh with lovely minerality, as well as flavors of lime and stone.

"Melodie de Vieilles Vignes" is the appropriately lyrical name for the cuvée made from 60 year old vines on Kimmeridgian marl soils. It spends eight months on its fine lees and is bottled without filtration. The 2010, with a truly vigorous thread of sur lie marrow, was deep and racy, with ingratiating flavors of lemon, ginger and mint. Bright and fresh, it definitely qualified as PMG. The 2006, tasted in 2009, was a Sancerre for *haute cuisine*: big, fresh, textured, quite mineral with appetizing flavors of lemon zests.

Then there's Mi-Chemin, another white, which is not made every year. It comes from grapes grown on silex-rich soils and consists of a single barrique – 300 bottles. The barrel is positioned at a specific point in the cellar that induces it to give off energy which, in turn, translates into a singular sappiness and minerality in the wine. (I asked Gaudry if he was applying principles of *Feng Shui* but he didn't seem to know what I was talking about.) Gaudry hopes the energy produced by this barrel will permeate his entire cellar. This bottling is neither fined nor filtered.

The 2009 was yet another example of Chablis GC in Sancerre – even though these wines grew on flinty soils. The grape variety disappeared. The wine was entirely terroir-driven, with flavors of minerals, lemon, and lime and a very long citrus-mineral finish. Another PMG.

Gaudry has one hectare of pinot noir. Vincengetorix is the name of Gaudry's red Sancerre. The grapes are destemmed and ferment in resin tanks. Gaudry simply adds a layer of co2 and then covers the tanks. There's no temperature control and Gaudry does nothing other than "regulate the energy" – for example, by opening a door. The wine ages for ten months or a year in old oak barrels. It is bottled without filtration. The 2009 was *sui generis*: light in color and saturation, it was dense, pure, cool, and lightly tannic, with flavors of spice and black tea. Characterful and mesmerizing. The 2005, tasted in 2009, needed a bit more time to digest its oak but the wine was still admirable – fresh, with lovely ripe strawberry and plum fruit, and fine balance.

"Le Sang des Serfs" corresponds to another red. The grapes are not destemmed, ferment in barrel, and the wine is not filtered at bottling. The pun in the name is deliberate. Gaudry is not talking about venison; he's talking about "the people" and there is an old-fashioned aspect to the wine in the best sense of the word. The 2008, tasted in January 2011, was utterly seductive, like a enthralling woman who becomes more beautiful the more you know her. On a more prosaic level: muted cherry and cherry pit flavors mixed with black tea, dried fruit and sweet spices. Yes, PMG.

❧ Domaine la Gemière/Daniel Millet & Fils

18300 Crézancy-en-Sancerre: 02.48.79.07.96;
daniel.millet5@wanadoo.fr

❧ Recommended

In 2000, Daniel Millet was joined on his 18 hectare domaine by his two sons, Sebastien and Nicolas. The Millet's practice sustainable farming, keep yields in the 60 hl/ha range and harvest by machine. Soils are chiefly calcareous.

The 2006 Sancerre *blanc* Cuvée Initiale was pungent, highstrung and more than a bit green, with loud vegetal and cat pee flavors. The "Louis/Cuvée d'Exception" bottling from the same year was riper and fuller, with flavors of peach and minerals. The grapes for this cuvée undergo skin contact and the wine displays the thick texture of this technique. It needs to be well chilled to avoid seeming flat. The 2006 rosé Cuvée Initiale was as pale as it was delicate. Somewhat watery but not at all unpleasant. The Cuvée Intiale red from 2006 was soft but not flabby, an easy-going, two-dimensional red with pleasant strawberry notes.

❧ Domaine Fernand Girard & Fils

18300 Verdigny-en-Sancerre; 02.48.79.37.33; f:02.48.79.38.18

❧ Recommended

Alain Girard succeeded his father Fernand about 20 years ago on this 12 hectare family domaine. Their vines, located in the communes of Sancerre, Verdigny, Sury-en-Vaux and Saint Satur, grow on a mix of the appellation's three principle soil types – *caillottes, terres blanches* and silex. The Girards practice sustainable farming, harvest both by hand and machine, and the wines ferment in temperature controlled stainless steel tanks. No commercial yeasts are added, and the wines are filtered lightly before bottling.

The Girards bottle only a portion of their wine, selling the rest to négociants. Perhaps their finest wine is the Sancerre *blanc* "La Garenne" which comes from a 2.5 hectare parcel, an east-facing slope with rocky limestone soils. The 2006, tasted in 2008, opened with attractive lime, mineral, and tropical fruit notes. Ample and fresh, it was very attractive. Later in the day, it developed earthy flavors and its texture roughened. By the glass? The domaine Sancerre *rouge* 2005, also tasted in 2008, seemed rather light for the vintage but was a supple, nicely focused, pleasant, medium-bodied red.

Recommended

Gitton Pere & Fils

18300 Ménétréol-sous-Sancerre; 02.48.54.38.84; gitton@wanadoo.fr; www.gitton.fr

I said it before and I'll say it again:If only Pascal Gitton weren't overextended! An enthusiastic world-traveler, a linguist, Gitton talks really good wine (with Est-like emotionalism) but seems overwhelmed by the six-ring circus he runs: a total of 36.5 hectares of vines in the Loire Valley, of which 27 are located in the Sancerre appellation (with four hectares planted to Pinot Noir); and the rest situated in Pouilly, where Gitton produces both Pouilly Fumé and Pouilly-sur-Loire, and the Coteaux du Giennois. Far to the southwest of Sancerre, Gitton owns the 13 hectare vineyard of Château Lafon, in the Côtes du Duras, an hour east of Bordeaux.

Viticulture is conventional, the average age of the vines is thirty years old, and grapes are harvested chiefly by machine. Gitton vinifies and bottles by parcel, offering more than fifteen different cuvées. Sancerre bottlings include les Belles Dames, la Vigne de Larrey, les Herses, Galinot, les Montachins, les Cris, les Romains, la Rey and les Fredins; in Pouilly, Jeanne d'Orion, and les Péchignolles. Despite evidence of distinctive raw material, there's a sameness in most of the wines, as well as a sense of dilution and lack of structure. I have, however, appreciated various vintages of le Galinot, les Belles Dames and les Herses. And I loved the 1970 les Montachins when I tasted it in 1990. Made by Gitton's father, Marcel, it was a structured, elegant wine, a weave of wax and herbs.

Herewith, notes on two 2006s and two 2005s, tasted in the summer of 2008.

Les Montachins comes from a four hectare parcel with Portlandian soils. The wine ferments in stainless steel tanks. The 2006 was mineral with light cat pee notes. It seemed somewhat confected and a bit watery.

Les Belles Dames comes from a five hectare vineyard with silex soils. Half of the wine ferments and ages in stainless steel, the other half in used oak barrels of varying sizes. More mineral than Les Montachins, the 2006 Les Belles Dames was more extracty, more focused, and revivifying. It, too, seemed slightly confected but that aspect was outweighed by attractive minerality. Much preferable.

Les Herses, one of Gitton's top cuvées, comes from a 1.2 hectare parcel with silex rich soils and ferments in new oak barrels. The 2005, 14.2 alcohol, was pale gold, creamy, both ample and fresh, with flavors of ripe fruit, minerals and oak. With aeration, it seemed to become borderline flabby but still, evidently, a crowd pleaser. (I brought it to the birthday dinner of a wine friend and all the guests – 100% wine pros – loved it.)

Solely owned by the Gittons, La Vigne de Larrey comes from a 1.7 hectare vineyard with limestone soils. The wine ferments in new oak demi-muids and comes in a heavy bottle. The 2005, 13.5 alcohol, was lightly oxidized, oaky, and nearly viscous. (The wine tasted as if the grapes had been harvested just at the point of over-ripeness). It, too, lost some of its freshness after having been opened but would surely appeal to those who like that combination of Loire freshness and New World overstatement.

&. Recommended

&. Vincent Grall

149, Avenue Nationale 18300 Sancerre; 02 48 78 00 42 06 75 48 12
46; www.grall-vigneron-sancerre.com

Vincent Grall, who comes from a vigneron family and started his own winery less than twenty years ago, has all of 3.2 hectares, making his one of the smallest domaines in the appellation. Most of his land is located on a plateau with silex-rich soils. Grall's viticultural practices – from the treatments and fertilizers he uses to the ways in which works the land — seem to lack only official accreditation to be called organic. Harvest is by hand. There are two cuvées of Sancerre *blanc*, each fermented using indigenous yeasts.

Grall's Sancerre *blanc* "Tradition" ferments in tanks at low temperatures. The 2008 displayed the acidity of that vintage energetically. Invigorating and lively, it was a breezy white, a waft of lemon zests and minerals. I brought it with me for the oyster course on Christmas day 2010.

Grall's "Le Manoir" bottling comes from the center of a southeast-facing slope with marl soils which are particularly rich in clay. Fermentation occurs in three to four year old oak barrels.

In December 2010, the 2008 seemed somewhat disjointed, with acidity in one corner, new oak flavors in another, more or less joined by strong flavors of citrus zest and lemon curd. I'd give it a bit of time and drink the "Tradition" bottling while waiting.

🍷 By the Glass

🍷 Domaine des Grandes Perrieres/Jerôme Gueneau
18300 Sury-en-Vaux; 02.48.79.39.31; f:02.48.79.40.27

Jérôme Gueneau created this 13.5 hectare domaine in 1993. Viticulture is conventional, grapes are machine harvested and the wines generally ferment in tank, at low temperatures. Gueneau's 2006 Sancerre *blanc*, tasted in 2008, was a quick "Hail and Farewell" of a wine; the 2006 Vieilles Vignes was somewhat crude but flavorful. Casual bistro drinking. There is also a cuvée "Silex" as well as a red and a rosé.

🍷 Excellent

🍷 Domaine Pascal Jolivet
Route de Chavignol, 18300 Sancerre; 02 48 78 60 01;
www.pascal-jolivet.com

The son of a wine broker (for Savour Club) and the grandson and great-grandson of the cellarmaster of the Château de Tracy, Pascal Jolivet created his own firm in 1987 and is now the third largest exporter of Sancerre and Pouilly, selling 750,000 bottles a year — 600,000 in Sancerre/Pouilly and 150,000 Vin de Pays "Attitude," more than 85% of it white —, from France to Japan, the United Arab Emirates and Russia. Jolivet's wines are stocked in duty free shops throughout Europe, are served in business and first class on numerous airlines and are poured on such luxury liners as the Queen Mary.

In 1990 Jolivet completed Napa-style cellars on the outskirts of the town of Sancerre and he has been acquiring vineyards. As of now, the firm manages 34 hectares in Sancerre, 8 in Pouilly and 23 in Touraine. Half of Jolivet's wines now come from his own vines. The balance comes from purchased grapes and juice from about 35 different growers, including a number of exclusive contracts with specific properties such as Château du Nozay.

The Jolivet wines I particularly admired back in the 1990s were Château du Nozay, Les Caillottes, Le Chêne Marchand and Grande Cuvée, an old vines bottling made only in good years. At a blind tasting of Loire whites in 2005, I sampled a number of Jolivet's wines then on the market. Predominantly from the 2004 vintage, with the oldest being a wine from 2001, they did not impress. When I tasted a full range of Jolivet's 2006s in 2009 I was delighted. I loved every single one of them.

What, however, could explain such a discrepancy? According to Jolivet, 2004 was one of his weakest vintages. The quality of the harvest was such that Jolivet was obliged to adapt his work methods, for example, by adding sulfur to the grape musts. Additionally, many things have changed at the domaine. He practices sustainable farming on 90% of his land and has converted 10% — in Chêne Marchand, the Clos du Roy, and Bondenotte — to organic farming. While Jolivet is considering harvesting entirely by hand, for the moment he harvests all the Pinot Noir and all the top-cuvée of Sancerre blanc by hand, the rest by machine. The grapes ferment slowly in temperature controlled stainless steel tanks, without added yeast, and age on their lees.

Jolivet currently makes six ranges of wine. At the high end, there is "Metis," a Sauvignon Blanc from Hawkes Bay in New Zealand. A joint venture between Jolivet and Trinity Hill, the grapes come from Esprit Vineyards, a 23 hectare plot in Hawkes Bay, New Zealand. The wine is vinified in Hawkes Bay by John Hancock, Trinity Hill's winemaker, and Jean-Luc Soty, the winemaker at Domaine Jolivet. But this is a book on Loire wines and in the Loire we shall stay.

Herewith, tasting notes on the 2006s, tasted in 2009, and 2007s, 2008s and 2009s, tasted in 2011.

Jolivet's simplest wine is his Vin de Pays "Attitude" made from vines in the Sancerre area and in Touraine. From the Sauvignon Blanc, to the Pinot Noir, to the rosé, a blend of Cabernet, Gamay and Pinot Noir, these would make pleasant house wines in a neighborhood restaurant – if the price reflects the honest but modest ambitions of the wines.

The grapes for Jolivet's basic Sancerre *blanc* come from 20 hectares of vines on a mix of the appellation's classic *terroirs* in the communes of Bué, Verdigny and St. Gemmes. Vivacious, full and ripe, the 2006 displayed a lovely balance of fruit (particularly kiwi) and minerality. An appetizing wine. The 2009, plump and redolent of peach and gooseberry, could have used a bit more zing but it finished on an acidulated note and, frankly, was true to its vintage.

The basic red comes from vines on clay and limestone soils. The grapes cold soak for ten days before fermenting and aging in tank. The 2008 was a pretty, three-dimensional wine, well balanced, with attractive griotte cherry flavors.

Next in Jolivet's Sancerre range come five whites and a red from selected plots, each representing specific soil types or the expression of a single parcel or lieu-dit.

The first, Les Caillottes, comes from 40+ year old grapes, hand harvested, from 3.5 hectares of limestone soils. The 2006 was seductive, indeed. The nose was very mineral, the focus, tight, the texture, near viscous, with the freshness and marrowy feel of lees aging. A fleeting note of vanilla merged with keen flavors of grapefruit zests and minerals. The 2009, with 13.5%

alcohol, was a mouthfilling wine – zaftig and tender. But it was also fresh, floral and juicy, with flavors of lime, tropical fruit, herbal tea, and stone. A tinge of 2009 heat, yes, but the wine slipped down the gullet very easily.

Roughly four hectares of old vines in Ste.Gemme provide the fruit for Jolivet's Château de Nozay. The lightly exotic 2006 was tangy and flavorful, its whiff of foxyness overshadowed by juicy grapefruit flavors.

My favorite may be the eponymously named bottling made from grapes grown on a 1.2-hectare plot with full southern exposure on Le Chêne Marchand. The racy and elegant 2006 was crystalline, tight, fresh, and pure as a mountain stream flowing over stones, with flavors of white fleshed peaches, white flowers and ginger. The 2008, at 12.5% alcohol, tasted so ripe, its acidity so amiable, you could have taken it for a 2009. Grippy and dense, it was a tangy Sancerre with good flavors of lime and lime zests, stone, and tropical fruit.

"Clos du Roy" is made from selected grapes on a 1.5 hectare, south-facing parcel on the calcareous soils of that famous lieu-dit. The 2009, 13.5% alcohol, was a plump but muscular and pedigreed wine with flavors of stone and *tilleul*.

La Bondenotte, the red Sancerre in this line-up, comes from a 1.5 hectare south-facing parcel with clay and limestone soils. The 2008, which I tasted twice in the spring of 2011, was pleasant but a bit thin and quite bland. An underachiever. I expect more from Jolivet than this.

As of 2011, a new bottling will join this group. It comes from a recently acquired 2 hectare plot with pure, flinty soils in the lieu-dit "Le Roc."

Moving up the scale of bottlings, we arrive at what Jolivet categorizes as "Pure Expression." In Pouilly, this is the "Indigène" cuvée. In Sancerre it is "Sauvage" – in three colors. It replaces Jolivet's "Grande Cuvée" and is, in fact, an entirely different wine. The Sauvignon Blanc comes from a one-hectare parcel in Champtin that Jolivet farms organically. The wine does not undergo malolactic fermentation, as Grande Cuvée had, but ages on its lees for a year, and is bottling without being filtered.

Simultaneously mellow and sprightly, the 2006 was an intriguing wine that seemed full of contradictions – or, if you will, organoleptic oxymorons: Ample, and seemingly riper than its 12.5% alcohol, it was also highstrung and edgy. Additionally, it was fresh and sappy, with toothsome notes of lime, ripe fruit, and stone, yet also a wee bit oxidized. Fascinating. The savory 2008, tasted in 2011 was *soigné* and mouthwatering, with flavors of mineral, apples, sour lemon, slate, and stone and remarkably tame acidity for the vintage.

The rosé, from old vines, macerates before being pressed, resulting in a wine the color of pale, raw silk. The 2009 was textured and vinous, with flavors of lemon and pineapple. Slightly hot – no surprise at 13 degrees alcohol – it's a big rosé, made for meals.

The red, made from vines planted in 1952, spends 15 months in barrel and is bottled unfiltered. The 2005, tasted in 2011, was smooth, spicy and oaky, with ripe cherry flavors. With aeration, a worrisome note of gaminess emerged. A night in the fridge, served a bit more chilled than normal, and the gaminess disappeared while the cherry flavors deepened.

Finally, we reach "Exception" in red and white which come from Jolivet's own parcels on such lieux-dits as Chêne Marchand, Monts Damnés, Clos du Roy and les Bouffants.

The 2007 white was almost viscous, distinctly salty and a powerful presence. With its flavors of preserved lemon, lemon zest and stone, as well as a hint of oxidation, and a tangy finish, I'd pair it with shellfish – from batter-fried calamari to lobster.

Grapes for the red Exception come from vines over 50 years old. The wine ages in oak and is bottled unfiltered. The supple 2005, tasted along with the 2006 whites, displayed an adept balance of fruit and oak and admirable purity of flavor. Good work.

✿ Serge Laloue

Excellent

18300 Thauvenay; 02.48.79.94.10; www.serge-lalou.fr

Founded in the 1930s by François and Simone Laloue, the domaine originally consisted of mixed agriculture – vines, livestock, cereal crops and tobacco production. The Laloues also ran a small café in the village. In 1960, son Serge took over and began to concentrate on winemaking, slowly building up the vineyard holdings. Today the domaine consists of 21 hectares and is run by two of Serge's children – Franck (Lycée Viticole de Beaune) who tends the vines, vinification and sales, and Christine, who manages the domaine and helps with sales.

The Laloues practice sustainable farming; they renovated the cellars – replacing concrete tanks with stainless steel – in the 1990s. Harvest is principally by machine.

The domaine's main Sancerre *blanc* grows on chiefly Kimmeridgian marl soils. The 2006, tasted in 2010, was pungent, tangy and fresh, a grapey-foxy Sauvignon. The Cuvée Reservée comes from two hectares of flinty-clay soils. The 2006, 14 degrees alcohol, was nicely ripe, ample yet fresh and pure-fruited, with alluring flavors of minerals, stone and grapefruit zests. A lovely meal wine, perfect for what the French call *un poisson noble en sauce.*

Laloue makes 900 bottles of a Sancerre *blanc* called "1166". The vines — exactly 1166 plants — grow on a .20 hectare parcel with silex topsoils over limestone. The grapes are hand harvested and ferment in 600 litre French oak vats. The wine is lightly fined but not filtered before bottling.

The 2008, an alluring yellow-gold, was ripe, with very mild suggestions of oak. It was pure and crystalline. All mellowness and minerality, the concept of "varietal" was irrelevant. Beautifully balanced, it was simultaneously transparent and rich, classy, yet without pretension. A real pleasure.

At the end of 2008, Laloue took over his cousin's one hectare on the Cul de Beaujeu, with its Kimmeridgian marl soils and inclines so steep (45 degrees) that all work must be done by hand. Yields are 35 hl/ha. In October of 2010 I tasted the 2009 which had been bottled a month earlier. It's a good idea to serve this wine well chilled, which tempers both the heaviness and the heat that might come from the wine's 14.5 degrees alcohol. With that in mind, the wine is ripe, with seductive aromas of tropical fruit such as mangoes, livened by notes of lemon zests and herbal tea. Ample and mellow, it's Alsace meets the Loire with none of Sauvignon's caricatural traits. The finish is pleasantly tangy, with an appetizing bitter thread.

The rosé ferments in temperature controlled stainless steel tanks and spends two months on its fine lees before bottling. The 2009 was a big (13.5 % alcohol), dry, appetizing rosé with fragrant notes of rose petal. Paired with a perfumed chicken bsteeya in a Berber restaurant in Paris, it disappeared in a flash.

The domaine's red comes from a 3.10 hectare parcel with half flinty clay and half clay-limestone soils. Yields average 42 hl/ha and grapes are harvested by hand. Half ferments in demi-muids of French oak and half in termperature-controlled stainless steel tanks. Vatting lasts about 20 days with regular punching down and pumping over of the fermenting mass. The wine is bottled without being fined or filtered. The 2008, tasted in 2010, was an utter delight with its inviting cherry-plum nose and its seductive flavors of morello cherries and black tea. The vibrant acidity characteristic of the 2008 vintage was there and, in this case, nicely integrated with the whole. A comfort wine on a rainy November night.

&. Excellent

&. Domaine Laporte (Bourgeois)
Cave de la Cresle, Route de Sury-en-Vaux, 18300 Saint Satur; 02.48.78.54.20; www.domaine-laporte.com

Domaine Laporte, created in 1850, consists of roughly twenty hectares of vines, of which 80% is planted to Sauvignon Blanc and the rest to Pinot

Noir. In 1986 Réné Laporte, then the president of Sancerre's growers *syndicat*, asked Jean-Marie Bourgeois to take over everything – the vines, the vinification and sales. (Laporte had three sons but none wanted to run the domaine.)

The Laporte portfolio of wines, including negociant bottlings, is as extensive as that of Domaine Bourgeois. Negociant bottlings include a Sauvignon Blanc and a Cabernet Franc Vin de Pays labeled "Bouquet;" Sancerres labeled "Le Comte de Charme" and "Richard Bourgeois;" as well as bottlings from Quincy, Menetou-Salon, Châteaumeillant, and the Giennois. Laporte, from its own vines, produces several wines not reviewed here, including the Sancerre *blanc* "Jean-Pierre Laporte" and a new world Sauvignon from their New Zealand outpost, Chapel Peak.

Laporte is hardly an afterthought for Bourgeois. Stylistically, its wines are quite different from those from Domaine Bourgeois: though equally appealing and masterly, they are more streamlined and austere. I happen to love this style but, if you like a tender Sauvignon, stick with Bourgeois. Additionally, all Laporte vineyards are in the process of being converted to organic farming and should be so accredited by 2013.

Harvest is by hand and by machine. In Sancerre, the grapes for the following wines are hand harvested: the red and the rosé Grandmontains, the whites Le Rochoy, Le Grand Rochoy, and La Comtesse, and the red Les Royaux.

All wines are vinified by terroir, ferment in stainless steel tanks, and, with the exception of Le Grand Rochoy and Les Royaux which age in oak barrels, remain, in tank, on their lees, until spring bottling.

Laporte's basic Sancerre in all three colors used to be called La Cresle de Laporte. No longer. The wine now bears the historic name Grandmontains. In the 12th century, Etienne, Count of Sancerre, gave a slope in Ménétréol to the religious order of Grandmontains who subsequently developed the vineyard. In 1997 Domaine Laporte acquired a 4.8 hectare at the heart of the slope with soils that are essentially *terres blanches* with some flint. The wine made from these vines is bottled under the name Grandmontains. The 2008 *blanc*, tasted in 2010, was highstrung and mineral, with vivid grapefruit zest and gooseberry flavors. The 2008 red, tasted in 2011, was relatively lean, cool and smooth, with flavors of black tea accented with cherry.

The La Comtesse bottling comes from 22 *ares* of Kimmeridgian marl soils on the heart of Les Monts Damnés. The 2003, tasted in 2007, was rich, deep and unctuous, another Chablis ringer. Tasted in 2010, the 2006 was pedigreed and long, with flavors of minerals and gooseberry mixed with a definite chalkiness. The 2008, tasted in 2011, was fresh and vinous, with a good sense of place. It also faithfully expressed the vintage, mixing flavors of gooseberry, a whiff of cat pee and resonant notes of minerals and lemon zests.

The Le Rochoy bottling comes from a flinty, stony, ten-hectare slope that had been quarried in Gallo-Roman times when it was called "Rochetum." The 2005, tasted in 2007, was pure and rectilinear, extremely mineral, marvelously fresh, and adamantly flinty. Tasted in 2010, the 2008 was a tall, racy, and stoic wine, a proud, flinty warrior. Le Grand Rochoy, which is not made every year, comes from a 2.5 hectare parcel of 45-plus year-old vines in Rochoy. Hand harvested, at 40 hl/ha, part ferments in barrel, and the wine ages on its lees for six months with regular *batonnage*. The 2006 was complex, tight and commanding.

Ah, vignerons, God love 'em! When, in 2011, I asked for a sample of the most recent Grand Rochoy, Bourgeois sent me the 2005. The wine was certainly drinking well, a textured white with lime, light gooseberry and mint flavors underscored by minerals and steel. A mellow Sancerre with a zingy, citric finish.

Yet another, very different and compelling expression of the soils of Rochoy can be found in Les Royaux, Laporte's red Sancerre. The grapes, hand-harvested at 30 to 35 hl/ha, come from a flinty, south-facing parcel. They vat for two weeks or more and are punched down and pumped over twice daily. The wine is then transferred to barriques for malolactic and ages in barrel for twelve months. The last three vintages marketed of this cuvée were the 2005, 2006, and 2008. The 2005, tasted in 2010, was, quite simply, a royal delight, a *gourmandise*, a smooth stream of black cherry and black tea. Somewhat less distinguished was the substantial 2008, tasted in 2011. It came on with a warm, spicy, Pinot nose. With aeration, the wine straightened up, found its steely edge and flavors of cherry emerged as well as oak and acidity (the latter not surprising for 2008). But persistant notes of gaminess emerged as well, not my favorite flavor. With its combination of tartness and stuffing, however, this was a red that could handily take on a *tête de veau* with a pungent *sauce gribiche*.

By the Glass

Eric Louis/Celliers de la Pauline
Place du Bourg - 26 rue de la Mairie, 18300 Thauvenay; 02 48 79 91 46; www.sancerre-ericlouis.com

It all started in the 1860s when Eric's great grandmother, Pauline, sold her wine in the market. Since that time the domaine has expanded considerably. Eric Louis now produces five different bottlings of Sancerre – the

Cuvée Pauline in red and white age in barrel – as well as Pouilly-Fumé, Menetou-Salon, Quincy and Sauvignon Blanc and Pinot Noir as Vin de Pays. His 2008 Sancerre blanc is a good representative of the domaine's production: relatively ripe, with the vintage's acidity held in check, it was a good commercial product.

🎗 Château de Maimbray/Georges Roblin & Fils

18300 Maimbray; 02 48 79 34 51;
château.de.maimbray@wanadoo.fr

🎗 Recommended

This venerable family domaine harvested its last grapes in 2009. The vineyards were split – over time – among members of the Roblin family. You may still find Château de Maimbray wines on lists and they are well worth ordering. The 2006 white, tasted in late December 2010, was lightly rustic but not haphazard, with penetrating flavors of gooseberry. The 2006 rosé offered delicate fruit against a backdrop of minerals. A nice food wine.

🎗 Domaine Masson-Blondelet

(See Pouilly)

🎗 Recommended

In order to add red wines to his line, grandfather Blondelet bought four hectares of vines in Thauvenay, the Sancerre commune closest to Pouilly. Each granddaughter inherited two hectares. Today the Masson-Blondelets produce both a red and a white on this land. The 2008 red, tasted in January 2011, is made in the fruit-forward, user-friendly style. And that's exactly what it is. The 2009 white was ample and vibrant with vivid gooseberry flavors.

🎗 Domaine Alphonse Mellot

Domaine de la Moussière, 18300 Sancerre; 02.48.54.07.41;
www.mellot.com

🎗 Excellent

Now run by Alphonse Mellot *père* and Alphonse Mellot *fils*, generations 18 and 19 respectively, this venerable house traces its roots back to 1513. It became one of the ambassadors of the appellation under the stewardship of the previous two generations who got the wines into Paris restaurants, began the firm's negociant arm — at first to supply their own auberge in Sancerre, later to satisfy demands of Paris bistros, including their own wine bar, le Sancerre (no longer in the family) — and began building up the domaine's vineyard holdings.

Until the mid '90s, the domaine was mostly known as a negociant. Alphonse *père*, significantly influenced by Didier Dagueneau, began to put the emphasis on domaine wines and to cut back on negociant bottlings. After he was joined by Alphonse jr. some twenty years ago, the negociant line was all but eliminated and the focus was on ever finer wines from the Mellot's own vineyards which now consist of 49 hectares of Sancerre, mostly on the la Moussière vineyard, 18 hectares in Côtes de la Charité (a Vin de Pays). And recently, Aphonse #18's daughter, Emmanuelle, has inaugurated a negociant line from two hectares of vines in the Pouilly Fumé appellation.

As part of the restructuring process, the vineyards are now farmed bio-dynamically, vine density has been increased to well above the legal man-dated minimum, grapes are harvested by hand, and a good half dozen new cuvées – tiny in quantity, sky-high in price — have been added, including some luscious red Sancerres.

The mainstays of the domaine are the "La Moussière" bottlings which come from a mix of 4 to 40 year old vines on the St. Doulchard marl soils of a 34 hectare vineyard of the same name.

I never used to be a fan of Mellot's basic Sancerre blanc, "La Moussière." Back in the ancient 1990s, the wine always seemed blowsy to me. No longer. With a change of century, came a change of style: half of the grapes ferment in tank, half in new oak casks. The wine ages on its fine lees for seven to eight months before bottling.

Working backwards, the 2007, tasted on several occasions in 2010, was savory, mineral and tart, with good citrus zest flavors and a thread of sur lie marrow. When tasted in 2008, the wine was friskier, very pure, very min-eral and very tart. Either expression would have made a fine bistro white. The 2006, tasted in early 2007, was pungent and fresh, a well-made basic Sancerre. Tasted in 2006, the 2005 was rich, round, mineral and fresh; the 2004, fragrant, ripe, balanced, and fairly discreet.

Grapes for the red La Moussière are cold soaked for five to ten days before being transferred to 60 hl tronconic wood vats for fermentation. The wine is then placed in oak barrels – 80 to 100% new – for malolactic fermentation and aged for ten to eighteen months on its fine lees before bottling.

When young, the La Moussière *rouge* is often dominated by oak and has worrisome gamy notes. With age, the wines seem to settle down into a charming little package of red. Tasted in 2010, the 2008 fit the less than enthusiastic part of the above description to a T; the 2006, however, though still oaky, was a crowd pleaser – smooth, solid, with attractive flavors of ripe cherry. The 2007, tasted in early 2008, seemed a bit lean for all the oak but the fruit quality was quite fine and precise.

The Mellots produce about 40,000 cases of La Moussière (red and white) a year as compared to their special cuvées which run from 3000 to 6000 bottles yearly.

First among these is "Les Romains," a Sancerre *blanc* that comes from vines planted in 1951 on a 1.14 hectare south-southeast facing parcel with flinty-clay soils. The grapes ferment in 13 hl tronconic vats, and the wine stays on its fine lees for between eight and twelve months before bottling. The 2008, tasted twice in 2010, was sufficiently well-upholstered to offset the strident acidity of the vintage. A good wine, needing only time. My first tasting of the 2007, in 2008, revealed an extremely fresh, mineral wine with flavors of grapefruit zests and petrol and ample acidity. When tasted in June 2010, it seemed either to be going through an awkward phase or was beginning to come apart: there was a light sense of oxidation, the acidity seemed more aggressive than previously – more like the crude acidity of 2008 than of refined acidity of 2007. That said, the wine went down very easily.

Alphonse #19 created what may be the domaine's most celebrated bottling, Génération XIX. The white version is made from 87+ year old vines on the La Moussière vineyard. It ferments and ages in 900 litre tronconic barrels.

The 2009, tasted in December 2010, weighed in at 15.6 degrees alcohol with over 6 g/l acidity. Not surprisingly the wine was plump and rich but had adequate acidity. Oak, again, was a major presence, and only time will tell whether the various parts will unite into a splendid whole. The 2007, tasted in June 2010, was slightly less heady – with a mere 13 degrees alcohol. Fresh from the fridge, it charmed with aromas and flavors of lime, verbena, and an appetizing saltiness. Tingly and elegant, with very fine acidity, it was savory, stylish and real. Later, as the wine warmed up, mellow oak flavors emerged but so did worrisome signs of oxidation which made me think of the current "premox" (premature oxidation) problems causing so much consternation in white Burgundies. Looking over my notes, I see that oxidation was also an issue when I tasted the wine in 2008 at a Paris event, even though the wine was otherwise tight, bright and mouthwatering.

When push comes to shove, however, I think my favorite of all the Mellot wines is the Cuvée Edmond, named after Alphonse *père*'s father. Cuvée Edmond comes from the oldest vines – between 40 and 87 years old – on the south-southeast facing slope of Mellot's main vineyard, La Moussière. The soils are composed of *caillottes* over Kimmeridgean marl. Yields are low – roughly 40 hl/ha – and the grapes are hand harvested in small bas-kets. The wine ferments in small oak barrels, 60% of which are new, 40% the barrels of one or two wines, and ages on its lees for up to 14 months. (Increasingly opposed to the use of new and newish oak, I admire the mas-tery of the barrel aging here: the oak doesn't mask the fruit or the terroir. This represents a major step forward as I recall a 2002 of the same cuvée that, tasted in 2007, was still dominated by oak. That said, I've always loved the 2001. Go figure.)

The 2005 Cuvée Edmond, tasted in 2009, was elegant, crystalline, and emphatically racy, its texture, sleek and satiny. The wine is both mouthwa-teringly fresh yet lusciously layered, with mingled with notes of verbena, lime, and light toast from the oak. All about pedigree, this was, quite simply, a very fine wine. The 2006, tasted in December 2008, was young, tight and oaky, but there was a sense of great race and minerality underneath. A wine to wait for. Excellent.Tasted in December 2010, the 2008 (14 degrees alcohol with over 6 g/l in acid) was fresh, full and tasty. Both citric (grapefruit zests), chalky, and racy, it's admirably austere, stoic, with a long finish playing every variation on the theme of grapefruit.

As of the 2008 vintage, however, Cuvée Edmond has competition in my short list of preferred Mellot bottlings: it is "Satellite": This is a new cuvée, from two hectares of vines in Chavignol on the Cul de Beaujeu and les Monts Damnés. Alphonse #19 told me that the family had had these vines for 50 years, and own an additional two, but had either assembled the grapes with other lots or sold them. (The latter is hard to understand but *ipse dixit*.) To anyone, like me, who loves the Sancerres from Chavignol, this is a cuvée to follow – though I wonder if the name will change from "Satel-lite" to something that more specifically reflects its privileged origins. The 2008 acidity was there, particularly in mid-palate, but the wine was never shrill. Very good ripeness for the year, with flavors of lime and grapefruit zest.

Alphonse #19, who studied viticulture and enology at both Dijon and Montpellier, has contributed in no small way to the evolution of Domaine Mellot. He is widely respected as a wizard in the cellar and he is the man to be credited with the firm's commitment to making not only Sancerre *rouge* but Sancerre *rouge* of high quality: Even more than the white version of Génération XIX, the red bottling is the wine that should be considered the signature of Alphonse #19.

All the domaine's reds are vinified in a similar fashion: after a cold-soak-ing of 8 to 10 days, the wines ferment. Vatting lasts for about four weeks, during which time the mass is punched down and pumped over once a day.

All the cuvées below are transferred to new oak barrels for malolactic fermentation and age in barrel for roughly 14 months before being bottled without fining or filtration.

The grapes for the Génération XIX red come from low yielding (eg 21 hl/ha) 62+ year old vines on the Saint Doulchard marl soils of a one-hectare parcel of land. The 2008, tasted at a Paris event in 2010, was plush and oaky. I prefered the more discreet expression of En Grand Champs (see below) but this was a soigné red, very stylish, accomplished, and eager to please. I wanted to spend more time with the wine, to do a "Slow Tasting" and asked Alphonse #19 to send me a sample, along with a sample of the "Satellite." Herewith, the results:

Day One: 11 am: deeply colored. (Cold soaking?) Fragrant. Oak, sweet spices, cinnamon, cherry. Right now the wine is dominated by oak but time will surely help. The wine is fresh, the acidity good (and not violent), a tad furry, but nicely balanced and urbane.

Day One: 7pm: The wine has smoothed out considerably and the oak is beginning to blend in with the other flavors but, for my palate, still dominates.

Day Two: 6 pm: Mellow, rich cherry and sweet spices. The oak continues to integrate into the whole, attractive acidity. The wine is beginning to define itself. It's coming across as graceful and *gourmand*. After some aeration, the 2008 acidity reveals itself.

Day Three: 6pm: The oak still dominates but it's softer; the wine is more refined, more transparent, more of a whole.

In other words, worth the wait. In June 2010 I put the 2006 through the same paces, the results of which I'll summarize: smooth, stylish, well-focused and well-made, the wine was succulent, and offered flavors of cinnamon, cherry and, of course, plenty of oak. For me, it lacked a sense of place but it was undeniably a pretty glass of red and I don't know many people who wouldn't have been happy to drink it. My tasting notes on the 2005 and the 2004 are so similar to the above, I won't try your patience by including them.

My favorite among the Mellot reds is always the En Grand Champs bottling. This comes from the low yielding (24 hl/ha), 60+ year old vines in a parcel at the top of La Moussière. The soils are composed of Buzançais limestone – particular to this zone – over Kimmeridgian marl.

I "slow" tasted the 2006 in 2009 during a week when I'd been sampling quite a few red Burgundies — eg at the tasting of the Domaines Familiaux de Bourgogne – and this Sancerre could have held its own in that very prestigious crowd. It had more stuffing – by which I do not mean overextraction

– than many of those Burgundies. When first uncorked, the oak was a bit too dominant. Several hours later it had blended in nicely. There was nothing rustic about this wine. The balance was beautiful, the flavors lovely, sinuous and pure. Sheer lipsmacking pleasure. The 2004, tasted in February 2006, was characterful, *gourmand*, and bordered on elegant. It was lightly tart, too; not a surprise in 2004, and would find a perfect home in a *bistrot gourmand*. The 2005, tasted in February 2007, was young, meaty, fresh and a bit furry. Oak made the finish a bit drying – much like the 2006 at the same point in its evolution — but there was also an intriguing chalkiness in the mix. A wine that should be scrumptious today, to wit: March 2011. The 2008, tasted at the above-mentioned Paris event in December 2010, was structured, with fine definition. Oak dominated but I was convinced that if I could have followed the wine for several days as with the 2006, it would have melted into the whole – as it will surely do as it ages.

Another appetizing Sancerre rouge is Mellot's "La Demoiselle" from 50+ year old vines on the silex-rich soils of a 1.2 hectare parcel, a south-southeast facing slope. I tasted the 2004 in early 2006, shortly after it had been bottled. Well structured and tasty, it had notes reminiscent of pencil shavings. Surely ephemeral but not bothersome, in any event. The 2006, tasted in December 2008, was pure fruited, with lively cherry flavors, and satisfyingly mellow. Here, again, however, the wine needed time to digest its oak. When tasted again, in June 2010, the wine exhibited a bright, mellow, cherry and spice nose, with a palate to match. The oak still stood out and made for a drying finish. That was Day One. On Day Two, the nose was more exuberant – crushed ripe cherries and berries. The oak was still a presence but it was less drying; the wine was juicier and, once chilled slightly, the oak began to slink into the background where it belonged.

❧ Recommended

❧ Joseph Mellot
Route de Ménétréol BP 13, 18300 Sancerre; 02.48.78.54.55;
www.josephmellot.com

The House of Mellot traces its roots back to 1513 when César Mellot served as Louis IV's wine advisor. In the 1920s Alphonse Mellot became the region's unofficial ambassador, seducing Parisians with the wine. His sons, Edmond and Joseph, divided the domaine in the 1960s, and in 1984, Alexandre, Joseph's son, took over the running of the domaine. After Alexandre's death in 1987 Catherine Corbeau Mellot, his wife, took control.

The firm owns 90 hectares throughout the *Région Centre*, having purchased the Domaine Joseph Marchand in Pouilly in '94, the Domaine Pierre

Duret in Quincy in '95, re-assuming control over the Clos du Pressoir in Menetou-Salon, and a vineyard in the Giennois in '99, and buying the Quincy and the Reuilly properties of Jean-Michel Sorbe in 2001. New cellars have been built, sustainable farming is practiced in the vineyards. The negociant arm of Mellot also purchases grapes.

While they'd never be my desert island Sancerres, the wines from this important grower-negociant have improved dramatically over the past 20 years.

Among Mellot's five white Sancerres, "Chatellerie," which comes from silex-rich soils, ferments in temperature controlled stainless steel tanks and ages on its fine lees, seems to be the basic cuvée. And, based on the 2006, tasted in 2008, it's a pretty good one. The 2006 was fresh and lively, with appetizing flavors of lemon and grapefruit zests set against a backdrop of steel and minerals. "La Grande Châtelaine," in a heavy, prestige bottle, comes from older vines on a slope with a mix of *terres blanches* and *caillottes* soils. The wine ferments for from two to seven months in barrel, a third of which are new. It then ages in barrel for another twenty months. The 2005 wasn't bad but the oak came on a bit strong and the wine, like many 2005 Sancerres and Pouillys, was less than phenolically ripe, with flavors of *pipi de chat* and gooseberry.

Mellot also makes a direct-press rosé and two cuvées of red Sancerre, "Le Rabault", a tank-fermented bottling from silex-rich soils and, from similar soils but older (25 to 30 years) vines, "Le Connetable," which ferments in tank and is transferred to barrels made from local oak for malolactic fermentation. The wine ages in barrel, one-third of which are new, for ten months before bottling. The 2005, tasted in 2008, was dominated by flavors of oak and vanilla. Food helped, however, and the bottle was finished with dispatch.

ஃ Domaine Merlin-Cherrier

ஃ Highly Recommended

18300 Bué; 02.48.54.06.31; f:02.48.54.01.78

Thierry Merlin, whose vines come from his mother's side of the family, works 14 hectares, mostly in Bué, on a mix of *caillottes* and *terres blanches* soils. He practices sustainable farming and harvests by machine but says he'd gladly harvest by hand, if he could find a team. Merlin makes two whites, a rosé, and a red, and is a good example of the evolution of consciousness and quality in the appellation over the past twenty years. I expect him to continue improving.

His basic white is a blend of grapes from all his parcels. Fermented in temperature controlled tanks, with some stirring up of the lees, the 2009, tasted in January 2011, was textbook Sancerre, pleasantly fresh, with good balance and tasty lemon flavors. Not grandiose but good and solid. Merlin's vines on the cru Chêne Marchand are relatively young – a maximum of twenty years. For this bottling, Merlin uses only indigenous yeasts and leaves the wine on its lees for ten to sixteen months. The 2008 mixed aromas of creamed corn, lemon and lime. Good acid control here, and another good, middle of the road Sancerre.

Merlin says he really started working on his red wines in 2005: he changed his method of pruning as well as his canopy management; he debuds and maintains yields no higher than 60 hl/ha. As a result, the grapes ripen better, he says. I tasted the 2009 a month after it had been bottled. With its lovely griotte and cherry pit flavors, mingled with black tea, it was smooth and easy drinking. A strong Quiet Red. The 2008, less earnest than the 2009, was a cool, black tea, bing cherry charmer with light tannins.

≀➤ Outstanding

≀➤ Gérard & Pierre Morin
18300 Bué, 02.48.54.36.75; morin.perfils@orange.fr

The Salon des Vins de Loire reminds me of Brigadoon: it is a village that springs to life once a year – rather more frequently than Brigadoon's once-every-hundred-year incarnation – and picks up as though no time had passed since last we met.

For journalists, a buffet lunch is served in the pressroom every day. Not surprisingly, producers leave bottles of wine to be tasted. I only let myself drink wine at lunch on the last day and that was when I made the happy discovery of this very special producer in 2008. It was Morin's standard bottling of 2007 Sancerre *blanc*, so beautifully balanced and deeply mineral. When I got home, I contacted them for samples and for information about the domaine.

Gérard Morin took over his family's 1.5 hectares over twenty years ago. He was joined by his son, Pierre, in 1994 and, together, they have extended the domaine's holdings to 9.5 hectares, 90% of which are in the commune of Bué, 10% in Sancerre. The Morin's practice sustainable farming, have not used weed killers for the past three years, keep yields moderate with debudding and, if needed, cluster thinning. Grapes are harvested by hand, often by successive passes through the vineyard, and only indigenous yeasts are used for fermentation.

Abandon any clichés you may have about Sauvignon Blanc when you taste Morin's savory, appetite-whetting cuvée "Ovide." Made from 60 year old vines on *caillottes* soils, fermented in tank for two months, then aged on its fine lees for nine months, with a regular stirring up of those lees, and bottled without filtration, the 2007 Ovide is a cold, pure mountain stream, stony and steely, with full, long citrus-mineral-stone flavors as well as a fleeting hint of pear. Once again: Chablis in the Sancerrois.

And what a fine mouthful of white is Morin's 2007 blanc from the *caillottes* soils of Bué's most prestigious slope, Chêne Marchand, also bottled without filtration. The wine's mouthwatering vivacity combined with a textural meatiness recalled Dagueneau's best Pouillys. Profound minerality, flavors of gooseberry, grapefruit zest and pulp underscored the wine's raciness, its pedigree, as the wine slid across the palate like so much taffeta.

Morin's red Sancerre comes from vines ranging from 6 to 50 years old vines from various parcels in Bué with a mix of *terres blanches, caillottes* and heavier marl soils. After a three-week whole-cluster fermentation (semi-carbonic to start, then with regular punching down), two thirds of the wine ages in tank, one-third in oak casks for twenty-two months. The wine is bottled without having been fined or filtered. The 2006, tasted in 2009, was firm, tight and decisive, despite its pastel delicacy. Its flavors of plum, griotte cherries and black tea were downright lipsmacking. PMG for sure! The 2005 Sancerre, tasted in December 2010, was cool, discreet and delicious. An understated wine, with light tannins, so pure and transparent, I can't help but love it. Definitely PMG. I polished off the entire bottle.

ૐ Domaine Henry Natter   ૐ Highly Recommended
Place de l'Eglise 18250 Montigny; 02.48.69.58.85;
www.henrynatter.com

When Henry and Cécile Natter created their domaine in the 1970s, they were new to both the region and to wine. Somewhat prim and didactic, their style of wine is more austere than most – but not less alluring – and there is always a whiff of the *recherché* or the exotic in the air. The Natters appear to be outliers both by nature and by choice of location. Their 23 hectares of vines lie in Montigny, the southwestern limit of Sancerre, where that appellation meets Menetou-Salon.

Soils are Kimmeridgian marl and vine density is a relatively high 8500 plants per hectares. Juggling concepts of sustainable, organic, and biodynamic farming, the Natters work with an agronomist and, for the past 25 years or so, with a team of Hmong workers from the mountains of Laos. Grapes are machine harvested.

There are two basic bottlings of Sancerre *blanc* — the entry level and Cuvée de la Grange de Montigny. The first is made from vines with an average age of thirty years, yielding roughly 60 hl/ha. It ages for six months in large barrels made of the choicest oak (merrain). The second comes from older vines – 50 + years – with slightly lower yields (55 hl/ha). It ages in merrain barrels for 12 months.

I brought the 2008 to go with the oyster course of Christmas dinner in 2010. Creamy, not aggressively varietal, it was simply a good tasting Sancerre and everyone enjoyed it.

I tasted the 2006 Cuvée de la Grange de Montigny in October 2009. Refined and lissome, the wine offered flavors of lemon and preserved lemon, backed by light grassiness. Pure and elegant. The 2005, tasted at about the same time, had good grip and focus. Fresh and discreet, its flavors of minerals, preserved lemon, and lemon zests married beautifully with *vitello tonnato*.

Natter's rosé is made like a white, with no oak aging. I found the 2007 rather bland but the 2006 was a pleasure. Graceful and gracious, it was mildly mineral with light notes of strawberry.

The basic red ages for 18 months in oak barrels. The 2008, tasted in December 2010, was pale, rather fine-boned and delicate, recalling lightly infused black tea. The 2005, somewhat more evolved, was lean and steely. Firm and not very generous, it nevertheless grabbed your attention.

Natter's "l'Enchantement" bottling is a red Sancerre that ages in local oak. A back label speaks enigmatically of a "new generation dynamizing the old." I have no idea what that means. The 2005, however, was firm, with attractive flavors of cherry, plum and black tea. With aeration, the oak became more prominent. Nevertheless, the wine remained nicely balanced. A soft-spoken red but it spoke nicely.

From time to time the Natters bottle select lots of red or white Sancerre in magnum under the "L'Expression de Cécile" label.

෫ Highly Recommended

෫ Domaine Henry Pellé
(See Menetou-Salon)

The Pellé's, true ambassadors of the Menetou-Salon appellation, have five hectares of Sancerre in the commune of Montigny, labeled "La Croix au Garde." The 2009 *blanc*, sweeter tasting than its Menetou counterparts, was chewy and fresh. Worth following. Paul-Henry Pellé says he finds the 2009s somewhat "cooked" in flavor and that many of the grapes looked roasted at harvest. Though the nose of the 2009 rouge exhibited notes of hard candy

– sometimes a sign of youth – the wine had attractive flavors of cherry and black tea.

🐌 Recommended

🐌 Jean-Paul Picard
11 chemin de Marloup 18300 Bué; 02.48.54.16.13;
jean-paul.picard18@wanadoo.fr

Passed from father to son since the 18th century, this family domaine is currently run by Jean-Paul Picard and son Mickaël. They practice sustainable farming on their 12 hectares on the limestone soils of slopes in the commune of Bué. Harvest is by hand and only natural yeasts are used.

The basic white ferments at cold temperatures and ages on its fine lees for a minimum of four months. The 2006, tasted in 2009, was as much of a wake-up call as the most vividly acidic 2008. It reminded me of the style of Sancerre whites typical of the 1980s.

Much better is their Cuvée Prestige, produced only in the best vintages. Made from 55+ year old vines, hand harvested by successive passes through the vineyard, fermented slowly using only natural yeasts, and aged on its lees, the 2005, tasted in December 2010, was the color of florentined gold. (I credit new oak aging of 10 to 20% of the wine for the lovely hue.) Smooth and creamy, and very slightly vegetal, it was a mineral white with saliva-inducing tartness. The quality was high and there was a true sense of place.

The Picards let the grapes for their rosé macerate for 24 to 48 hours before pressing.

The 2006 was as tart as its white counterpart. More successful was the 2006 red, the grapes for which are cold soaked for 48 to 72 hours and ferment and age in tank. Though relatively light in color and saturation, verging on thin, with some green notes and bitter tannins, it had attractive flavors reminiscent of menthol, strawberry and strawberry coulis.

🐌 Excellent

🐌 Vincent Pinard
18300 Bué; 02.48.54.33.89; www.domaine-pinard.com

Pinard, in French, is one of the many words for plonk — precisely what this serious domaine does not make. Sons Florent and Clément Pinard have seamlessly succeeded father Vincent – after having done stints in wineries in New Zealand as well as in other parts of France. Their eco-serious, hand-harvested, handcrafted Sancerres from the family's 16 hectares include nicely structured rosés; scrumptious reds; and what seems like an ever-increasing number of beautiful whites, including minuscule amounts of Le

Chêne Marchand and Clémence, from vines in Thauvenay (neither of which I've tasted).

The Florès and Nuance bottlings both come from 25+ year-old vines on rocky *caillottes* soils in the village of Bué. Yields are roughly between 40 and 50 hl/ha and, as with the other whites, the Pinards harvest the grapes by hand after an initial *tri*.

Florès, the basic bottling, ferments and ages in tank, on its lees. Bottling begins the spring following the harvest. The 2006, tasted in 2009, was a beautifully integrated and rather elegant Sancerre, combining flavors of lemon and grapefruit zests, fine minerality and a long finish. The 2010, tasted in 2011, opened with aromas of peach and pear, light gooseberry, and a blast of lemon zest. Ramrod straight, clean as a whistle, it was extremely fresh, and finished on notes of lemon, steel and chalk. I'd drink this one on the fruit.

A third of the Nuance cuvée ages in once-used barrels. The excellent 2006, tasted in 2009, was a crystalline wine with full, fresh flavors of grapefruit pulp and zest and minor appearances of oak and gooseberry. The 2009, tasted in 2011, was mellow and tangy. Its lively acidity recalled neither the refined acidity of 2007 nor the aggressive acidity of 2008; it fell somewhere between the two, and the fullness of the wine balanced the tartness. A vigorous wine, with flavors of preserved lemon and a very mild suggestion of oak, it was not exactly elegant but it was classy. I'd pair it with sole *meunière* or a delicately seasoned fish or chicken tagine.

Pinard's cuvée "Harmonie" comes from 45+ year old vines grown in the lieux-dits of Chêne Marchand and Grand Chemarin. Two-thirds of the wine ages in new barrels, one-third in tank. The 2005, tasted in 2009, was full, rich and textured. A pellucid wine, with subtle flavors of oak and minerals, it fully merited being paired with *haute cuisine*. Not a single misstep here. Ditto for the shimmering 2008, tasted in 2011, a crystalline Sancerre, limned with fine acidity and flavors of lemon, lime, and chalk.

In 2007 Pinard added two new white, single vineyard cuvées to his stable – Chêne Marchand and Le Petit Chemarin. The latter comes from vines planted in 1968. Made much like the other whites, it ages in four barrels, one of which is new, and in tank. The 2009, tasted in 2011, combined delicate peach, lime, lemon curd, and mineral aromas with vivacious acidity. As the wine breathed, the oak became more apparent but the citrus tang lifted the whole. It was a self-assured wine which would benefit from a year or two of cellaring or an hour in a carafe before serving.

The domaine has always been known for its reds – and for good reason. The Pinards have 4.5 hectares planted to pinot noir. Their two traditional cuvées of red – the basic Sancerre (now called Pinot Noir) and Charlouise – come from a parcel in Bué with *terres blanches* over limestone subsoils. Yields average 30 to 35 hl/ha. After harvest and destemming, the grapes undergo a cold soaking and ferment, using only indigenous yeasts, in tronconic oak vats. They are lightly punched down and pumped over. The basic Sancerre ages in used barriques; Charlouise, in barriques on a three-year rotation. Each spends from 11 to 18 months in barrel and is bottled without fining or filtration.

The basic red, from vines averaging 28 years old, always benefits from a bit of chilling. The 2006, tasted in 2009, was pure, focused and accurate, with light caramel notes and juicy cherry fruit. The smooth 2009, tasted in 2011, offered rich, warm, succulent cherry fruit. Despite its 14% alcohol, it wasn't heavy, though it *was* soft, with notes of cooked cherries and prunes.

Charlouise comes from vines averaging 50 years old. The 2005, tasted in 2009, was a fluid weave of vibrant, dark cherry, sweet spices and mild oak. Well balanced and nicely focused, it was a perfect meal wine and one that could be easily taken for, say, a very good Mercurey. The 2007, tasted in 2010, was lightly tannic, very fresh, with tangy, pure flavors of griotte cherries. *Gourmand* and PMG. The 2008, tasted in 2011, mixed black and griotte cherries with sweet spices and muted oak. Very seductive and very pretty.

৯ Domaine Paul Prieur/ La Croix de Perthuis

Route des Monts Damnés, 18300 Verdigny; 02 48 79 35 86; paul-prieurfils@wanadoo.fr

ৡ Highly Recommended

Now run by Didier, Paul's son, and Didier's son, Philippe, who studied enology at Beaune, this venerable domaine has 18 hectares of vines in and around Verdigny. The Prieurs practice sustainable farming, keep yields within the 60 hl/ha range, and harvest by hand. The wines ferment in tank, using only natural yeasts.

The domaine's white comes from a number of parcels of south-facing slopes with a mix of Sancerre's classic soils: 40% *caillottes*, 40% *terres blanches* and 20% silex. A vibrant wine, not tyrannized by the acidity characteristic of the vintage, the 2008 was a fine bistro Sancerre – floral, with grapefruit and white-fleshed peach flavors as well as a whiff of creamed corn. The 2006, tasted in December 2010, still had some CO_2. Youthful and zesty, its acidity more resembled 2008 than the acidity of the actual 2008. Clean as a whistle, it had good texture and minerality. There were some vegetal notes typical of less-than-ripe Sauvignon Blanc but they were minor. And the wine displayed a real sense of place. I preferred it to the

2005 which was ampler but, like quite a few of its confrères, it was sharp and slightly shrill, with cooked vegetal flavors. It was still youthful in late 2010 but I'd serve this one in a noisy brasserie or at an exuberant dinner party.

The domaine has five hectares of Pinot Noir with an average age of 35 years old. I have been trying to taste one for almost a year but our signals keep getting crossed. When the happy day arrives, I'll post my tasting notes on my website.

Highly Recommended

*Roger & Didier Raimbault
Chaudenay 18300 Verdigny; 02.48.79. 32.87;
www.raimbault-sancerre.com

Here is a rather archetypal Sancerre domaine. The family has been making wine in the commune of Verdigny for about a century. By 1995 Roger Raimbault was overseeing a property consisting of 7 hectares. When son Didier joined him in 1996, they were able to add an additional 6.5 hectares belonging to family members who had recently retired. Today they have 17 hectares, 65% of which are on *terres blanches* and 35% on *caillottes*. (Most of their bottlings represent a blend of grapes from the two terroirs.)

The Raimbaults practice sustainable farming, maintain moderate yields, harvest by machine, and ferment their wines in temperature controlled stainless steel tanks.

The wines, too, embody the good, solid middle ground of Sancerre today. The 2008 white had a smooth, creamy attack. The tartness characteristic of the vintage emerged mid-palate, revealing a fresh, vigorous white with accents of grapefruit, citrus zest and lemon and a satisfactory sense of place. The 2005 *blanc* Vieilles Vignes was quite full, self-assured, and crystalline. Aromas of menthol, lime, and verbena joined saline and stony notes on the palate. Hard to know who wouldn't like it.

The grapes for Raimbaults Sancerre *rouge* ferment for 8 to 15 days in stainless steel tanks. They are lightly filtered before bottling. Tasted in December 2010, the 2007, with 12.5 % alcohol, had an inviting berry nose. It was light and tart, vintage *oblige*, but all of a piece, with faint tannins blending into flavors of black tea. The 2006, slightly more alcoholic, was also slightly firmer, with persistant flavors of black and red cherries. The domaine's *Vieilles Vignes* bottling – from 35 year-old vines – ages in oak for a year. The barrels range from one to seven years old, a sensible decision, which may explain why the 2005, tasted in 2010, was not dominated by flavors of oak. Rather, it displayed a toothsome cherry-black tea weave quite similar to the normal red bottling. All of these wines would be fine partners for *oeufs en meurette* or a *salade aux gésiers*, informal, tasty fare.

&. Highly Recommended

&. Domaine Bernard Reverdy & Fils
Chaudoux 18300 Verdigny; 02.48.79.33.08;
reverdybernard@orange.fr; www.reverdy-sancerre.fr

The Reverdys — Noel, his wife Claudine, and their son, Romain, who recently graduated from viticultural school in Burgundy — run an eco-friendly domaine of 12 hectares, mostly planted to Sauvignon Blanc, on twentyseven different parcels. Soils are a mix of Kimmeridgian marl and Portlandian clay-limestone.

The domaine was always known for its alluring rosés. Made from a direct press of Pinot Noir and vinified like a white, the tea-rose colored rosés were mouthfilling, lightly floral and appetizingly dry. The Reverdy rosés are as delectable as ever. The 2008, tasted in January 2011, was taut and focused, a real presence. Delicate notes of fruit and blossoms were there but minerals dominated. A hard wine not to love.

It's heartening to report that the reds, which cold soak before fermentation and age for ten months in oak barrels, are now as delicious as the rosés. The 2007 opened with aromas of cotton candy, cherry and strawberry. On the palate, black tea dominated, mixed with a variety of black and sour cherries. Several hours later, the wine had opened up and fleshed out, and the cool yet luscious cherry flavors took center stage. Really lovely.

The 2008 white, while tasty and admirable, was not quite up to the deliciousness of the red and the rosé but offered fine flavors of citrus zest and lemon.

&. Highly Recommended

&. Hippolyte Reverdy
18300 Chaudoux-Verdigny; 02.48.79.36.16;
domaine.hreverdy@wanadoo.fr

Another domaine with deep roots in the region, the Reverdys have 14 hectares of vines, three-fourths of which are planted to Sauvignon, one-fourth to Pinot Noir.

The 2006 Sancerre *blanc*, tasted in 2009, was zingy and vibrant, with good focus and texture. A perfect bistro Sancerre, its gooseberry-grapefruit flavors and invigorating freshness fit the classic image of nervy Sancerres – in the best sense. If you couldn't recognize this on a sommelier's exam, you deserve to fail. I served it with oysters at Christmas and the most fervent wine lover present was totally knocked out. The 2003, tasted in 2005, was rich and ripe, with flavors of tropical fruit. Taut structure and a thread of CO2 gave it the vitality it needed in such a rich vintage.

Limpid and fresh, the 2006 rosé, tasted in 2009, was made from a direct press of the harvest. Mouthfilling, it had a hint of strawberry and bitter almond but was not what anyone would call fruity. I liked it a lot.

Reverdy's Sancerre *rouge* ages in oak casks. The 2006, tasted in 2009, was not a showy wine and it didn't set out to seduce. Its flavors of cooked cherries, prunes and tobacco took a backseat to notes of stone and mineral. I love this style. All I needed was a nice omelette.

🍇 Excellent

🍇 Pascal & Nicolas Reverdy
18300 Maimbray; 02 48 79 37 31; reverdypn@wanadoo.fr

Pascal took over the family property in 1985. He was joined by brother Nicolas in 1993 and both worked together until 1997 when Nicolas was fatally injured while the two were felling a tree. Pascal has continued, along with his wife, Nathalie, and Nicolas' widow, Sophie.

Over the years they have built the domaine's holdings from 3.5 hectares up to 14 hectares, chiefly on *terres blanches* – 11 planted to Sauvignon Blanc and 3 planted to Pinot Noir — which they cultivate using their own very strict definition of sustainable farming. Grapes are hand harvested and hand sorted, ferment in tank and, depending on the cuvée, age in tank, casks or demi-muids. There are two whites, a rosé, and two reds.

Terre de Maimbray is the name given to entry level Sancerres in all colors. The white, which is called Cuvée les Coûtes in the USA, ferments in stainless steel tanks and ages on its fine lees for about six months. The 2006, tasted in 2009, was pungent and bouncy, full and fresh, with heady scents of white-fleshed peaches and blossoms. It was the kind of white Sancerre that could unify a jury. The 2008 was so buoyant it practically vibrated. Full of character, it was a great bistro white. The 2009, tasted in January 2011, exuded aromas of mango and other tropical fruit, ripe and creamy, it was lightly hot but, overall, masterly.

The Les Anges Lots bottling, a white formerly labeled Vieilles Vignes, takes its name from a vineyard with vines over 60 years old. It ferments in old barrels and is bottled unfiltered. Tasted in 2010, the 2007 was fine-boned and fresh, with aromas of mint, grapefruit and gooseberry under a mantle of oak so delicate as to be barely perceptible. It was all about the wine. Tasted again in January 2011, it was very lightly oxidized, quite mineral, with flavors of lemon and lemon zest. Beautifully pellucid, it had a cleansing, citrus-accented finish. The 2008, tasted at the same time, was in its adolescence, with strong creamed corn aromas and vivid but well-cushioned acidity. The 2009 was layered and fresh, with mouthwatering flavors of lime and verbena. The 2005, tasted in 2010, was an unctuous wine with almost syrupy texture, and flavors of lime, minerals and white-fleshed peaches. Fresh, vivid, racy, and elegant, it was another example of Chablis in Sancerre.

The 2010 rosé had been bottled for a month when tasted in January 2011. With its delicate rose petal and mint flavors, it was the vinous incarnation of a summer afternoon.

The red Terre de Maimbray comes from vines on *terres blanches*. The grapes are cold-soaked for five to seven days before fermenting in wood uprights and stainless steel tanks. Like the Cuvée à Nicolas, it is bottled without filtration. The 2009, tasted in January 2011, was slightly gamey, fleshy and lightly tannic. It needed a good two years cellaring. The 2006, tasted in 2010, was fragrant and simultaneously firm yet supple as a caress, with flavors of cherry and sweet spices.

Cuvée à Nicolas is the top-of-the-line red. It comes from vines on gravelly *caillottes* soils and ages in demi-muids which include a percentage of new oak. Tasted in January 2011, the 2007 had an alluring nose of cherries. With aeration, the oak emerged but in no way diminished the overall charm of the wine. The 2008 was vibrant, energetic and spicy, with light oak flavors.

❧ Domaine Reverdy-Ducroux

❧ Highly Recommended

Rue du Pressoir 18300 Verdigny; 02.48.79.31.33; reverdy.
ducroux.sancerre@wanadoo.fr; www.reverdy-ducroux.fr.

Alain and son Laurent, with roughly 21 hectares distributed over many different parcels, represent the most recent generations of the Reverdy-Ducroux tribe to continue a winemaking tradition that dates from 1550. Viticulture tends towards the eco-friendly but this is a fairly traditional Sancerrois operation, which has, nevertheless, improved impressively over the past 15 years. Yields are relatively moderate; harvest is by machine. The domaine's principal bottling is the Cuvée Beau Roy. Made from 20 year - old vines growing on a mix of *caillottes* and *terres blanches* soils, the grapes ferment in temperature-controlled tanks. The 2006, tasted in 2009, was crystalline and focused, with fine balance, a core of steel, and toothsome flavors of lime, white-fleshed peaches and minerals. Montée de Bouffant is the name given to a cuvée made from a small parcel (40 *ares)* of vines over 50 years old. Fermented in barrel, one third of which are new, the wine ages in oak for an additional ten months before being transferred to heavy, deluxe bottles. The 2005, showing hints of over-ripeness, was simultaneously fleshy and bracing. A very good wine, but I prefer to Beauroy because the oakiness of the Montée de Bouffant masked the terroir. The domaine's top red is the Cuvée Louys Marie which comes from a half hectare of 40 year-old vines growing on *terres blanches* soils. After a twelve day vatting at 30 degrees, the wine is put in new oak barrels to undergo malolactic fermenation. It ages in barrel for a year before bottling. Oak was the dominant flavor in an otherwise admirable 2005. Overall, it was a gentle wine, low key, with notes of vanilla and sweet spices and an appetizing bitterness. It went down very easily.

&⋄ Outstanding

&⋄ Domaine Claude & Stéphane Riffault
Maison Sallé, 18300 Sury-en-Vaux; 02.48.79.38.22;
claude.riffault@wanadoo.fr

Stéphane Riffault, who has just turned 30, is one of my favorite "discoveries". Before succeeding his father in 2002, he earned a degree in viticulture and enology in Beaune and worked with Olivier Leflaive and at Château l'Angélus. (His brother has married one of the Sauzet girls.)

Since taking over the family's 13.5 hectares, Riffault has begun converting the domaine to organic viticulture, entirely eliminating machine harvesting, and, in general, pampering his vines, as well as experimenting with partial oak aging for some of his wines. All of his wines except his rosé are bottled without filtration. He also seems constantly to change his cuvées; keeping up with him is a Sisyphean task.

White Sancerre accounts for 80% of Riffault's production. There are, for the moment, five distinct bottlings. Riffault's vines are spread out in 33 different parcels, chiefly mid-slope, in four villages, so he vinifies each parcel separately to respect the geological origins.

Half of Riffault's Sauvignon is planted on the *terres blanches* soils of the Les Boucauds vineyard which is also the name of his basic Sancerre blanc. After harvest, hand sorting and a four-hour pressing, 88% of the wine ferments in tank and 12% in barrel, then spends eight months on its lees before being bottled without filtration. The 2006 "Les Boucauds" was the first Riffault wine I'd ever tasted. It blew me away. A pungent, grapefruit and gooseberry attack gave way to flavors of stone, salt and minerals. Beautifully racy, it had extraordinary texture. The 2009, tasted in spring 2011, was simultaneously supple and crystalline. A joy.

"Les Chasseignes," a local term for *caillottes* soils, gives its name to Riffault's cuvée made from grapes ranging from five to forty years old grown on a high, well ventilated, southeast facing vineyard whose shallow limestone soils cover subsoils of overlapping stones. Seventy percent ferments in tank, the rest in barrel. The wine spends eight months on its lees before being bottled without filtration. The 2006 was strong and structured, with good traction and grip and focused flavors of minerals and peach. Downright ambassadorial.

In 2009 Riffault eliminated two of my favorite cuvées of his white Sancerre, "Les Pierrottes" and "Antique." For those of you lucky enough to still find them in shops or on lists, here are some notes.

"Les Pierrottes" came from the silex soils of two parcels within the lieudit "Les Bois". The 2006 was edgier than either the Boucauds or the Chasseignes of the same year. Stony and mineral, it was impressively racy, with fine grapefruit zest flavors along with notes of ginger. It recalled Chablis – even more so than the bottling from *terres blanches* soils. An excellent wine, it was lipsmacking and characterful. The 2007 was more tender, with flavors of preserved lemon, lime, caramel, and a savory saltiness. Each flavor was like a window opening onto another.

With his "Antique" *blanc* bottling, Riffault was clearly entering Didier Dagueneau territory. Made from three parcels of vines, all planted on *terres blanches* soils in 1959, the grapes ferment either in temperature controlled tanks or barrels. (About half and half.) The wine ages for eleven or twelve months, eight of them on its lees, which are regularly stirred up. The 2006 was statuesque, mellow and greatly mineral, an elegant, pedigreed wine with a refined stone and citrus zest flavors. The 2007, both ample and steely, had mouthwatering flavors of lemon and lime and exquisite acidity. Both nervy and racy, it was PMG.

Riffault has replaced those cuvées with Les Denisottes, Les Desmalets and Les Chailloux. Les Denisottes is made from 36 to 45 year-old vines on *terres blanches* soils with a southeastern exposure. Sixty-five percent ferments in tank, the rest in barrel. The wine ages on its lees for nine months before being bottled without filtration. The chiseled, crystalline 2009 was a textured beauty with flavors of minerals, lemon, lemon zest, and a whiff of gooseberry to give it a little punch. Excellent.

Les Desmalets comes from a 45 *are* parcel of vines aged from 16 to 37 years growing on the *terres blanches* soils of a southfacing hillside. After a long, slow pressing and decantation, the wine is put into large wood casks for fermentation. There it remains until it is assembled and, after an additional two months, bottled without having been filtered. The 2009 was a knock-out. Devastatingly fine, fresh, and pure as a mountain stream, it propels Sauvignon Blanc to great heights. The race, the sublety, the lingering flavors of lemon and lime, with an edge of salinity, is so mouthwatering you never tire of tasting it. And it's only when the wine warms up that you sense its 14% alcohol. Exceptional.

Ditto for the 2009 "Les Chailloux. Made from vines ranging from 13 to 40 years old on the silex soils of a slope with southwestern exposure, the wine ferments in large wood vats where it ages for seven months on its lees, before being assembled and aged for an additional two months, then bottled without filtration. Richly fragrant, the wine is more pungent than "Les Desmalets" but equally racy and crystalline, with a hint of oak. A bottle could disappear before you realized it.

All of Riffault's Pinot Noir is planted on the *terres blanches* and heavier marl soils of a parcel called La Noue which gives its name to Riffault's rosé and his basic red Sancerre.

Part of Riffault's rosé comes from wine bled from the tanks for the red Sancerre; the rest from grapes left to macerate for six to twelve hours before being pressed. The two are assembled for bottling. The 2007, tasted in January 2011, charmed with floral aromas mixed with those of peach, apricot, and crushed raspberry. It was a dry, delicate wine with a mineral core, and the fine acidity of the 2007 vintage. The 2006, tasted in 2009, was big, taut and very fresh – a serious, deeply colored rosé with aromas of rose petals and flavors of ripe strawberry and stone.

The grapes for the red version cold-soak for six to seven days and ferment for about three weeks with regular punching down and pumping over. From 30 to 50% is transferred to barrel while the rest ages in tank. After ten to twelve months, the two are assembled and bottled.

Based on my experience, La Noue *rouge* is a wine to be drunk in the near term, after having spent an hour or two in a carafe. After aeration, the 2008, tasted in December 2010, was cool, silken and fine of grain. Wonderfully fresh, pure and fluid, it had deep flavors of cherry and black tea. The 2006 was a bit less refined. Slightly chewy and tannic, it had flavors of sweet spices, mint, cassis and cherry. Wood never seems to be an interfering presence here.

As in Sancerre *blanc,* Riffault's top-of-the-line red was his "Antique" bottling but he has recently discontinued that, as well. As you may also come across this in shops and restaurants, here are some specifics. The wine comes from 40+ year old vines on clay-limestone soils. Yields are kept low by severe debudding and, depending on the year, successive cluster thinning. The grapes undergo a six to seven day cold-soaking before a three week vatting. The wine is transferred to oak barrels of one to four years for malolactic fermentation, and ages for four months without being fined or filtered.

Pure fruited and tantalizing, the 2007, tasted in 2010, had lipsmacking flavors of cherry and black tea, a real *gourmandise.* It would be considered a stellar Sancerre rouge in any vintage but for 2007 it was simply outstanding and, despite its 13 degrees alcohol, light on its feet. I watched the beautiful 2006 evolve over two days. Delicious, focused and admirable, it was a fresh, structured, suave Pinot Noir with succulent flavors of griotte and black cherries. A perfect example of why I go ballistic when people claim Sancerre can't make good pinot noir. After aeration, the 2005 fit this mouthwatering description as well. Bravo.

ॐ Sebastien Riffault

18300 Sury-en-Vaux; 02.48.79.32.57; 06.09.63.48.35

ॐ Hypernatural

Sebastien Riffault is an amiable young man who is a firm advocate of the non-interventionist school of wine making. On the three hectares of vines carved from his father's property (Domaine des Quarterons), Riffault farms organically. In the cellar, he uses no sulfur ("if possible"), adds no yeast, lets all his wines go through malolactic and ages them in old oak barrels.

The most mainstream of Riffault's wines is his Sancerre *blanc* "Les Quarterons". Fermented in tank, aged on its lees, lightly filtered, and treated to a small dose of so2, the 2007, at one tasting, was both tart and creamy with flavors reminiscent of ivy. On another day, it was fragrant – recalling both Chenin and the perfumes of Alsace. It had 2007's elegant acidity, and a grand statement of terroir. The 2007 red "Les Quarterons," also tank fermented, was smooth, a bit soft and somewhat volatile.

The heart of Riffault's production consists of cuvées with Lithuanian names – for his girlfriend – all related to soil types or stages of ripeness. "Akemine," which means stony, is the name of a white Sancerre from *caillottes* soils. It ferments in old oak barrels. Both hot and tart, the 2007, tasted in 2010, was concentrated, somewhat salty, quite oxidized and lightly caramelized. Riper Sauvignon, based on lower yielding vines, goes into the cuvée "Auksinis". More concentrated than the previous bottling, it also spends a longer time in barrel. The 2007, too, was oxidized and had a hot finish. But it was my favorite of Riffault's Lithuanian-named wines, both livelier and deeper, with notes of minerals and ginger. "Skeveldra" comes from silex soils. The 2007 was a bit foxy, with brazen flavors of ivy and cat pee. Tasted again, on another day, it was oaky and oxidized but interesting, based on good raw material. "Raudonas" is Riffault's red Sancerre from low yielding vines on limestone soils. It spends 18 months in old barrels. The 2007 was a tad hot and tasted of herbs and black tea, at one tasting; sampled again, it was a bit gasy but fluid and charming, light and fresh, with delicate pinot noir flavors.

🐚 Highly Recommended

🐚 Domaine Matthias & Emile Roblin
Maimbray 18300 Sancerre; 02.48.79.48.85;
matthias.emile.roblin@orange.fr

Matthias Roblin, whose father owns the Château de Maimbray, created his domaine roughly in 2000. He was joined by brother Emile in 2006. Their eight hectares of vines are chiefly on Kimmeridgian marl soils, and were augmented by another seven hectares on similar soils when the Château de Maimbray ceased activity after the 2009 vintage. The Roblins practice sustainable farming, yields are moderate, harvest is by machine save for the Ammonites and the Sancerre *rouge* bottlings. The Roblins produce three whites, two reds and a rosé.

The following wines were tasted in January 2011. The 2009 Sancerre *blanc* was creamy, with flavors of lemon, lime, and the zests of each. Like many 2009s, there's a bit of heat in the finish. Serve very cold. The 2006 Sancerre *blanc* was smooth and nicely balanced, *bien dans sa peau*. Its upfront citrus zest and grapefruit flavors were gently evolving in the direction of Chenin. A very good Loire Chenin-Sauvignon, fine for a bistrot dinner.

Ammonites are the shell-shaped fossils found in the limestone soils of the Sancerrois. The Roblins gave this name to a bottling of Sancerre *blanc*. Born in 2006, the cuvée comes from a *tri* of 20 year-old vines on the domaine's best parcels. The wine ages on its lees and is bottled without fining or filtration. With its aromas of creamed corn, the 2008 seemed to have entered its adolescence. A textured and tangy wine, it needed a bit of time to flesh out. The 2007, despite a whiff of ivy, was more discreet, evolved, and very mineral, with satisfying flavors of lemon, lime, and herbal tea. The 2006 gave off an initial whiff of ginger, followed by grapefruit and cassis bud. Pure and nuanced, it was also substantial and fairly deep. I'd have paired it with *sole meunière* or crab. Or a million other things.

The newest bottling, born with the 2010 vintage, is "l'Enclos de Maimbray," a blend of Sauvignon from all their parcels. The debut vintage, an infant when tasted, was a pungent, gooseberry flavored Sancerre.

The 2006 rosé, though slightly bland, was taut and dry, with very light hints of strawberries and minerals. The Roblins made no rosé in 2009 but their 2010 promises to be charming, with its tart peach flavors.

The Roblin's basic red comes from young vines (8 to 10 years old) on silt and clay-limestone soils. Sixty percent of the wine ages in stainless steel tanks, 40% in *demi-muids* of one to four wines. The 2008 had an alluring Pinot Noir nose. Somewhat drying on the palate and lightly gamy, it needed time to settle down. Firm but gentle, the 2006 was aging nicely: its color edging toward brick; its flavors entering the realm of dried fruit, spice, light hay, leather, and black tea. It was simply lovely with cèpe-stuffed ravioli tossed with sweet butter and parmesan.

The Roblins make a minute amount — about 12 hectolitres a year – of red called Grande Côte de la Vallée from hand-harvested, fifteen year old vines on a south-facing slope with silt and limestone over clay soils. The vintages I tasted fermented partially in demi-muids and partially in stainless steel tanks but the aim is to ferment all in oak casks. The 2009, though quite similar to the basic griotte-and-spice scented 2009 (each drawn from tank), was deeper, more tannic, and had richer flavors of black tea. The 2008 was all of a piece, its oak aging adding sweet spice notes to flavors of dried cherries.

᧞ Jean-Max Roger   ᧞ Highly Recommended

11, place du Carrou 18300 Bué:02 48 54 32 20;
jean-max.roger@wanadoo.fr; www.jean-max-roger.fr

Jean-Max Roger, a reliably good grower-negociant, took over the family's four hectares of vines in the early 1970s and expanded the estate to 26 hectares in Sancerre, and 5 in Menetou-Salon and Pouilly. He has been joined by two of his sons, Etienne and Thibault.

Roger produces five different Sancerre *blancs*. With the exception of the Vieilles Vignes bottling, all ferment in tank for several weeks, using indigenous yeasts, and are racked and fined in January or February, after which most are bottled.

The 2006 "Les Caillottes" cuvée, named for its soils, was textured and nicely structured, with pungent notes of grapefruit and gooseberry. Another 2006, the Cuvée GC, made mostly from grapes grown on the privileged slopes of Le Grand Chemarin, was my clear favorite of the line up. Pure and transparent, with a thread of sur lie bubbles, it was perfectly ripe, crystalline, with lovely citrus zest and mineral flavors. Downright racy. On the other hand, the 2005 Sancerre *blanc* Vieilles Vignes was curiously foxy and green. (A portion of this cuvée ferments in 400-litre oak barrels and ages in barrel for a year before being assembled, filtered, and packaged in a heavy, deluxe bottle.) The firm makes two additional whites, "CD" and "C.M."

Roger also makes a Sancerre rosé and two reds — a Vielles Vignes bottling which spends 15 to 18 months in barrel; and "La Grange Dimière," the entry-level red which takes its name from an ancient tithe barn. Twenty to thirty per cent ages in oak barrels for a year; the rest in temperature-controlled stainless steel tanks. The 2005 Grange Dimière, tasted in 2008, greeted me with a strong whiff reminiscent of the rind of a St. Nectaire, which I don't find disagreeable. It came across rather hard, with cool, lean fruit. Food helped immensely. My dinner guests and I had no trouble polishing off the bottle.

᠅ Highly Recommended

᠅ Domaine de la Rossignole/Pierre Cherrier & Fils:
Rue de la Croix Michaud, Chaudoux 18300 Verdigny-en-Sancerre; 02.48.79.33.41; cherrier@easynet.fr

Created in 1927, this domaine was taken over and expanded in 1923 by Pierre Cherrier. In the early '80s Pierre was joined by sons François and Jean-Marie, each of whom spent three years studying at the Lycée Viticole de Beaune.

The Cherrier's practice sustainable farming on their 19 hectares – vineyards with a mix of Sancerre's classic soils: *caillottes, terres blanches* and silex. Yields average 60 hl/ha. Harvest is by machine, and the grapes ferment in thermoregulated tanks.

Tasted in January 2011, the 2006 Sancerre Vieilles Vignes was a vivid, textured wine whose fresh, grapefruit flavors made your mouth water. It was cool as a pure, mineral, mountain stream. The cuvée "l'Essentiel" is a Sancerre *blanc* made from a single hectare of 30 year old vines on clay-limestone and flinty-clay soils. It is bottled unfined and unfiltered. A characterful wine with a true sense of place, the 2006 was alluringly structured, vibrant, with mouthwatering flavors of grapefruit, stone and flint. And it was just all around nice.

The Cuvée Grand Picot ages in barrel. The 2008 benefited from a bit of aeration during which time the wine seemed to refine itself into a fresh, mineral, pellucid Sancerre, lightly tart, with appetizing flavors of gooseberry and fresh lemon juice.

❧ Domaine de Saint Pierre/Pierre Prieur & Fils

Rue Saint Vincent, 18300 Verdigny; 02.48.79.31.70;
www.prieur-pierre-sancerre.com

Another reliable and venerable family domaine. Thierry and Bruno, the
sons of Pierre, having taken over from their father, are the tenth generation
to work the family vines. Gaël Prieur, 21, who studied viticulture at
Fondettes (outside of Tours) is the 11th.

The Prieurs have 17 hectares of vines spread out over 30-plus parcels,
with 12 hectares planted to Sauvignon Blanc and five to Pinot Noir. Soils
are chiefly *terres blanches* and *caillottes* with 10% flint. The Prieurs practice
sustainable farming, and the harvest is conducted by hand.

There seems to be an ever-expanding number of white cuvées, starting
with the "domaine" bottling, a blend of all three soil types. The 2009, tasted
in January 2011, was full, textured, and lightly varietal, with flavors of citrus
and gooseberry.

"Les Coinches" comes from ten year-old vines on a 1.5 hectare south-facing parcel. Both this and the previous bottling ferment in stainless steel
tanks and spend three to four months on their lees. The sample I tasted
was *brut de cuve* but already extremely promising. Textured, racy and elegant, it had lovely flavors of minerals and citrus — for drinkers like me —
and sufficient gooseberry and herbaceous notes to please admirers of the
old, unreconstructed "varietal" style.

"Les Monts Damnés", from 30 year-old vines, made its debut in the 2010
vintage. It had a broader nose than "Les Coinches" and impressed with its
stature, length and depth, combined with flavors of grapefruit, citrus zests,
and a hint of gooseberry. Very nice.

The "Maréchal Prieur" bottling comes from the domaine's oldest vines
on *terres blanches* soils. The grapes are hand harvested and 25% ferments
and ages in oak – some new and some once-used. The 2008 displayed light
but definite oak. It was creamy, mineral and very appealing, but I preferred
the *lieux-dits*. The 2005 was ripe, layered and almost viscous but not heavy.
It was not a ringer for Chablis though you might have taken it for a more
southerly Burgundy. Clearly a Sancerre for fine dining, it was ample and
flavorful, and the oak came across as a delicate seasoning. The 2003, by
2011, had clearly started the oxidation phase of its life. An interesting wine,
I'd serve it with cheese.

The domaine's rosé comes from 10 to 20 year old vines on chiefly flinty
soils. Most of the harvest is pressed directly and ferments in tank. The
lightly floral 2010 was taut but tender. A pleasure.

The domaine's basic red comes from ten to forty year old wines, half of which grow on *terres blanches* soils and half on flinty soils. The grapes are cold soaked for three days and ferment in stainless steel tanks. A fraction – 15% — ages in barriques on a four-year rotation. The seductive 2008 had clear aromas of raspberry mixed with light oak. The French would call it *gourmand* and would say *ça se boit sans soif* (one drinks it without being thirsty).

The red version of "Maréchal Prieur" comes from a selection of old vines on *terres blanches* and *caillottes* soils. It ages in barriques of one wine for a year. The 2007, impressively structured for a red from that vintage, had a textbook, classic Pinot nose, mingled with oak, spices, dried fruit and leather. The 2008, tasted in June 2011, was a smooth, balanced, and very pretty Sancerre *rouge* with juicy black cherry flavors. Just perfect with pan-fried duck breast.

Recommended

David Sautereau
18300 Crézancy-en-Sancerre; 02.48.79.42.52;
david.sautereau@wanadoo.fr

Ninth generation vigneron David Sautereau rented the family's six hectares of vineyards – predominantly *terres blanches* with 25% *caillottes* — in 1998 and began replanting and practicing sustainable farming. Yields are moderate – 63 hl/ha – and grapes are harvested by machine. White wine makes up most of the production. It ferments at cool temperatures and spends three months on its lees before bottling. The 2006, tasted in December 2010, offered a straightforward gooseberry-grapefruit nose. Coherent and well made, with an appetizing scent of lime, it was a good middle of the road, solid bistro white. Sautereau also makes a small amount of pleasant red and rosé. The wines may appear under different labels in different markets.

Highly Recommended

Domaine Michel Thomas
Les Argots 18300 Sury-en-Vaux; 02.48.79.35.46;
thomas.mld@wanadoo.fr

Michel and Laurent Thomas practice sustainable farming on their 17 hectares of vines. Grapes are machine harvested, ferment in temperature-controlled stainless steel tanks, and age on their fine lees. The basic white bottling is made from 30 year old vines on Sancerre's tyical mix of soils — *caillottes, terres blanches* (40% each) and silex (20%). Though slightly off-dry, the 2009, tasted in January 2011, was fresh and floral with distinct ripe peach flavors. The 2006, tasted in 2009, was tart, green and a bit stiff. The "Silex" bottling comes from 25 year-old vines from silex soils and is bottled unfiltered. The 2009 was tight, focused, fresh and flinty. It, too, had ripe peach flavors, here mingled with fine minerality. Not only very admirable but very definitely PMG. The 2006 was very mineral, rather racy and truly flinty, with an ample mouth feel. Its flavors included grapefruit and cat pee as well as hints of tar, and a sweetish note in the finish. Very appealing. The "Terres Blanches" cuvée, not made every year, comes from old (45 to 50 years) vines, ages in barrels on a three-year rotation, and is bottled unfiltered. Creamy and vanilla-scented, the 2009 is a wine worth cellaring for at least three years. The domaine's basic red ferments and ages in tank. The 2009 was plump, with toothsome flavors of cherry and black tea. Charming. The "Alexis" bottling comes from vines over 50 years old, yielding 45 to 50 hl/ha. It ferments in stainless steel tanks and ages in barriques on a three year rotation. Sweet vanilla-oak flavors dominated the 2009 when tasted in January 2011, but fine Pinot Noir fruit was perceptible beneath. Put this one away for three years, alongside the "Terres Blanches".

ɶ Domaine Claude & Florence Thomas-Labaille   ɶ Excellent
18300 Sancerre; 02.48.54.06.95; thomas.labaille@wanadoo.fr

In 1994 Jean-Paul Labaille quit his job as a civil servant and he and his wife, Florence Thomas, took over her father's 9.3 hectare domaine. (Labaille is from Sury-en-Vaux and stands to inherit 1.5 hectares in that commune.) Labaille cleaned up the cellars and bought new – but not brand new – barrels, but otherwise continued to make wines as his father-in-law had done. (He had assisted during harvest for ten vintages.) He practices sustainable farming. The location of most of the vines on the steep slopes of Monts Damnés necessitates that most work be done by hand. Yields are low and, depending on the cuvée, wines ferment in barrel, stainless steel tanks, or concrete vats. They are bottled unfiltered. There are three white bottlings and a red.

I usually start with the most accessible cuvée. Here, however, I'll start with the domaine's superb bottling from "Les Monts Damnés", the 2006, which I first "encountered" in July 2008. (NB: this bottling is sometimes sold under the name "Aristides" rather than "Monts Damnés".) When tasting this majestic Sancerre (unfiltered), from one of the best sites with the best soils (*terres blanches*) in one of the best communes (Chavignol) in the appellation, I thought 'Chablis in the Loire.' An achingly regal wine, it is fresh, focused, and tight yet layered; its flavors, all minerals, chalk, stone and citrus zests — grapefruit, lemon and lime. It goes beautifully with food and yet it's so racy that it's almost a *vin de méditation*. It certainly put me in a reflective mood! (It is, in fact, one of the wines that made me reconsider my opinion of Sauvignon Blanc as a grape variety.)

As for the 2006 of the more accessible "L'Authentique" bottling, well, it's a beauty too: A tight, focused wine with lots of grip and heady aromas and flavors of white-fleshed peaches, blossoms, grapefruit zests and minerals, it is racy and delicious.

The excellence of these two wines made me want to visit the domaine which I was able to do in the spring of 2009 where I tasted the 2008s. My notes from that visit as well as from the Salon des Vins de Loire in 2011, where I tasted the 2009s, follow.

The first wine tasted during my visit to the domaine was the 2008 "L'Authentique." Fermented and aged in tank, it was floral and tart, a well-mannered Sancerre, dominated by flavors of lemon, lime, lime zest and herbal tea. The 2009 was creamy, tangy, full of lemon and herbal tea flavors. Pure Chavignol.

The 2008 "Monts Damnés" aka "Cuvée Aristide", ages half in tank and half in barrel and was to be bottled – unfiltered – during the week of our visit. So we tasted four different lots. Racy and powerful, the first sample, from 7 to 8 year old barrels, exploded with intense lime flavors, light gooseberry, minerals, and seemed enveloped by a glaze of ginger, verbena and tilleul. The next barrel sample brought a marrowy, textured wine, full of oak and citrus flavors. The oak seemed more integrated in the third sample which was zesty and lipsmacking. Barrel number four had already been assembled for bottling. All I wrote was: The Force is with you. The 2009 was pellucid, deep and racy. Mineral and complex, you completely forgot about the grape variety. Another GC Chablis in the Loire.

Then came another bottling from "Monts Damnés" which, in the United States, goes by the name "Cuvée Buster" (after the importer's late dog) or "Fleur de Gallifard", its lieu-dit. The low yielding (25 hl/ha) vines are over 80 years old and grow on soils rich in both chalk and the kind of clay used in pottery making. (The greater Sancerrois region is also known for its pottery.) Fermented in barrel, with natural yeasts, neither racked, nor fined, nor filtered, it weighed in at 14.7 alcohol with a gram of residual sugar. A dense wine, yet straight as an arrow, with notes of ginger and soft oak, the 2008 was simply excellent. A 2007 disappointed slightly with flavors of green pea mixed with lime and verbena, but I'd love to taste it again. The 2009 was deep, creamy and regal, its oak well-integrated. What a pity Labaille makes only two barriques of it!

Labaille has two hectares of Pinot Noir, not all of the same quality. Some, he says are "Pinot Droit, a terrible vine, but used only in the rosé." Labaille presses his red grapes immediately for his rosé. The 2008, with notes of rose petals, was mineral, tart, dry, lovely. He makes a small amount –one tank – of red. The 2007 recalled Pineau d'Aunis with its black and white pepper accents and pretty fruit. Chalky, spicy, charming and *gourmand*. The 2008 had just been bottled but was as charming as the 2007, and another lip-smacker.

❧ Domaine Tinel-Blondelet/La Croix Canat
(See Pouilly)

❧ Highly Recommended

A solid producer of Pouilly-Fumé since 1985, Tinel-Blondelet also makes an admirable Sancerre. The 2006 *blanc*, tasted in December 2010, was as fresh as a spring morning. A racy wine, with a thread of sur lie carbonation, it was extremely mineral and evolving gently toward Chenin-like flavors. Whites from 2006 can sometimes seem flatfooted. Not this one. It soared.

❧ Domaine Roland Tissier
Le Petit Morice 18300 Sancerre; 02.48.54.02.93;
sanerretissier@wanadoo.fr; www.domaine-tissier.fr

❧ Recommended

In 1972 Roland Tessier combined the vineyard holdings of his father and his father-in-law into a single domaine of 11 hectares, 80% of which is planted to Sauvignon, 20% to Pinot Noir. After having worked with their father, Rodolphe and Florent took over the property and built new cellars in 2004. They make a rosé by bleeding the vats of fermenting red wines, two cuvées of red Sancerre, including an old vines bottling, and two of white. I have only tasted the whites.

The first is the domaine bottling. It comes from 30 year old vines grown on a mix of Sancerre's typical soils — *caillottes, terres blanches* and silex. The grapes are machine harvested and ferment in enamel-lined tanks at 15 degrees celcius for 15 to 20 days. The wine is aged on its fine lees for a time before being fined, clarified and lightly filtered for bottling.

The 2006, tasted in 2010, seemed very generic, shallow and only marginally ripe – foxy, with aromas of cat pee – though it weighed in at 13 degrees alcohol. That said, it won the Liger d'Or, a gold medal at the Salon des Vins de Loire competition. Similarly generic was the 2006 "Cuvée Saint-Benoît". Made from 60 year old vines grown on *terres blanches*, the wine ferments and ages in oak barrels. It is lightly filtered before bottling. Relatively ample and a bit sour, the 2006 wasn't bad and will please those who like oak flavors.

𝄞 Outstanding

𝄞 Domaine Vacheron

Rue du Puits Poulton, BP 49, 18300 Sancerre; 02.48.54.09.93; vacheron.sa@wanadoo.fr

Here is a domaine that goes from strength to strength. And shows no signs of stopping. Certified biodynamic, the domaine consists of 34 hectares of Sauvignon Blanc and 11 hectares of Pinot Noir, many of them located on Sancerre's most privileged *lieux-dits*.

Run by brothers Jean-Louis and Denis and their sons Jean-Dominique (Lycée de Beaune) and Jean-Laurent, the Vacherons pamper their vineyards — debudding in spring, strictly limiting yields, brewing home-infused homeopathic treatments, and hoeing by hand. And they continue to fine tune their work: they seem constantly to redefine the use of oak, for example, using both larger and older barrels, and have worked out a legally approved method of repropagating their own selection massale vines.

Some twenty years ago, Vacheron was known mostly for its red wines, though its whites were highly regarded as well. Today one would be hard pressed to choose between the two colors – the entire line in each is top notch – and the rosés are mighty tempting too.

The domaine's entry level Sancerre *blanc* comes from vines planted along a fault line in Sancerre, giving it a mix of chiefly of silex and *caillottes* soils, with about 10% marl. As I may have said before, it drives me nuts when people dismiss a wine – or refuse to try it – because of the high alcohol level. To me, it's all about balance, coherence and freshness. The 2009 Sancerre blanc weighed in at 14.5 alcohol and you didn't feel it. At least I didn't. Tasted in December 2010, my first notes were "C-ductive!" And then some minor observations, to wit that it seemed to have some residual sugar, but that sense of sweetness might have come from the alcohol; it was fresh, despite the alcohol, and its grapefruit-dominated flavors mixed deliciously with an appetizing chalkiness.

Tasted in the fall of 2009, the 2008 was tangy and vibrantly fruity, with spirited yet ample 2008 structure, and flavors of gooseberry and grapefruit. There was a whiff of cat pee, too, but also minerals, chalkiness, and an abundance of citrus zests. Lipsmacking. Tasted in December 2008, the 2007 was thoroughly admirable, nicely ripe, with fine acidity, lovely balance, and savory minerality. The 2006, tasted at the same time, was classic in the best sense of the word: ripe, tight, mineral and fresh, with lively grapefruit flavors. There was a wee touch of heat in the finish but nothing to worry about.

"En Grands Champs" is a new single-vineyard bottling. The grapes come from a plateau with clay-rich, calcareous soils dating back to the Oxfordian and Kimmeridgian eras, in other words, 150 to 130 million years. The 2009, tasted in December 2010, was very fresh, very chalky, and very promising. While not at all vegetal, it tasted lightly "green" and was yet another Chablis ringer.

Another new cuvée is "Paradis" which comes from a south-facing parcel of the same name whose stony, calcareous soils also date back to the Oxfordian and Kimmeridgian eras. The 2009 drank like a blend of the juices of grapefruit, lemon and passion fruit. It was a touch hot but lively and fairly intense without being vulgar.

"Les Romains" comes from the Vacheron's two-hectare parcel of this seven hectare lieu-dit reputed for its superb exposition as well as for its pure silex soils. The wine ferments at low temperatures, without added yeasts. Half ages in tank and half in barrels of one to three wines. The 2009, tasted in December 2010, was reduced and in serious need of aeration. Nevertheless, minerals and citrus zest flavors were perceptible. The 2008, tasted at the same time, was true to its vintage: its vigorous acidity well cushioned by ample fruit and alcohol. The most typically "varietal" of the Vacheron-line-up, it fell just short of phenolic ripeness but was mighty tasty. The 2007, tasted in late 2008, was a high octane, terroir-driven Sancerre. Lightly foxy, it was steely, forceful, saline, with a long finish. Another sample was all crystalline elegance, an ice sculpture of citrus zests. Excellent. The 2005, tasted in 2009, was tight yet so full it bordered on unctuous. It was also slightly foxy. Behind a scrim of fruit there was a racy and alluringly pellucid backdrop of herbal tea, rock crystal, and steel that I wished would come to the fore. I'll be eager to try it again.

The Vacherons make a toothsome direct press, barrel-aged rosé. The 2008 was a welcoming wine, taut, with no jagged acidity, and delicate fruit. Tasted both in 2009 and 2010, it was a bit oaky but quite appetizing.

The 2007 entry level red, tasted in late 2009, was a fragrant charmer; the 2006, tasted a year earlier, disappointed; it was a bit gamy and somewhat drying.

"Belle Dame" is the name of the deluxe red bottling. The wine macerates and ferments for thirty days in stainless steel tanks equipped with pneumatic punching down mechanisms, and spends a year in barriques and another in 25 hl oak casks. The 2007, tasted in December 2010, was light but perfectly formed. It was discreet, charming and *gourmand*. Beautiful lady, indeed. The 2006, tasted on several occasions between 2007 and 2009, was nuanced and gentle, with flavors of mulled cherries and sweet spices along with mild oak and a whiff of gameyness. Simultaneously steely and supple, the 2005 was a fine red for an upscale bistro, a mouthwatering wine, full and fresh, with flavors of rich spices, cherries and light tannins.

🐾 Recommended

🐾 Domaine André Vatan
Route des Petite Perrières, Chaudoux 18300 Verdigny;
02.48.79.33.07; avatan@terre-net.fr

Now represented by the fourth generation — grand father was a barrel maker, a winemaker, a cultivator of cereal crops and a shepherd; André's father, having no talent for barrel making, concentrated on wine and cereal – the domaine, now purely *viticole,* has 12 hectares of vines and makes three different bottlings of Sancerre and a bit of Vin de Pays. Viticulture is conventional, yields are 50 to 60 hl/ha, and harvest is by machine.

There are two bottlings of white Sancerre. The first, "Les Charmes", comes from 20+ year-old vines on Sancerre's three classic soil types. It ferments in tank. The 2005, tasted early in 2006, was vibrant and bracing, a bit herbaceous, a lot mineral, with a tangy grapefruit zest finish. The 2006, tasted in January 2011, was ripe, lightly evolving toward mellow Alsace and Chenin-like flavors, yet still tangy. Time to drink up, however, and it would be very nice with Alsace classics such as *flammenküche.* The second cuvée, "St. François," comes from 30+ year-old vines on silex soils. Two-thirds ferments in tank, one-third in oak casks. The 2005, tasted in early 2006, was lightly pungent, varietal, rich, and just a bit too tender for me, though I liked the kick of lemon zest in the finish.

"Maulin Bèle" is Vatan's name for a red bottling made from 25+ year old vines on limestone and clay-limestone soils. The 2006, tasted in January 2011, should probably have been drunk in 2009. Brick-colored around the rim, it was quite dry, a bit thin, with flavors of game, dried fruit, and spices as well as unripe tannins.

🐾 To Follow

Michel Vattan
18300 Sury-en-Vaux; 02.48.79.40.98; www.michel-vattan.com

Pascal Joulin, who worked alongside Michel Vattan on this 9-hectare property since 2002, has recently taken over the reins. Having worked at such Bordeaux properties as Meyney, Biston-Brillette and Gruaud Larose, as well as having helped create a vineyard in Quebec, Joulin sought work in his native Sancerre when his father fell ill.

Since his arrival at Domaine Michel Vattan, Joulin has been adopting eco-friendly methods of farming and has focused on vinification by terroir. I have tasted only one of the domaine's several bottlings, the 2008 "Cuvée Argile", from 42 year-old vines planted on *terres blanches*. In 2010, the wine was ample and saline, with vivid acidity and notes of creamed corn and hard candy. I had the sense of a good job done with less than exalted raw material. Promising stuff. And I expect we'll be hearing more good things about Joulin – and tasting some very nice wines – in the years to come.

🍇 Domaine des Vieux Pruniers/ Christian Thirot-Fournier

18300 Bué-en-Sancerre; 02.48.54.09.40;
www.domaine-des-vieux-pruniers.com

🍇 Recommended

Christian Thiriot is the most recent generation to head this 10-hectare family domaine. The seven hectares planted to Sauvignon Blanc grow on *caillottes* soils; the three hectares of Pinot Noir, on *terres blanches*. Viticulture and vinification are rather conventional.

The basic wine ferments in tank at low temperatures for about two weeks and ages on its lees. The 2008 was vigorous, pungent, and distinctly foxy. The fresh, pleasant 2008 rosé, made from bleeding the vats of fermenting red, had candy-like strawberry flavors. There is also a special cuvée of white, "la P'tite Coûte," and two reds, one of which is oak-aged.

Chapter Three
Pouilly-Fumé &
Pouilly-Sur-Loire

Status: AOCs Pouilly-Fumé; Pouilly-sur-Loire 1937.

Types of Wine: dry white.

Grapes: Sauvignon Blanc for Pouilly-Fumé; Chasselas for Pouilly-sur-Loire.

Zone: 1,232 hectares (3,043 acres) for Pouilly-Fumé and 30 hectares (74 acres) for Pouilly-sur-Loire in seven villages on the right bank of the Loire in the Nièvre départemente. The villages are Pouilly-sur-Loire, Tracy-sur-Loire, St. Andelain, St. Martin-sur-Nohain, St. Laurent, Garchy, and Mesves-sur-Loire. Well-known hamlets include Les Loges and Les Berthiers.

Production: For the 2010 vintage: 75,115 hl for Pouilly Fumé; 1,785 hl for Pouilly-sur-Loire.

Soils: Two types of *caillottes* (pebbly, compact limestone): Villiers from the Oxfordian and Barrois from the Portlandian periods; *terres blanches* or Kimmeridgian marl with small oyster shells; and Silex, or flinty clay from the Cretaceous period.

When to Drink: For Pouilly-Fumé, depending on your taste, now, later, much later; for Pouilly-sur-Loire, unless made by Serge Dagueneau & Fils, DYA.

Price: Pouilly Fumé: $$ to $$$$; Pouilly-sur-Loire: $ to $$

Pouilly-Fumé

Situated between Burgundy and Berry, the Pouilly appellations face Sancerre across the Loire. The name Pouilly is derived from the Roman Paulica Villa or Villa Paulus though its vineyards predate the Roman era and have been continuously cultivated since that time. Vines covered nearly 2000 hectares by 1832 when Jullien issued his *Topographie de tous les vignobles connus* (1832) in which he wrote, "Pouilly sur Loire produces white wines which have body and spirit, a light scent of gunflint and an extremely agreeable flavor. They don't turn yellow and they keep their douceur for a long time."

The wine Jullien describes was a blend of Sauvignon Blanc and Chasse-las, the two grapes which, bottled pure, make today's Pouilly-Fumé and Pouilly-sur-Loire, respectively. Pouilly-Fumé is by far the more important —and the finer — wine. But Sauvignon, or Blanc Fumé, as it is often called, was rarely bottled on its own until the '30s and did not overtake Chasselas in the region's vineyards until the last thirty-five years. It now represents more than 90% of planting. And the wine it makes here bears a strong resemblance to Jullien's Pouilly —full, spirited, flinty, tasty and tender.

Vibrant and forceful when young, with flavors ranging from the herba-ceous (including *pipi de chat*) to full-fruited – from citrus to peach, fig and apricot, to exotic fruit like mangos — to mineral and stone, it evolves much like Chenin Blanc (albeit not as long-lived), when, after four or five years in bottle, apple, quince, quinine, and herbal tea flavors like chamomile, ver-bena and tilleul become part of the weave.

The threat of frost, which is more of a problem in Pouilly than in Sancerre, has concentrated production within three communes, Pouilly, St. Andelain and Tracy/Maltaverne, a sheltered microclimate with the best soils, which runs north of Pouilly for about seven kilometers on either side of RN7.

Kimmeridgian marl, called *terres blanches,* underlies much of Pouillys vineyards; around St. Andelain (excepting La Butte), for example, and in parts of le Bouchot. Rich in clay, these soils take longer to heat up and pro-duce heavier, longer-lived wines.

Two types of compact limestone (*caillottes*) are also common: *calcaire de Villiers* is found mostly in the eastern part of the appellation and at the southern and eastern limits of le Bouchot; composed of harder, larger stones, *Calcaires de Barrois* are dry, poor soils, found on the western border of the appellation; in Boisfleury and Boisgibault, for example, and the ham-let of Les Loges. These soils tend to make aromatic, earlier drinking wines. The fourth major soil type is the flinty-clay from the Cretaceous era, or silex, to be found on the Butte of St. Andelain, in St. Laurent L'Abbaye and on the hillsides of Tracy.

Many of the same soil types exist in Sancerre though Pouilly's have more clay. Thus, its wines take longer to express themselves but they are richer, weightier, broader in flavor, and more alcoholic.

What is the difference between Sancerre and Pouilly Fumé? "Hard to say," was the answer I habitually received from growers, followed by

"Sancerre's soils are more varied; there's a greater difference between a Sancerre from Bué and one from Crézancy than there is between Sancerre and Pouilly."

An after-image says Pouilly is more reminiscent of southern Burgundy than Sancerre. The best of the "regular" cuvées have a weight and texture that recalls Burgundy's Pouilly-Fuissé. The best of the best, Domaine Didier Dagueneau's "Silex", for example, or Jonathan Pabiot's cuvée "Prédilection", are deep, structured, whites with none of Sauvignon's characteristic edginess and little of its green bean-*pipi de chat* aromas. In weight and style, they recall Côte d'Or, the Côte Maconnais and the Côte Chalonnaise as well as Chablis.

A further observation: I have found that a number of Pouillys – particularly those from the Les Berthiers/St. Andelain and Les Loges areas – sometimes have foxy notes reminiscent of the characteristic scents of *vitis labrusca* grapes like Concord and Noah. I have no idea where or why this particular expression developed in these wines.

Note that a number of producers choose to label some or all of their Pouilly-Fumé as Blanc Fumé de Pouilly. There is no difference.

Pouilly Sur Loire

With the arrival of the Bourbonnais railroad in 1858, Paris fruiterers came to the Pouilly region in search of Chasselas to sell as table grapes — for which they were willing to pay higher prices than they paid for wine. Sales boomed. In 1865 the railway station of Pouilly, one of three in the area, sent 3000 metric tons of Chasselas to Paris. By 1890, however, Parisian produce merchants had abandoned the Chasselas of Pouilly for grapes from the Midi, which the creation of new rail-lines linking Paris with the south of France had made more accessible. The Chasselas crop was turned into wine but, as growers realized that Sauvignon did a better job in that department, they began replacing their Chasselas with Blanc Fumé.

Wine made from Chasselas in the Pouilly Fumé zone is entitled to the appellation Pouilly-sur-Loire. But it is an endangered species. Generally planted on heavy, clay-siliceous soils, its acreage diminishes with each vintage. A bland, creamy white, it nevertheless has its fans. Certainly no one tasting Domaine Serge Dagueneau & Filles old vines Pouilly-sur-Loire would want to see this special wine disappear.

Serge Dagueneau, and now his daughter, Valerie, have always made a bit of old vines Pinot Noir for home consumption. It's pure gourmandise, nothing less than a *cru,* and it bears witness to the fact that the soils of

Pouilly could very well accommodate the Pinot Noir vine – as has been amply proven in two neighboring appellations, Sancerre, across the river, and the Coteaux du Giennois, a northern extension of Pouilly.

Producers

There are 130 winemakers, 10 grower-négociants and one cooperative. Many are grouped in two hamlets — Les Loges in Pouilly, and Les Berthiers in St. Andelain. Additionally, quite a few domaines located in other appellations make wine in Pouilly. Some are reviewed below. Others include: Gitton, and Jean Max Roger, both in Sancerre; Langlois-Château in Saumur, and Hubert Veneau in the Giennois.

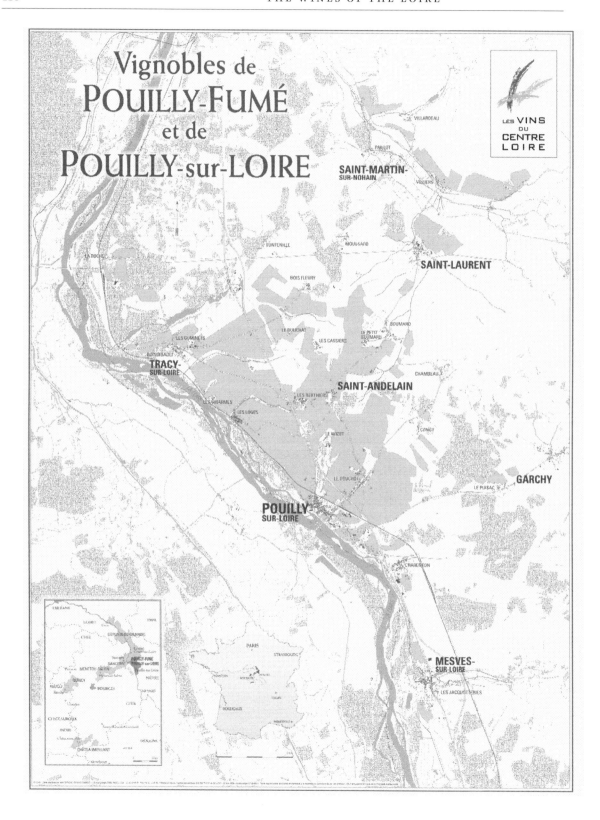

Vignobles de
POUILLY-FUMÉ
et de
POUILLY-sur-LOIRE

LES VINS
DU
CENTRE
LOIRE

VILLARDEAU

PAILLOT

SAINT-MARTIN-
SUR-NOHAIN

VILLIERS

FONTENILLE

MOUSSARD

LA ROCHE

SAINT-LAURENT

BOIS FLEURY

LE BURCHAT

LES CASSIERS

SOUMARD

LE PETIT
SOUMARD

LES OUMINETS

BOISBRADET

TRACY-
SUR-LOIRE

CHAMBLAU

SAINT-ANDELAIN

LES CHARMLS

LES BERTHIERS

LES LOGES

LE NOZET

CONGY

GARCHY

LE POUCHO

LE PURSAC

POUILLY-
SUR-LOIRE

CHARENTON

MESVES-
SUR-LOIRE

LES JACQUOTTERIES

Pouilly-Fumé et Pouilly-sur-loire

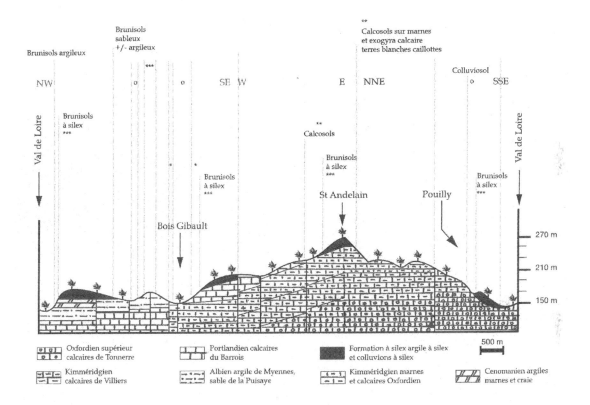

Brunisols argileux

Brunisols
sableux
+/- argileux

Calcosols sur marnes
et exogyra calcaire
terres blanches caillottes

Colluviosol

NW   o   o   SE W   E   NNE   SSE

Val de Loire

Brunisols
à silex
***

Calcosols

Brunisols
à silex
***

Brunisols
à silex
***

Brunisols
à silex
***

St Andelain   Pouilly

Bois Gibault

Val de Loire

270 m

210 m

150 m

500 m

Oxfordien supérieur calcaires de Tonnerre	Portlandien calcaires du Barrois	Formation à silex argile à silex et colluvions à silex	
Kimméridgien calcaires de Villiers	Albien argile de Myennes, sable de la Puisaye	Kimméridgien marnes et calcaires Oxfordien	Cenomanien argiles marnes et craie

🎗 Outstanding

Domaine Didier Dagueneau 🎗 Jonathan Pabiot

🎗 Excellent

Henri Bourgeois 🎗 Alain Cailbourdin 🎗
Serge Dagueneau et Filles 🎗 Pascal Jolivet 🎗 Domaine Laporte
🎗 Domaine Michel Redde 🎗 Château de Tracy

🎗 To follow

Alexandre Bain

🎗 Highly Recommended

Michel & David Bailly 🎗 Domaine Francis Blanchet 🎗
Domaine Bouchié-Chatellier 🎗 Caves de Pouilly sur Loire 🎗
Domaine Jean-Claude Chatelain 🎗
Andre Dezat & Fils/ Domaine Thibault 🎗 Château Favray 🎗
Domaine Masson-Blondelet 🎗 Régis Minet 🎗
Domaine de Riaux/Jeannot Pere & Fils 🎗 Domaine Tinel-Blondelet
🎗 Domaine Sébastien Treuillet

🎗 Recommended

Domaine Gilles Blanchet 🎗 Jacques Carroy et Fils 🎗
Domaine de l'Epineau/ Emmanuel Charrier 🎗
Domaine Hervé Seguin

🎗 By the Glasss

Gilles Chollet 🎗 Pomaine Dominique PabiotDomaine 🎗
Domaine Nicolas Gaudry 🎗 Eric Louis 🎗 Pierre Marchand & Fils
🎗 Joseph Mellot 🎗 Domaine Guy Saget

🎗 Other

Baron de Ladoucette/Château du Nozet

✍ Michel & David Bailly

3, Rue Saint Vincent Les Loges 58150 Pouilly-sur-Loire;
03.86.39.04.78; domaine.michel.bailly@wanadoo.fr

✍ Highly Recommended

The Bailly family has been making wine in Pouilly for over 200 years. Initially exclusively in the village of Les Loges, they have since extended their reach to Tracy and further north, to the Coteaux du Giennois where they have 1.50 hectares planted to Pinot Noir and Gamay. A half a hectare is planted to Chasselas for their Pouilly-sur-Loire and the rest is planted to Sauvignon Blanc. David Bailly joined father Michel in 1998 and seems to have introduced more than a breath of fresh air into the domaine. The Baillys practice sustainable farming. They harvest by machine and all their wines ferment in thermoregulated tanks and age sur lie.

I was introduced to the domaine's wines at the ViniBGood stand at the Salon des Vins de Loire in 2004. They were pouring a tank fermented 2003 from Kimmeridgian marl soils. A pungent cat's pee aroma gave way to a wine that was full and on the verge of over-ripe on the palate, much in the bosomy style of "M," made by Touraine's indefatigable Henry Marionnet. It was a big, low acid wine with what seemed like 2 grams of residual sugar. Not perfect but ambitious and I made a note to follow their progress.

A range of 2006s, tasted in 2009 and 2010, confirmed my optimism. The cuvée "Les Vallons" comes from 15 year-old vines on limestone and Kimmeridgian marl soils. The 2006 was vibrant and gold-hued with flavors of preserved lemon, lemon zest, and verbena. Savory and mouthwatering, it was an envigorating wine with notes of melon and fig in the finish.

The cuvée "les Bines" represents a selection made from their best parcels, 35 year-old vines on limestone soils. It is fermented with indigenous yeasts and ages in tank, on its lees, for eleven months without racking. The 2006 was mineral and citric, with light blackcurrant bud notes. An appetizing wine, it had good focus, good grip, and an appetizing mineral core.

The cuvée "Les Tonnes", in a Burgundy bottle, comes from 35 year-old vines on a mix of limestone and Kimmeridgian marl soils. After fermenting in tank, the wine is aged on its lees in new 500 litre barrels. The 2006 was gold, mellow, and simultaneously full and fresh, with light but definite oak flavors. Savory and textured, it was an ambitious wine.

🐌 To Follow

🐌 Alexandre Bain

Boisfleury 18, Rue des Levées, 58150 Tracy sur Loire;
06.77.11.13.05; alexandre.bain@orange.fr

Touraine maverick Thierry Puzelat is not a secretive man. When I asked him where he sourced the grapes for the Pouilly Fumé he sells as a negociant, he gave me Bain's name. Puzelat is always an interesting reference and young Bain, who created his 7.5 hectare domaine in 2007, is definitely someone to watch.

Bain specifically wanted a domaine on a "human scale." Soils are Kimmeridgian marl and Portlandian limestone. Viticulture is organic and biodynamic, and Bain's wines are entitled to both the Ecocert and the Demeter labels. Grapes are hand harvested.

A 2009, tasted in early 2010, was perfumed and mineral, more Alsace than Loire – which is not unusual. Worth following. A 2008 was pure fruited, with aromas of creamed corn. A vibrant wine, it was a full-throated expression of 2008's quilt-wrapped acidity.

"Mademoiselle M" is named for Madeleine, Bain's daughter who was born on the day of the harvest. I found the 2008 too oxidized to taste but expect Bain to do better in the name of his little girl in future vintages.

Generally, Bain makes two cuvées of Pouilly-Fumé. In 2008 he made a third, partially barrel-fermented wine from grapes grown on a small parcel with Kimmeridgian soil. The wine wasn't dominated by oak flavors. It seemed to have some residual sugar and full-blown, vigorous 2008 structure.

🐌 Highly Recommended

🐌 Domaine Francis Blanchet

Le Bouchot 58150 Pouilly-sur-Loire;03.86.39.05.90;
www.vins-francis-blanchet.fr; francisblanchet@orange.fr

Francis Blanchet, whose family has been making wine in Pouilly since the 18th century, cultivates 9.5 hectares of vines spread out over three communes – Pouilly, Saint Andelain and Tracy – with the corresponding mix of soils. Blanchet adheres to the principles of sustainable farming. He does not use weed killers, favoring mechanical plows and hoes to work his vines. Yields are generally around 60 hl/ha and the grapes, for the most part, are hand harvested. Fermentation takes place in temperature controlled stainless steel tanks, with yeasts selected on the basis of soil type and grape variety. The wines age on their lees for a minimum of seven months before being fined and lightly filtered.

Tasted in September 2010, the 2006 Vieilles Vignes was textured and rather brawny with flavors of grapefruit zest and a whisper of gooseberry. A potent, well-balanced food wine with specificity. Tasted in 2005, the 2002 was highstrung and clear as a mountain stream, with grapey, foxy flavors mixed with grapefruit. The 2004 was a bit foxy, too, and every bit as edgy as the 2002 but more nuanced, with flavors of mineral and stone interwoven with those of grapefruit and grapefruit zest.

Tasted in September 2010, the 2006 Cuvée Silice, from young vines on hillsides with flinty-clay soils, was more floral than the Vieilles Vignes bottling, with flavors of white fleshed peaches and stone. It was also svelter and more elegant, a cool stream of flavor. Tasted in 2009, the 2005 exhibited the same foxy, cat's pee characteristics as I've found in many of the Pouillys from that vintage. It would be a good choice for a loud bistro. The 2004 seemed layered with minerals, completely terroir-driven. The 2002 Silice seemed chiseled, cut like a diamond, extremely mineral, with notes of grapefruit and grass.

The "Calcite" bottling, created in 2005, corresponds to young vines from slopes with southern or western exposures and soils composed of Kimmeridgian marl. The 2005 was a full, brawny, Serge-Dagueneau-style Pouilly, with lots of grapefruit, a hint of minerals and a whiff of cat's pee. The 2006, again in the Serge-Daguneau camp, revealed flavors of lime and verbena. It was a bit heavy, fitting squarely into the 2006 profile.

"Kriotine" is Blanchet's newest bottling. Some fifteen years ago, he selected prunings from his grandparents' vines and had them grafted by a specialized nursery. He planted these vines in a 1.6 hectare vineyard with Barrois and Villiers limestone soils. The vines are now ten years old.

The wines ferment in stainless steel tanks, starting at 14 degrees Celsius and ending fermentation at 20 degrees, and stay on their lees for seven months before bottling. I tasted the first two vintages, each with 13% alcohol, in May 2011. The 2009 was a punchy wine with full gooseberry flavors and subdued minerality. I much preferred the aerodynamic 2010, a cool, lean, lemon, grapefruit, and gooseberry wine with a hint of foxiness. Mineral and slatey, it was rectilinear, with an exciting, spine-stiffening iciness.

≈ Domaine Gilles Blanchet

Le Bourg 58150 Saint Andelain:03.86.39.14.03;
gilles.blanchet@wanadoo.fr

This family domaine is situated at the entry to the hamlet of Les Berthiers. Its eight hectares of vines lie within a three-hectare radius around the winery.

Tasted in the summer of 2010, the 2006 Pouilly Fumé was smooth, simultaneously tart and ripe, still youthful, but with some of the depth that comes with aging. I much preferred it to the rather green 2006 "Les Champs des Plantes". From a two-hectare parcel with limestone soils, it seemed confected and was marked by the pungent odor of cat's pee. On the other hand, the 2008 "Champs des Plantes" was delightful – glowing, stony and mineral, with 2008's vivid acidity enveloped by ripe fruit.

Highly Recommended   ### ≈ Domaine Bouchié-Chatellier

La Renardière 58150 Saint Andelain; 03.86.39.14.01;
www.bouchié-chatellier.fr;
pouilly.fumé.bouchie.chatellier@wanadoo.fr

I first met Bernard Bouchié in 1990 at the Cave Cooperative where he was – and still is – the director of winemaking. I later tasted wines he made at his own domaine, on his own time, in the hamlet of Les Berthiers. Consistently well-made, they were tasty and satifying Pouillys.

As a young man, Bernard worked the vines of the Hospices de Beaune and earned a diploma in enology at the Ecole d'Agronomie de Montpellier. His son Arnaud, who worked and studied in Burgundy, has joined him on the family domaine consisting of 23 hectares on silex-rich soils on and around the Butte of St. Andelain.

Viticulture is conventional with some nods toward eco-friendliness, such as plowing and the sowing of grasses between the hillside vines. Most of the vines are 35 years old and have, since the 1930s, been propagated by *séléction massalle*. Grapes, generally yielding about 50 hl/ha, are machine harvested and are transferred from harvest bin to fermentation tank to bottling line by gravity.

The cuvée "La Renardière" represents the major part of the domaine's production. The 2006 was a savory Pouilly, ripe and mineral with accents of citrus zest and almond and a distinctly saline note. The cuvée "Premier Millésime" corresponds to a selection of the best grapes given some skin contact in the press. The big, brawny, flavor-packed 2006 seemed on the verge of over-ripeness but was nicely acid, rich and textured, with flavors of lime zest and preserved lemon. It recalled the wines of neighboring Domaine Serge Dagueneau & ses Filles."Argile a S" (the S is for Silex) corresponds to a selection from the domaine's best parcels. The 2010, tasted in May 2011, was a vivid, plump wine with flavors of freshly squeezed grapefruit juice and a hint of foxiness. Envigorating and bracing, it struts its varietal character – but in a very winning way. It's a wine that could unify a jury.

Animal activists may be pleased to know that the Bouchiés do not allow hunting on their property.

ﾠ Domaine Henri Bourgeois

(See Sancerre)

ﾠ Excellent

This excellent grower-negociant house brings the same care and attention to its Pouilly-Fumés as it does to its Sancerres. The basic domaine bottling, "En Travertin", comes both from vines owned by Bourgeois (45%) and purchased grapes and must (55%). All come from the *terres blanches* slopes at the base of Saint Andelain. It is exemplary. The 2008 was tightly focused with appealing chalkiness and appetizing flavors of lemon and lime. My guess is that the 2009 was picked early – when it had reached 13% alcohol but had not yet achieved aromatic ripeness, as evidenced by the lightly unripe gooseberry flavors as well as by the admirable tartness and freshness.

The top-of-the-line Pouilly is "La Demoiselle de Bourgeois". A selection of the best grapes from the domaine's own five hectare parcel in Saint Laurent l'Abbaye, the vines grow on Kimmeridgian marl soils and are between 20 and 30 years old. Yields average 44 hl/ha. A small percentage of the wine – about 15% — ferments in oak, the rest in thermoregulated stainless steel tanks. The tank-fermented wine ages on its fine lees for seven to eight months; the barrel-fermented portion ages on its gross lees. A 2002, tasted in 2011 (from a friend's cellar that had been flooded), was a bit lumbering and vegetal, but the 2004, tasted on a number of occasions, was airy, lacy and mineral. A style I love. The 2008, tasted twice, was racy and manifestly pedigreed. Tense, focused and crystalline, with flavors of lemon zest and lemon curd, it would be perfectly at home in any Michelin-starred restaurant.

❧ Domaine Alain Cailbourdin

RN7 Maltaverne, 58150 Tracy-sur-Loire 03.86.26.17.73
www.domaine-cailbourdin.com; domaine-
cailbourdin@wanadoo.fr

As a teenager Cailbourdin came down from Paris to work harvests. He studied in Beaune and at Cosne, worked for some large Pouilly producers, and,
in 1980 bought two hectares, rented seven more, and began building his
cellars. Today he has 17 hectares.

Always reflective, he made measured, reasoned investments and progressed steadily, following the better angels of mainstream viticulture and
vinification. To those standards he has remained true.

In this vein, he practices sustainable farming. When it comes to canopy
management, he uses the *Taille Guyot* and the *cordon de Royat* to allow sufficient space for the grapes. He follows this by severe debudding both to
keep yields low and to ensure adequate distance between clusters. Vineyards are plowed and the rows between young vines are seeded with grass
to limit vigor.

Cailbourdin has always harvested by machine – at first with some degree
of skepticism, later, with no hesitation, as it allows him the freedom to pick
when he wants. The grapes, with exception of those for the cuvée" Trip-
tych", ferment in thermoregulated stainless steel tanks. There are four or
five cuvées, the principal three are described below.

Boisfleury is the appropriately spring-like name of both the bottling and
the vineyard that make Cailbourdin's early-drinking Pouilly. Called Le
Plateau de Boisfleury, the calcareous soils of this vineyard at the foot of the
Saint Andelain hill were formed during the Portlandian period. According
to Cailbourdin, the soils are also composed of Barrois limestone and contain a multitude of hard, white pebbles which store heat during the day and
release it at night. During the Pliocene period, part of this plateau was covered by sandy silica alluvial soils which bring freshness and floral aromas
to the wines. The "Cuvée de Boisfleury" is made from 20 year old vines. The
2006, with 13 degrees alcohol, was creamy, slightly foxy, tangy, fresh and
well-balanced.

"Les Cris" is both the local term for pebbly Barrois limestone soils and
the name of Cailbourdin's signature cuvée. Forty-five year old vines on a
slope with southwestern exposure, overlooking the Loire, the wine is usually racy and fine and can compete with some of the best of the appellation.
The excellent 2006 was an urbane wine, extremely stony, zesty and mineral
with flavors of citrus zests and herbal tea.

Born in 1998 "Tritych" comes from a selected parcel of vines over 70 years old grown on St. Andelain's best soils – a mix of clay, marl and flint. Yields are low – 35 hl/ha — and the wine is vinified in 300 to 600 liter barrels on a four year rotation. The oak, itself, is fairly local: it comes from the Bertrange forest about 20 kilometers from Pouilly. The wine ages in these barrels, on its fine lees, for a year. The 2006 was light on its feet, despite weighing in at over 13 degrees alcohol. Less phenolically ripe than "Les Cris," its aromas recalled grass and *pipi de chat*. Mercifully, the wine was not dominated by oak. It was rather elegant and a pleasure to drink.

🐌 Jacques Carroy et Fils

Le Bouchot du Haut, 9 rue Joseph Renaud 58150 Pouilly-sur-Loire; 03 86 39 17 01; carroy-jacquesetfils@wanadoo.fr

🐌 Recommended

This traditional family domaine is run by father Jacques and sons Christophe and Sebastien. Located in the hamlet of Le Bouchot, the 9 hectares of vines grow on limestone soils. Grapes are machine harvested and ferment and age in tank. Only Pouilly-Fumé is made.

The 2008 "L'Eclat" lived up to its name. Eclat means brightness or brilliance in French, and this wine was highstrung, mineral, with 2008's characteristic penetrating acidity. Lightly grassy and steely, it had a sour edge. The traditional cuvée of 2008 was tangy and extremely fresh, with flavors of grapefruit, gooseberry, mineral, and stone. Both would pair well with traditional bistro entrées such as *museau vinaigrette* and *hareng pomme à l'huile*.

🐌 Caves de Pouilly sur Loire

"Les Moulins à Vent" 39, Avenue de la Tuilerie - BP 9 58150 Pouilly-sur-Loire; 03.86.39.10.99; www.cavespouillysurloire.com; caves.pouilly.loire@wanadoo.fr

🐌 Highly Recommended

Founded in 1948, the cooperative today has 93 members, covering both the appellations of Pouilly and the Giennois. Creditable versions of both Pouilly-sur-Loire — the 2008 was fresh and vinous, with vibrant 2008 acidity — and several cuvées of Pouilly Fumé. Among the latter, I particularly liked the 2007 "Les Vieillottes", made from vines averaging forty years old grown on a mix of *terres blanches* and flinty soils. A grippy Pouilly with flavors of white-fleshed peaches and Badoit-like minerals, refined acidity, and a thread of salinity, it was not a grandiose but a precise wine, with a clean, lingering finish. I shared the wine with friends who preferred the "Tonelum" bottling, a small percentage of which ferments in Nivernais oak.

Also from the 2007 vintage, it was fleshier yet tarter than the "Vieillottes", with attractive lemon zest and mineral flavors which, to my mind/palate, were ill-served by dominating oak flavors. The basic 2008 was textbook: very fresh and envigorating, with flavors of grapefruit, gooseberry, verbena, slate, and minerals.

&. Highly Recommended

&. Domaine Jean-Claude Chatelain

Les Berthiers 58150 Pouilly-sur-Loire; 03 86 39 17 46;
www.domaine-chatelain.fr

No folklore here. No romance either. But Chatelain, an entrepreneurial winemaker and negociant who affects paisley ascots and LL Bean-style lumberjack shirts, has been making good, and consistently good, sometimes very good, Pouilly for over 25 years. Recently he has been joined by his son, Vincent, and his son-in-law Vincent Vatan.

The domaine has 30 hectares of vines spread out through six of the seven communes within the Pouilly appellation. Most grapes are machine harvested; only very young and very old vines (those over 50) are harvested by hand. Grapes from similar soils are assembled for vinification at low temperatures in stainless steel tanks. There are at least five different bottlings, including "Pilou", an oak-aged late harvest Sauvignon as well as a Pouilly-sur-Loire. The wines you are most likely to find are the three below.

Chatelain's basic Pouilly-Fumé comes from an assemblage of 23 to 30 year old vines grown on the appellation's three principal *terroirs*. The 2008, tasted in 2010, had pungent aromas of creamed corn, accents of herbal tea and black tea set against a backdrop of lemon-lime. 2008's acidity was present but well-managed. The wine was not at all shrill or strident.

The grapes for the "Vignes de St. Laurent l'Abbaye" – similarly between 23 and 30 years old – come from predominantly Kimmeridgian marl soils combined with 30% flinty clay. Tasted in 2011, the 2008 opened with notes of banana, creamed corn and vigorous acidity which was as well-managed as the acidity in the Domaine bottling. A nicely structured wine, its texture was suave, and it seemed to have a backbone of minerals and steel.

"Les Chailloux" comes from a 3.5-hectare parcel on stony silex with clay subsoils. Discreet, salty, and mineral, the 2009, tasted in spring 2011, was delightfully fresh, with a strong thread of sur lie marrow. (The wine is aged in tank for three months with a regular stirring up of the lees.)

🎗 Gilles Chollet

6 bis, Rue Joseph Renaud – Le Bouchot 58150 Pouilly-sur-Loire;
03.86.39.02.19 gilleschollet@orange.fr

🎗 By the Glass

The Chollet family's ten hectares of vines are planted on the sandy, limestone soils of a southwest-facing plateau in Le Bouchot. The vines, between
20 and 30 years old, are farmed traditionally. Grapes are machine harvested.
Tasted in 2010, the 2006 domaine bottling was lightly vegetal and saline,
somewhat short and bland. Acceptable. The 2005 "Cuvée Opaline" was
more vinous and not unpleasant to drink.

🎗 Domaine Didier Dagueneau

Le Bourg 58150 Saint Andelain; 03 86 39 15 62; silex@wanadoo.fr

🎗 Outstanding

When he died during a light plane crash in September 2008, Didier Dagueneau, then 52, had already become a legend in his own time in the world of
wine. A perfectionist with a Platonic ideal of the wines he wanted to make,
he almost single-handedly changed the image of Sauvignon Blancs from
Pouilly-Fumé and Sancerre. When I began my research in the Loire over
20 years ago, we were all still judging grape ripeness by sugars and potential
alcohol. One person alone was talking about phenolic maturity. That was
Didier Dagueneau. It made so much sense. And now it's part of our daily
vocabulary. Rather than shrill, feisty whites tasting of grass, green beans,
gooseberry or *pipi de chat*, Dagueneau's Sauvignons were statuesque, beautifully balanced wines, with flavors reminiscent of citrus zests, apricot, fig,
passion fruit, and minerals. Didier's best cuvées – "Silex" and "Pur Sang" –
were more evocative of stones and minerals than fruit. And that's the
expression I truly adore. They cost as much as a Grand Cru from Burgundy's Côte d'Or and consumers did not hesitate to pay: a Dagueneau wine
was a work of art.

   The man, himself, was famously controversial – capable of brutal honesty, stunning rudeness, and vast generosity. Central casting's dream of a
rebel, with his tangled mane of flame-red hair, his ice-blue stare, his grunge
garb (logger shirt, baggy jeans, trucker's cap), Dagueneau crusaded for his
idea of authentic Pouilly Fumé, denouncing its infidels anywhere he found
an audience.

   On French national tv Dagueneau inveighed against over-production.
At home he typically led visitors on tours of Pouilly's vineyards like a pros-
ecutor marshalling evidence, showing not just his own impeccable plots,
but a sampling of neighbors' high-yielding, weed-infested parcels as well.

In 1990 he made a succulent sweet sauvignon. It was denied the Pouilly appellation because it was deemed "atypical". Didier named the cuvée "Maudite" – the cursed one – and created a label picturing a hairy arm giving what the French call *le bras d'honneur*. (It has now become an all-purpose logo for the domaine.) He also sent journalists his declarations of harvest, covering yields, chaptalization, and his bill for harvesters. Like a politician revealing his tax returns, he was providing proof of purity. And like a politician, he was throwing down the gauntlet to his confrères. Lest anyone be confused by his meaning, he renamed his street Che Guevara.

At the same time, he rebuilt a crumbling church in his hamlet and used it for tastings, readings, and art exhibits. He regularly treated his cellar rats to meals in gastronomic restaurants so that they would understand where the wines they had had a hand in making would be drunk.

When he first met me in Charles Joguet's cellars outside of Chinon, he offered to put me up in what he called *la maison d'Henri* while I was doing my research – and whenever I visited. (It's a small house in front of the wine cellar with an office downstairs and several bedrooms upstairs.) And when many of the Loire's wine bureaucrats, its vintners, and négociants doubted I'd ever write the book — six Loire books were published between the time I started my research and the publication of my book in 1996 — Didier always believed in me. He "got it." When I held some post-publication tastings in New York he insisted that his importer donate all the bottles of "Silex" I would need.

At the time I lived there, Louis-Benjamin was a droll and dreamy little boy of 7. We called him Benjamin then. Now he's 27, tall, muscular, bearded and as opinionated as his father. In fact, whenever I speak to him, I feel that if I closed my eyes, I'd think it was Didier talking.

"I was always conditioned to be a *vigneron*," Louis-Benjamin told me. "I started working in the vineyards and tasting wines when I was 10. When Didier opened a great bottle – a Jayer, say, or an '89 Chinon Dioterie, or a Mas Jullien – we tasted, and I listened to what he said and tried to find what he described in the glass.

"When I was about 14 or 15," he continues, "I really started tasting Sauvignon Blanc. Our own wines. We'd taste those made from grapes that had been destemmed and from grapes that hadn't been destemmed, for example, wines that were filtered or not filtered, sulphured or not sulphured; wines aged in different types of barrels or barrels with different levels of toasting. We'd taste the lees, the grapes, oxidized wines."

Louis-Benjamin went to several different professional schools, earning a degree in viticulture and enology. Before returning to the family property in 2004, he apprenticed with vintners as exigent as his father, spending at least a year with François Chidaine in Montlouis and Vouvray in the Loire, and another year with Olivier Jullien at Mas Jullien in the Languedoc. He remains close to both. "But really," he notes," I learned everything from Didier,"

In fact, he worked side-by-side with his father vinifying the 2004, 2005, 2006 and 2007 vintages. So when the 2008 harvest started, several days after his father's funeral, Louis-Benjamin Dagueneau assumed the helm without hesitation. "It was easy. Everyone gave the best of themselves," he recalled, adding "I had a difficult moment of feeling that I was living Didier's life, that I'd stolen something. Then I realized that I was lucky. For me the hardest thing has been that my father didn't live to taste my first vintage. This is a regret that I'll always carry with me."

As someone who tasted with Didier over a period of twenty years, I can affirm that he would be extremely proud of his son – as will become evident in the tasting notes to follow. But first, at the time of this writing, some basics: Dagueneau has 11 hectares of Pouilly Fumé from which he makes four cuvées, starting with the bottling called "Blanc Fumé de Pouilly" which has an image of sheet music as its label. The only blended wine, this cuvée replaces "En Chailloux" – whose vines Didier lost – and comes from a small parcel of vines with two soil types – flinty clay and Kimmeridgian marl. Additionally, Dagueneau has .6 hectares in Sancerre and three in Jurançon in southwest France (which he visits once a month).

Father and son believe in hiring at least one person per hectare. In Pouilly, Dagueneau now has 15 employees, plus four horses trained to work the soil, and two weather monitors posted in key parcels in order to track temperatures, rainfall, humidity and so forth, and thereby to fine-tune treatment of vine maladies. (There is also a weather monitor in the Jurançon vineyard.)

Many people assume that the Dagueneaus practice organic viticulture. Not really. Here's what Louis-Benjamin told me: "We converted to organic farming back in the 1990s. We tried everything in the vineyards and the cellar. We kept what we liked and we ignored the rest. We're non-interventionist but it's not nature that prunes the vines or that presses the grapes," he asserts, and spells out some of the techniques they adopted and those they discarded, saying, "In essence, a wine must reflect its terroir and its vintage. Number One: Wine is made in the vineyard. Everybody says that but no one does it. You need to be rigorous and to have good sense. Second: Respect for nature: Working the soil – by plowing, sometimes with a horse – is something we kept. We don't use weed killers and we kept some of the infusions (essentially homeopathic vine treatments), others not. And we don't work with laboratory analysis. We decide the date of harvest by tasting the grapes. We decide if we've decanted the wine sufficiently by looking at the juice, and so forth."

Neither father nor son were believers in draconianly low yields. They like 45 hl/ha. Louis-Benjamin prunes hard and debuds. And, although they experimented with high density planting, they judged it a failure. This was the Clos du Calvaire which they planted with a vine density of 20,000 plants per hectare (40% of which were Sauvignon Rose). Benjamin felt the grapes could not ripen successfully at this density and ripped up the vines after the 2008 vintage. What Louis-Benjamin likes is 6.5 to 7 thousand plants per hectare. Harvest, no surprise, is by hand.

Dagueneau's cellar was built in 1989 and looks like a cathedral – or at least like a church in an affluent suburb. It operates on the gravity principle and is so clean you could eat off the floor at any time – even during harvest. Fermentation occurs in barrels whose temperatures (kept between 18 and 22) are carefully regulated to avoid thermic shock. (Each barrel has its own regulator.) Yeast is added. (In the 1990s, Didier experimented with different kinds of yeast as well as with no yeast at all. Louis-Benjamin feels you can't make dry white wine without yeast, saying, "We rejected working without sulphur or without added yeasts. You can't make dry wines without yeast. There'll always be some residual sugar or, if the fermentation goes too slowly for lack of yeast there may some off-flavors like volatile acidity.) Malolactic is blocked, the wines are not fined but are lightly filtered before bottling. (This, too, is a decision born of experience. Didier hadn't filtered the '89 Silex and, in 1990, he got reports that some had started refermenting in bottle. He repatriated every single bottle he could find, filtered the wines, rebottled them, and sent them back to their owners.)

The Dagueneau mastery of barrel aging has always made me shake my head in admiration. The oak *never* masks the wine; it's never an obtrusive presence. The Dagueneaus generally follow a four-year rotation of barrels for all the cuvées. The barrels come from various suppliers, among them Transault and Séguin Moreau, and include a 300 litre barrel shaped like a cigar that was custom made for Didier, Marc Kreydenweiss (Alsace) and Pascal Delbeck (Bordeaux).

During various conversations with Louis-Benjamin, he has talked about the future: an additional 20 *ares* in Sancerre, a dry Jurançon, but, "Fundamentally," he says, "I haven't changed anything but continue to experiment as we always did. I think we can evolve in the selection of the vines we plant. Now we're looking at five old varieties of Sauvignon Blanc that existed before cloning took hold. I think our vinification is ok but I'd like it to last a little longer. Now we have enough space in the cellars to keep the wines longer. So I'd like to age the wines twelve months in barrel and six months in tank."

Now, for the proof of the pudding:

During a visit in the summer of 2010 I tasted the entire range of 2009s in barrel, starting with samples from two different barriques that will form part of the "domaine" blend, "Blanc Fumé de Pouilly". The first, from 15 to 20 year old vines on flinty-clay soils had fermented in barrels of three or four wines. You could barely perceive the oak. Instead, it brought to mind a fine Viognier with its lively acidity, and ripe, exotic fruit flavors. Benjamin found it lacked acidity. I didn't. Its specifics: alcohol 12.7; acidity, 5.6 to 5.7. Next came a sample from marl soils. Calmer and less exuberant than the wine from the first barrel, with flavors of peach and aspergum, Benjamin said that Pouillys from these soils were always more tender.

The beautifully chiseled 2008, tasted from barrel in 2009, was a cascade of mint, ginger, and apricot, with a tart, lipsmacking, lemon curd finish. A year later it exuded lemons and lemon zests along with flavors of creamed corn which Benjamin felt would evolve into truffle-like notes. (He compared it to the 1996 which he described as 'the essence of truffles.') The 2007, tasted in 2009, after it had been in bottle for two months, was floral and lacy, a saliva-inducing wine whose flavors of peach, apricot, pear drops, and lemon zest seemed joined by a solid steel cord.

"Buisson Renard" comes from a parcel at the base of a hillside. Its rich soils are heavy with flinty-clay. The real (cadastral) name of this parcel is Buisson Menard. A French wine writer mistakenly called it "Buisson Renard" and the name stuck. I have always wondered whether the error was subliminal – as wines from this vineyard, to me, often have foxy flavors and "renard" means fox. According to Benjamin, it's the hardest to vinify, and its wines are always rich and opulent. Maybe, he says, that foxy quality comes from the soils.

"Buisson Renard" had suffered hail damage in 2008. Its 2009 yields were 30 hl/ha and the wine was the richest of Dagueneau's plots. Though plumper, more robust, and less high-spirited the other cuvées, it exuded flavors of white-fleshed peaches, melon and citrus zest. Despite its fleshiness, it was fresh, with fine acidity emerging at the finish. As a result of hail damage, the yields in 2008 were 15 hl/ha, with an alcohol level of 14.5. There was none of the foxiness I often find in this cuvée, though there were flavors of apple and beer which suggested an unfinished wine. The Dagueneaus regard the 2007 "Buisson Renard" as the best version they've made of that cuvée. It was lightly foxy but lovely, a crystalline white with fine balance and a mineral finish.

"Pur Sang" comes from "La Folie," a 3.2 hectare parcel in St. Laurent L'Abbaye, 5 kilometers from St. Andelain, with vein of pure flinty-clay. Wines coming from these exceptionally well-drained soils tend to be fine and elegant. Not marked on recent maps of the Pouilly vineyards, Didier had discovered it on an ancient document and succeeded in having it added to the appellation in 1989, and promptly planted.

The 2009, tasted from barrel in 2010, was voluptuous yet crystalline, as pure and exhilarating as a waterfall, its flavors of white-fleshed peaches, clementine and mango surrounded a solid mineral core. The finish was long and full. Here was a wine to inspire a chef. I immediately sent a Facebook message to Marie-Christine Clément (Hotel du Lion d'Or in Romorantin-Lanthenay) about it. Her husband Didier is a brilliant, sensitive chef and both had been close friends of Didier's.

Assembling my tasting notes, I was surprised and pleased to find that I had used very similar words to describe the 2008 when sampled from barrel in 2009, to wit: This is the apotheosis of the Loire: Voluptuous yet finely etched, it wraps its flavors of crystalized grapefruit and lemon zests around the tongue. Grandiose. A *vin de méditation*. Tasted a year later, two months after it had been bottled, it was clearly closed, a young beauty, complex, tender, and long. Oak was more evident in the 2007 but it hardly masked the wine's essence. Fresh as a spring morning, a waterfall of peach, grapefruit zests, a hint of salt, and a long finish.

"Silex", the most famous of all of Dageuneau's cuvées, comes from a north-facing vineyard near the woods of St. Andelain as well as from vines around Dagueneau's house in St. Andelain. Didier, who inherited the first parcel of vines from his mother, believed that silex-rich soils made the most structured, "intellectual" Pouillys.

With Benjamin, in the summer of 2010, I tasted samples of Silex from two different barrels. The first was from the custom-made cigar-shaped barrel. The wine was initially less expressive than the previous samples. Extremely mineral and stony, it was an iron fist in a peach-and-mandarine glove. The second barrel, an older *fût*, opened with discreet aromas of peach and mandarine, then exploded with flavors of peach and minerals and citrus zests. Amazing freshness, pedigree and beautiful balance.

Sixty to 70% of the 2008 harvest was lost to hail resulting in yields of 16 to 19 hl/ha. Tasting the 2008 "Silex" from barrel in 2009, we started with the most austere lot in the future blend. Very structured, very pure, very rectilinear, it was a weave of steel and lace, with flavors of minerals, stone, and grapefruit and lemon zests; Barrel #2: the largest percentage of the cuvée, weighed in at 14.2 alcohol with 6.2 acid: Stunning in its purity, full, yet astonishingly fresh, deep and racy, it had great tension and light flavors of oak that came across as a pleasant seasoning. Superb.

The 2007, rich, dense and textured, was closed and tight in the summer of 2009, tight like a Grand Cru from Marcel Deiss, with light oak notes, a whisper of gooseberry, vibrant flavors of grapefruit zests, steel, and flint, gorgeous balance. A monument.

And now for a *really slow* tasting:

On my website I like to select a Wine of the Year. In 2008 it was the 2006 Silex. Here's part of what I posted on the site.

"It's been cold this winter. So the wine was room temperature when I opened it, probably somewhere around 14C. As I pulled the cork, aromas of grapefruit and grapefruit zest drifted off its damp bottom.

Pale gold verging on platinum, the wine was rich, broad, and creamy, flowing over the palate, and finishing ever so slowly on notes of citrus zests, stone, and light, mellow flavors of oak.

It brought me back to a frequent reflection that Pouillys tend to be more expansive than Sancerres and that here was an example of the Loire in its most Côte d'Or expression. Though I hate saying that the Loire is anything but the Loire.

The wine was tight but supple, stern but generous. A tough-love Pouilly. As it opened, it revealed deep aromas of minerals and vibrant grapefruit juiciness along with the seductive herbaceousness of freshly mown spring grass. The discoveries kept on coming yet the wine was all of a piece.

There's also quite a bit of varietal character here. I'm wondering if that has anything to do with Didier's use of selected yeasts. I put the wine in the fridge to taste again in the evening and drink with dinner.

Evening of Day 1: the wine is tight and creamy, with a long mineral-stone-grapefruit finish. The colder temperature focuses it, and its race and power come to the fore. It's statuesque, big-boned, self-assured. The touch of oak is masterly. A superb wine.

I have decided to pair the wine with good store bought ravioli filled with pesto, pecorino and pine nuts, which I tossed with butter and parmesan. A full-force Loire Sauvignon is my first choice for pesto but I thought that straight pesto would have been too loud for a wine this elegant. But the ravioli preparation softened the expression. If anything, the ravioli was less forceful than the wine, but it didn't disappear. It graciously allowed the wine to star while playing the role of a delicious and appropriate partner. The flavors were complementary, the balance was perfect, and the gentle texture of the ravioli married well with the creamy, broad texture of the Pouilly. The wine's fresh finish revived the palate after each sip.

Day 2: If anything, the wine is more crystalline and the mineral expression even more potent. Tight, with lipsmacking viscosity, the flavors of grapefruit zests and grapefruit are oh-so subtly underscored by oak. The finish is slightly saline. The problem is that the wine is so damned good that, although I had been expected to drink it once again with dinner, I polished off the bottle then and there.

This is Didier demanding to be the best. And succeeding.

And then there are Dagueneau's outlier wines. Asteroid comes from two *ares* of ungrafted Sauvignon Blanc – regrettably now attacked by phylloxera. There was none in 2009 because of hail damage. The 2008, from barrel, was as tense as a high wire, chiseled. It was like taking a bite out of a glacier. All steel and herbal tea, it was majestic, achingly regal. Tasted again in 2009, from bottle, it was so pure, it seemed transparent, with deep citrus flavors and profound minerality, like tasting bedrock. There was none in 2007. The 2006 was so rich it seemed to have some residual sugar. It didn't, but 2006 dry whites in the Loire can fool you like that. Very textured, it had a long, saline-mineral finish.

As with the experimentation in vine density, Didier experimented with grapes not commonly found – indeed, mostly prohibited – in the appellation's vineyards. Benjamin continues this practice and I hope the law isn't such a ass that it will stop him.

Tasted from barrel, the 2008 Sauvignon Rose (from the vineyard that produces Silex): fresh, ample, and yet tart with light oak flavors. What's most intriguing are the rich, exotic fruit flavors which don't recall any one specific fruit but just a wave of lush yet subtle fruitiness. In 1989 Didier planted three rows of Riesling –a mass selection from Alsace's Marc Kreydenweiss. The 2008 Riesling was simply magnificent. Like bone dry ice wine. Majestic too. There have also been fascinating experiments with Petit Meslier (once used in the region to make sparkling wine) and Pinot Noir – each worthy of exploring further if the law would allow it. And there is the drop-dead gorgeous Jurançon which the author of a book on the wines of southwest France will have the pleasure of describing.

Suffice it to say that we winelovers can be both grateful and reassured that the future of this seminal Loire winery is in very capable hands.

☙ Serge Dagueneau et Filles

Les Berthiers, 58150 Saint-Andelain; 03 86 39 11 18;
sergedagueneau@wanadoo.fr

☙ Excellent

Way back in August 1990 I stopped by Didier Dagueneau's house in St. Andelain to leave off the better part of my belongings before heading south, to Saint Pourçain, the Auvergne and, ultimately, the source of the Loire.

As he often did, Didier had organized a tasting in his cellars that night. The theme of this tasting was Sauvignon Blanc. Most of the bottles came from France but there were a couple Didier had brought back from California.

That was where I met Didier's uncle, Serge, and where I first tasted his wine. I think it was my favorite in the tasting. Serge's daughter, Valérie, was there too. Her sister Florence was in California, working at the Peter Michel winery, where Valérie had also worked.

Serge and Valérie were always around, helping, tasting, schmoozing, joining us for meals. Serge was a very large, superficially gruff man of not too many words and I was amused and delighted to see that this dyed-in-the-wool good ol' boy was the first vigneron in the Loire with "& Filles" blazened across the winery. Valérie had studied at the Lycée de Macon; Florence, at the Lycée de Beaune.

Over the years I saw Valérie and Florence, generally at the Salon des Vins de Loire, and, of course, at Didier's funeral. It was with something very close to horror that I learned that Florence had died of cancer in the winter of 2009/2010. It seemed too much for the extended Dagueneau family to bear. When I visited in June 2010 there were picture-portraits of Florence hung in the cellar, in the tasting room, in Serge's workshop, and everyone was still very much in a state of mourning. Valérie, however, did have to carry on, and so she did. The weight of the family domaine was on her shoulders and she shouldered it heroically and humbly.

The Dagueneaus, who live in the hamlet of Les Berthiers, have 17.5 hectares in Pouilly Fumé, mostly on Kimmeridgian marl; .60 hectares in Pouilly-sur-Loire and nearly two hectares in Côte de la Charité (or Coteaux Charitois) Vin de Pays. They practice sustainable farming.

Serge always made brawny, flavorful, characterful Pouillys. This is still the case. Not a style that appeals to everyone, they are always honest, true to the appellation and to the vintage, and faultless. There's definitely a "there" there. I like them a lot.

If ever you need convincing that Chasselas has its rightful place in the vineyards of Pouilly, taste here. Dagueneau's Chasselas vines are over 100 years old and are replaced by *marcottage*. (Thus far, phylloxera has not been a problem.) The 2008, tasted in the summer of 2010, was delightfully fresh and textured, a weave of apricot, minerals, and nougat with a light saline edge. Always less alcoholic than Pouilly Fumé, it weighed in at 11.8 degrees but felt and tasted much ampler. Superb.

The traditional Pouilly Fumé comes from young vines on Kimmeridgian marl soils. Both machine and hand harvested, it is pressed immediately, ferments in tank, and ages on its lees for six months before being lightly fined and filtered, then bottled.

The 2009, just bottled when I tasted it, was a rich (above 13 degrees) blend of peach and fresh citrus flavors, textured, and pure. The 2005, tasted in early 2006, was ample with full-blown flavors of grass, minerals and grapefruit. The 2004, tasted in early 2005, was solid, ripe, and brawny; a rich presence.

The "Clos de Chaudoux" bottling comes from young vines on a 1.50-hectare parcel, Pentes (Slopes) des Chaudoux, also on Kimmeridgian marl. The grapes are hand harvested, sorted, and undergo skin contact for ten hours before being pressed. The wine ages on its lees for over a year and is bottled without being fined or filtered.

The 2007, tasted in June 2010, had spent two winters in tank and demi-muids before being bottled. It was nuanced and textured. Surprisingly crystalline – I generally don't associate that quality with skin contact – it was silky, mineral, and lightly vegetal, with good acidity, juicy peach flavors, and a long finish recalling herbal tea. The 2004, tasted two weeks after it had been bottled in early 2006, was ample, rather elegant, and very mineral. The 2003, tasted in early 2005, was highly perfumed, a strong presence with good freshness.

"Les Filles" is, obviously, the girls' cuvée. A late harvest wine, made only in certain vintages and when botrytis has just begun to attack the grapes, it is harvested by hand, ferments (to dryness) in tank and one new barrel (for tannins), and is bottled without being fined or filtered. The 2007, tasted in June 2010, was a big, dry white with a note of botrytis. It virtually ate its acid. The 2003, tasted in early 2006, was plump and seemed as if it would be sweet but was utterly dry. It recalled the "M" of Touraine's Marionnet and certain cuvées of Lucien Crochet.

La Léontine is a newcomer to the line-up. Named after Valérie's (and Didier's) great grandmother, the person who created the domaine. It's a small cuvée, initially an experiment, in which the wine ferments and ages in barrels of three to five wines and is bottled without having been fined or filtered. The 2008, tasted in June 2010, was smooth, plush but crystalline, and fresh. There was a hint of oxidation and of oak and grace notes of sweet spices. Very special.

In the years to come, if Valérie should create another cuvée, I believe she will name it after her sister Florence.

&. Andre Dezat & Fils/ Domaine Thibault
(See Sancerre)

&. Highly Recommended

This respected family domaine, situated in the commune of Verdigny, is noted principally for its delicious Sancerres. Its Pouilly-Fumé, Domaine Thibault, should not be overlooked, however. Made from sustainably farmed grapes grown on a mix of all the classic soils of Pouilly – *caillottes, terres blanches*, and flinty-clay – harvested both by hand and by machine, fermented in thermoregulated stainless steel tanks, the 2006, tasted in 2010, was a fleshy white with flavors of peach and lime. Ripe, solid and specific, it was a bit on the heavy side but that's not uncommon for a 2006 dry Loire white with a bit of age. All in all, a good, relaxed, meal wine.

&. Domaine de l'Epineau/ Emmanuel Charrier
Paillot 58150 Saint Martin sur Nohain; 03 86 22 57 15;
earl.charrier@free.fr www.domaine-charrier.com

&. Recommended

Charrier makes four different cuvées of Coteaux du Giennois and a single cuvée of Pouilly from sandy parcels located some 13 kms from his cellars. A 2006, from young vines, was a bit heavy and lightly oxidized when tasted in August 2010 – not surprising given the vintage and the location of the vines, at the northern limits of the appellation. It was well made, however, and had depth and good herbal tea flavors. I first tried it on my own, and then finished the bottle with some wine-loving neighbors in my village in the Loire. They liked it a lot.

&. Château Favray
58150 Saint Martin-sur-Nohan; 03.86.26.19.05;
www.château-favray.com

&. Highly Recommended

At the border of Cosne-sur-Loire, Quentin David cultivates 15 hectares of vines (following the principles of sustainable agriculture), another 230 of cereal crops, and raises horses as well. "Yes, we're at the northern limit of the appellation," he agrees, "but our soils are as interesting as those in the heart of Pouilly. Our vines are on one parcel, a well-exposed slope where there's very little topsoil and the subsoils are quite chalky. These are the oldest soils in the region, *calcaires de Villiers,* with a specific type of fossil. The soils drain quickly. The rain goes right through. The style of the wines from here is expressive and floral, earlier drinking than those on silex."

His Pouillys do seem less intense and complex than those from Pouilly *classico,* a soft fade of the appellation's power, but they are reliably well-made, the product of care and intelligence. The 2009, tasted in January 2011, was smooth and coherent, a well made wine with toothsome flavors of grapefruit and minerals. Lovely. As the French say, *à boire sans soif.* (You don't have to be thirsty to drink it.) The 2006, tasted in 2010, was tart but well knit, with good length, as well as flavor evolution recalling dry Chenin Blanc from Montlouis.

By the Glass

Domaine Nicolas Gaudry

58150 Pouilly-sur-Loire; 06.08.98.95.78;
domainenicolasgaudry@orange.fr

Nicolas Gaudry created his small domaine in 2003. His 5 hectares in the hamlet of Boisguibaut have soils composed of both Portlandian and Kimmeridgian marl. Gaudry adheres to the principles of sustainable farming and harvests by machine. He uses indigenous yeasts, ferments in tank, and ages the wine four months aging on their lees. His 2006 was fresh and smooth but lacked flavor. It seemed a tad confected and attenuated, as if he had harvested somewhat more than his stated 63 hl/ha. Nevertheless, the domaine and the vigneron are young. There's clearly room for improvement and, I think, reason for hope.

Excellent

Pascal Jolivet

(See Sancerre)

No reservations about the "Excellent" rating here. Jolivet's entry level Pouilly comes from 8 hectares of 15 to 25 year old vines growing on a variety of the appellation's soil types in Tracy and Les Loges. Harvest is both by hand and machine. The juice from the different soils ferment separately, in temperature controlled tanks, using indigenous yeasts. No sulphur is added until the end of fermentation. The wine ages on its lees until bottling. Discreet and mineral, the 2006 was a weave of grapefruit zest, peach, pineapple, mint and stone. It was tight, tangy, and fresh. Very appealing.

"Les Griottes" comes from a 1.5 hectare parcel in Les Loges first planted by the Benedictine monks in the 11th century. The vines are between

15 and 30 years old; the soils are "extremely limestone" – *griottes* is a local term for pure, tender limestone — and enjoy a south-south-east exposition overlooking the Loire. Yields are roughly 45 hl/ha. Harvest is by hand and the wine ferments in temperature controlled stainless steel tanks using only indigenous yeasts. The 2006, tasted in 2009, was deeper than the domaine bottling but equally discreet, with layers of verbena, mineral and grapefruit zest. Ample yet fresh and tight, it was racy and gracious. The 2009, tasted in 2011, opened with notes of pear and lemon above a foundation of mineral, steel and herbal tea. It was full (13.5% alcohol), without being heavy, fresh, and extremely food friendly.

"Indigène" is based on a selection from the best parcels. Yields are roughly 65 hl/ha and harvest is by both hand and machine. As with the other cuvées, only indigenous yeasts are used, and the wine ferments in temperature controlled tanks. Sulphur is added only at the end of fermentation. The wine ages on its lees and is bottled without filtration. The 2006 was ample, ripe and marrowy. Very rich and bordering on sweet – though it weighed in at 12.5 alcohol with 1.4 gms rs – it was zaftig and zesty, with flavors of fat ripe peaches accented with lemon and lime zest, finishing on an appetizing bitter note. The crystalline 2008 (12.5% alcohol) was as tart as fresh lemon juice, with tangy flavors of citrus, minerals and gooseberry. A fine reflection of the vintage.

ᠺ Baron de Ladoucette/Château du Nozet

Other

58150 Pouilly sur Loire; 03.86.39.18.33

Way back in the 1970s and 80s, the most famous name in Pouilly was de Ladoucette — the all-purpose basic cuvée for all normal white wine situations, and the "Baron de L", which made its debut in 1973, for special occasions.

And the home of this, the world's most omnipresent Pouilly was, appropriately, a showplace. Its Disney-esque château (you really do expect to see Tinkerbell soar above its pointy towers) is surrounded by vines so neat they look like garden shrubs. These, in turn, are bordered with hedges cut at exactly the same height. Versailles viticulture.

Baron Patrick de Ladoucette, the great-great grandson of Comte Lafon, the château's original owner, oversees the domaine which consists of about sixty-five hectares in Pouilly. He buys another 65 hectares worth of wine (including must and grapes) for both his Pouilly and his Sancerre, the latter sold under the Comte Lafon label. Add Marc Bredif in Vouvray ,and other Touraine appellations sold under the Baron Briare label, and Ladoucette emerges as one of the most important family firms — if not the most important — in the Loire. He also owns the Chablis house, Albert Pic, is co-partner with Gonzalez-Byass of a small Cognac company, directs his Bristol Distribution House (selling Latour, Antinori, and other brands within France) and owns vines in California.

Although I have tried to confirm all the above information, it is based on my interview with de Ladoucette in 1990. I have been unable to get any assistance from him or from his staff since then. And it seems as if the domaine's website has been removed – at least I couldn't access it when I tried (repeatedly) on August 16, 2010.

It does not suffice merely to say that I got no assistance from Ladoucette. I owe it to you, dear reader, to tell you the efforts made to get samples and information. First, the producers *syndicat*, the Bureau Interprofessional des Vins du Centre (BIVC) issued two general calls for samples and documents on my behalf. When various producers failed to respond, the BIVC called them personally.

When this approach failed, I attempted to contact de Ladoucette, first by the then-operational website. I received a call from a secretary who told me to try contacting de Ladoucette at his Paris office. I did this, with no response.

I then spoke with an American wine writer who told me he had no trouble getting samples and gave me the name of his contact, Heidi Donaldson Soldinger, who promised to send me samples and documentation. This was in October 2009. Despite repeated efforts to contact Ms. Donaldson Soldinger, I have yet to receive anything from de Ladoucette.

The one thing I can say – and I say this in all honesty: it never occurs to me to order a wine made by de Ladoucette. I have no doubt they pass commercial muster but, given the exciting developments in winemaking in the Loire (and elsewhere), I hope to find more than mere competence in a wine, particularly wines that cost as much as these do. (On the internet, the basic 2008 is listed at nearly 18 euros, an intermediary (I assume) bottling of 2008, Baron de la Doucette, at 21 euros 50, and the 2006 Baron de L at nearly 41 euros.)

Excellent

🍇 Domaine Laporte
(See Sancerre)

The "Les Duchesses" bottling comes from limestone subsoils covered with flint in the village of Les Loges. Sixty percent comes from purchased grapes and must; forty percent from vines managed but not owned by Laporte.

Harvested by machine, the wine ferments at between 15 and 20 degrees C in stainless steel tanks, using indigenous yeasts, for roughly ten days. It ages on its fine lees for five months before bottling. The 2008 was a tall white, albeit a bit foxy. (Duke Ellington, anyone?) The 2007 was a revivifying Pouilly with flavors of preserved lemon, fresh lemon pulp and a stony-citric finish.

"La Vigne de Beaussoppet", a lieu-dit already known as a vineyard site in 1492, is a 1.25- hectare parcel of low yielding (35 to 40 hl/ha) old vines on flinty soils. (Laporte owns 80% of the vines; the remaining 20% comes from purchased grapes or must from growers who work exclusively with Laporte and whose vines are supervised by the domaine's enologists and vineyard managers.) Hand harvested and partially barrel fermented (30%), the wine ages on its fine lees for nine months with regular *batonnage* during the first four months. It ages in bottle for six months before being offered for sale. The 2006, tasted in the summer of 2010, was brisk, racy and crystalline, with flavors of verbena, freshly grated coconut, and light oak accents. Burgundian in style, except for its lively acidity, it was all of a piece and beautifully integrated.

﷼ Eric Louis/Celliers de la Pauline

(See Sancerre)

﷼ By the Glass

Eric Louis calls his Pouilly Fumé "Les Affaubertis," explaining that it was Berrichon argot for "nutty" and his grandfather used it to refer to the vignerons of Pouilly as he thought their method of tending their vines was a bit bizarre and, he adds, "that made me laugh." Whatever. The 2007 "Les Affaubertis" was shrill and painfully acid, with full- blown *pipi de chat* flavors. Its texture was silky and the wine was fresh. Maybe a stinky cheese or an excruciatingly spicy dish would counterbalance that acidity.

﷼ Pierre Marchand & Fils

Les Loges 58150 Pouilly-sur-Loire; 03.86.39.14.61; f:03.86.39.17.21

﷼ By the Glass

Eric and Pascal Marchand have taken over this 16-hectare domaine from father Pierre. I've only tasted the 2006 which seemed far from ripe and quite acidic. Unrealized possibilities here.

🐚 Highly Recommended

🐚 Domaine Masson-Blondelet

1, Rue de Paris 58150 Pouilly-sur-Loire; 03.86.39.00.34;
www.masson-blondelet.com; masson.blondelet@wanadoo.fr

Jean-Michel Masson became a vigneron when he married Michelle
Blondelet in 1975. A law graduate, he learned his new trade from Michelle's
father Fernand who was 5th generation vigneron. Today Jean-Michel, now
president of Pouillys growers' *syndicat*, and Michelle work with their children, Pierre-François, a graduate of the Lycée Viticole de Mâcon-Davaye,
and Melanie, the 7th generation.

The domaine today consists of 21 hectares. Viticulture is eco-friendly,
generally following the principles of sustainable farming and eschewing
the use of weed killers and insecticides. Yields are moderate. All but one
wine ferment in temperature-controlled stainless steel tanks and age on
their lees until bottling.

The domaine produces a Pouilly-sur-Loire, four cuvées of Pouilly-Fumé,
Sancerre and, at Château de Tersac, a range of wines from Corbières. Having tasted Masson-Blondelet wines with some degree of regularity, I would
say that the domaine remains stable, the style of its wines dependable.

"Les Pierres de Pierre," Masson-Blondelet's most recent bottling,
comes from parcels acquired by Pierre-François in 2004 under provisions
favoring young vignerons. The land in question is a 1.50-hectare southwest facing parcel with flinty-clay soils (locally called *chailloux)* typical
of the butte of St. Andelain. Zingy and fresh, the 2009, tasted in January
2011, was the most mineral and flinty of the domaine's bottlings in that
rich vintage. The 2006, tasted in 2009, was a lovely meal wine; fresh, mineral, with deep lemon-slate-flint flavors and a fairly long citrus and stone
finish.

"Villa Paulus" comes from a 4.50 -hectare parcel near the old Roman
road. Its soils are chiefly Kimmeridgian marl, and the vines, on average, are
over 35 years old. The 2006 seemed the soprano to the baritone of "Les Pierres de Pierre", with flavors of blackcurrant buds and a vibrato (sorry!) of
lemon zest. Tender and supple, the wine was well made and serious. The
2009, savory and meal-friendly, was fresh and slightly slatey, with light
gooseberry accents.

"Les Angelots" practically abuts Château Favray and has similar *calcaires
de Villiers* soils. The 2009 was a mouthfilling presence – fresh and deep,
awash with flavors of gooseberry and citrus.

"Tradition Cullus" represents the top-of-the-line and is only made in the
best vintages. A tribute to Michelle's great grand father, it comes from the

domaine's oldest vines (40 to 70), planted on Kimmeridgian marl. Alone among the domaine's Pouilly bottlings, "Tradition Cullus" ferments in oak demi-muids. The 2005, tasted at the same time as the two previous wines, was my least favorite of the line up. It was shrill, somewhat saline, with strong flavors of cat's pee. That said, it was still a very good wine.

∞ Joseph Mellot
(See Sancerre)

∞ By the Glass

This important, Sancerre-based grower-negociant produces a Pouilly-sur-Loire and three cuvées of Pouilly-Fumé on its 32 hectares of vines. The top two cuvées, "Le Troncsec" and "La Grande Cuvée des Edvins", come from the Kimmeridgian marl soils of Saint Laurent de l'Abbaye. The samples I've tasted did not live up to the promise of the terroir.

The 2008 "Troncsec" was a shrill wake-up call, very acid, even for 2008, with flavors of ivy, grapefruit, and cassis buds. Aeration tamed the wine a bit. Lightly vegetal and a bit heavy handed, the 2006 came across as a wine made from high-yielding vines, vinified by the book. "La Grande Cuvée des Edvins", in its heavy bottle, comes from Mellot's best parcels, fermented in barrels from the oak of the Allogny forest. The 2005, tasted in 2010, seemed confected and was surprisingly acid. A pity. Both the "Tronsec" and "Grande Cuvée des Edvins", despite their shortcomings, reveal the potential to make truly distinctive wines.

∞ Domaine Régis Minet
Le Bouchot 58150 Pouilly sur Loire; 03 86 39 04 32;
minet.regis@wanadoo.fr

∞ Highly Recommended

This solid, 11-hectare family domaine turns out solid, savory Pouilly-Fumé. The Minets follow the principles of sustainable farming, they deleaf and cluster thin to keep yields around 50 hl/ha. Grapes are machine harvested and ferment in thermoregulated stainless steel tanks. When tasted in August 2010, the 2006 Vielles Vignes – twenty-year old vines on limestone soils – was a nicely evolving Pouilly, with aromas of wax, lime and citronelle, and a tangy finish. The cuvée called "Le Vin du Desert" had nothing Saharan about it. The wine had a hint of residual sugar (under 2 grams) and was nicely ripe, with flavors of citronelle and lime, and a mineral core. An appetizing wine with good grip and focus, it had a slightly bitter finish with a hint of alcohol. (The label on each of the wines listed alcohol as 13 degrees; the winemaker's notes said 14. No matter. Neither was heavy though there was a bit of heat in the finish of "Le Vin de Desert".) In any event, both wines went down very easily.

𝄢 Recommended

𝄢 Domaine Didier Pabiot

1, rue Saint-Vincent, Les Loges, 58150 Pouilly-sur-Loire;
03 86 39 01 32; didier-pabiot@wanadoo.fr

The father of rising star Jonathan Pabiot, Didier Pabiot recently joined forces with his son on 15 hectares of vines on the mix of *caillottes* and Kimmeridgian marl soils of Les Loges – which Jonathan is in the process of converting to organic farming. Prior to the partnership, Didier turned out admirable Pouillys though the last I tasted, his 2007, was not his best. Very green and unripe, the grapes were surely picked too soon but, given the nature of the 2007 growing season, Pabiot may not have had a choice. Pabiot's Pouilly's from 2006, when his son was still working with him, were top-notch: the 'Aubaine' was pungent, steely, and stony with vibrant gooseberry and grapefruit flavors; the "Prédilection" bottling was more discreet, an appetizing mix of minerals, citrus zests and pulp.

𝄢 By the Glass

𝄢 Dominique Pabiot

Place des Mariniers Les Loges 58150 Pouilly-sur-Loire;
03.86.39.19.09; dominiquepabiot.com

Vigneron de père en fils for five generations, 10 hectares of parcels on the *caillottes* or Kimmeridgian soils of Les Loges, vines between 7 and 80 years old, sustainably farmed, stated yields between 40 to 62 hl/ha, harvest by machine. Sounds more or less ok. Results? Not so convincing. At least not the 2006s I tasted in the summer of 2010: the cuvée "Les Vieilles Terres" had some flavor – mostly due to aging – but was short and inconsequential; the old vines bottling, "Cuvée Plaisir", produced only in the best years, was foxy, green and sharp.

𝄢 Outstanding

𝄢 Jonathan Pabiot

Les Loges 58150 Pouilly sur Loire; 03 86 39 01 32;
pabiot-jonathan@wanadoo.fr

The new Didier Dagueneau? That's easy: it's his son, Benjamin (or Louis-Benjamin). But Benjamin has a soul brother, Jonathan Pabiot, 26, whose first vintage of Pouilly-Fumé was 2005. Benjamin and Jonathan went through public school together, defied death in motocross races together and, together – well, each at his own domaine – are making the best, most probing, and most exciting Pouilly-Fumés.

Pabiot, who had always worked alongside his father, attended the local viticultural school at Cosne-sur-Loire but dropped out for a number of cogent reasons that anyone who rebelled in the 1960s will understand (by extrapolation): essentially it was all theory and no practice, but worse, still, was the routine of placing charts on the walls with everything that could go wrong in the vineyard and cellar accompanied by which industrial products you could buy to remedy the problem, and where to buy them.

Pabiot then started working with different vignerons around France. The most formative was the six months he spent working at Domaine Léon Barral in the Languedoc in 2004. Following that experience, he returned to Pouilly. Both his grandfather, Lucien, and his father gave him some vineyard land, and Jonathan bought an additional parcel, giving him a total of 3.5 hectares, which he immediately started converting to organic farming.

In the process, Jonathan also converted his father, not only to the benefits of organic farming, but to some of the theories of biodynamic farming – which Jonathan refers to as homeopathic. He's also, as he puts it, "a little bit astral".

Today, the two men work together, with a total of 15 hectares, most in Les Loges, some in St. Laurent l'Abbaye, all farmed according to Jonathan's philosophy – to the extent allowed by financial constraints.

Jonathan's philosophy is, thankfully, based on reflection, his own judgement, and not conformist. "I don't debud and I don't cluster thin. I prune and that's it. Some of our vines are three years old, some are 25 to 30. Our goal is to work the soils, to bring out the qualities of our soils. We make our own compost. Acidity is my thing. I taste all the grapes. My palate is very sensitive to sugar. Less so to other things but very sensitive to sugar."

Harvest is both by hand and by machine. And Jonathan calls on sommelier and chef friends from Paris to help bring in the grapes. Harvesters include the sommeliers from Lasserre, Magnolia, La Truffière, Versance, and Le Miroir – whose chef-owner comes to prepare the *cassecroûte*.

Each plot ferments separately – using both wild yeasts and neutral organic yeasts – for 8 to 10 days at low temperatures. The wines are then assembled and age on their lees until bottling.

Pabiot currently makes at least three cuvées of Pouilly Fumé as well as a very good, lightly floral Pouilly-sur-Loire. The first is an assemblage of grapes from all parcels. The 2009, plump, with perhaps a bit of residual sugar, was the kind of fresh, generous Pouilly that could unite a jury. So many 2009 whites were heavy and dull, I asked Pabiot how he managed to keep the lovely acidity. Answer: he was one of the first to harvest, around the 12th and 13th of September. The texture was silky, the flavors were lovely, chiseled, – a hint of gooseberry, ripe Mirabelle, mango, and lime zest, all of which persisted through the long, fairly regal finish. The 2008 was crystalline, ripe and focused, blending flavors of minerals, lime, verbena, and citrus zest. It had good grip and impressively refined acidity for 2008.

The first of Pabiot's special cuvées is "Aubaine" from Oxfordian and Portlandian soils. He makes between 1000 and 1200 bottles a year. The 2008 was beautifully ripe, with Alsace-like perfumes and flavors of white-fleshed peaches and mirabelle. Incredibly racy, it could have used a bit more acid (for me). This in 2008!

The cuvée "Prédilection" comes from a parcel with Kimmeridgian marl soils. Textured and gracious, it was pure and precise and revivifying as a cascade, virtually gleaming with freshness. A weave of minerals and quinine, lime and grapefruit, it was a beautiful food wine and would be at home at the grandest of tables.

"Eurythmie" debuted in 2008. It comes from the same parcel as "Prédilection" but from a segment directly on the limestone bedrock. Its grapes are so popular with the local boar and deer population that Pabiot is installing electrified fencing. "Eurythmie" ferments in new oak. Pabiot wanted to buy a demi-muid but that was too expensive so he settled for a less costly barrel. The wine fermented for 8 to 10 days and stayed in barrel, on its lees, until bottling – unfiltered, by hand, according to the phases of the moon. Economy was the mother of invention here: when the cellars got too cold, Pabiot covered the barrel with quilts. We all agreed the 2008 was too oaky but it was still delicious, quite Burgundian, with smooth flavors of caramel.

Excellent

Domaine Michel Redde
La Moynerie 58150 Pouilly-sur-Loire; 03.86.39.14.72; www.michel-redde.com

Michel Redde, 5th generation vigneron, was the person responsible for orienting this domaine exclusively to wine production and away from mixed farming. He bought, regrouped, and planted vineyards, and was one of the first in the appellation to systematically bottle his wines. And he built a cellar that is hard for the visitor to miss: it sits right on the beloved RN7, the old road from Paris to the Côte d'Azur, a thoroughfare that cuts a vertical path through Pouilly's vineyards.

To be honest, I doubted that following generations – Thierry (6th generation) and his sons Sebastien and Romain — would live up to his example. I'm delighted to say that they have not only done that, they have gone further in the pursuit of quality and authenticity and, after having spent an hour tasting and talking with the intense Sebastien, I fully expect them to go even further.

The Reddes built new, gravity-driven cellars in 2001. They practice sustainable farming on their 42 hectares. Harvest, which was once predominantly by machine, now is chiefly by hand, save for the "Petit Fumé" bottling. The Reddes also produce a white and a red Sancerre, "Les Tuileries."

The domaine, to its great credit, is one of the few that has always taken Chasselas seriously. Maintaining 1.5 hectares of the grape almost as a conservatory, the Reddes make two bottlings of Pouilly-sur-Loire. The traditional bottling, always good, is called "La Moynerie" and ferments and ages in stainless steel tanks. With the "Gustave Daudin", the Reddes have taken Chasselas to new heights. Named after Thierry's great grandfather, an early champion of Chasselas, the wine ferments and ages for eight to ten months in large (1500 to 2000 litre) oak vats. The 2005 Pouilly sur Loire "Gustave Daudin", tasted in December 2010, is vinous and seemed much ampler than its 12 % alcohol. The wine was creamy but not heavy and its light oxidation came across as butterscotch (nice). Bravo.

There are six cuvées of Pouilly-Fumé, starting with the bright and chipper "Petit Fumé", essentially a young vines bottling.

"La Moynerie Pouilly-Fumé" is the traditional Pouilly bottling. It comes from vines with an average age of 25 years, planted on three different soil types: a third comes of *argile à silex rouge Albien* in Saint Andelain; another third from Portlandian *argilo-calcaire* in Tracy-sur-Loire; and the final third from Kimmeridgian marl in Pouilly-sur-Loire. Yields average 50 hl/ha, the grapes are machine harvested and the wine ferments and ages on its lees in stainless steel tanks. The 2006, tasted in December 2010, was full and fresh, tart but not unripe, a savory Pouilly with good tension. Full of citrus and mineral flavors, the 2007 was nicely structured and bracingly tart.

Redde's top-of-the-line has historically been the Cuvée Majorum. Made only in the best vintages, it comes from the domaine's oldest vines – on average, 40 to 45 years old – chiefly grown on Kimmeridgian marl, with a third planted on *argiles à silex rouge*. The grapes are hand harvested, undergo skin contact, followed by a slow (eg two month) fermentation and aging for 18 months in stainless steel tanks or in *foudres* and *demi-muids*. The 2002, tasted in December 2010, was steely and vibrant. My only quibble is that it lacked phenolic maturity, mixing foxy notes as well as cat pee with attractive flavors of grapefruit and minerals. The 2006, tasted in January 2011, was, as the French say, *bien dans sa peau* (comfortable in its skin). Creamy and ripe, it had solid flavors of citrus and minerals and a whiff of gooseberry.

The next vintage of "Majorum" will be 2010. To this day, it is "Majorum", the creation of Michel Redde, that enjoys pride of place: it is always served last. However, I'm much more excited – and I think grandfather Redde would be too – by three new bottlings introduced in 2005.

Each is from a single vineyard and each is called Blanc Fumé de Pouilly. All are hand harvested, yields average 45 hl/ha and the wines ferment and age for ten months or more in stainless steel tanks. I found them among the best 2005 Pouillys I'd tasted and, simply, very exciting Pouillys.

First among equals is "Les Cornets," named after a parcel of pure Kimmeridgian marl soils in the village of Pouilly, along the old Roman road. The texture of the 2005 was entirely seductive, if hard to imagine: a blend of cream and satin. The flavors mixed lime, freshly grated coconut and long-steeped herbal tea, surrounding a strong mineral core. Elegant, with a lovely sense of place, it was an excellent wine.

"Les Champs de Billons" comes from vines on Portlandian soils in Tracy. Creamy and silken, the 2005 offered flavors of preserved lemon and a hint of butterscotch. Texture, structure, elegance and sense of place were the main characteristics of this thoroughly admirable Pouilly.

"Le Bois de Saint Andelain" comes from the highest vineyard in the appellation. It was acquired by Michel Redde in the early 1970s. Soils are *argile à silex rouge albien*. The most pungent of the three, the 2005 was also the freshest, tangiest and most varietal. A presence. Nervy, with flavors of quinine and herbal tea as well as a saline edge, it flaunted its pedigree. Very good indeed.

I was ever-so-slightly less enthused by the 2007s. Oh, they were very good: "Les Cornets", discreet, creamy and elegant, intermingled flavors of ginger, mint, and minerals with a slight note of oxidation and a hint of ivy; "Les Champs des Billons" came across a bit tenser and more site specific. It was also slightly more herbaceous than "Les Cornets", lightly hot and oxidized, with a savory saline finish. "Les Bois de Saint Andelain", flinty and strong, was a powerful presence.

These are three cuvées I want to follow very closely. And Sebastien would like to add two additional bottlings: a *cuvée Oxfordien* from a parcel called Les Toupées, and another from grapes they are currently planting on a site formerly used to quarry silex. For all these reasons, the Reddes merit an "Excellent" rating.

✌ Domaine de Riaux/Jeannot Pere & Fils
58150 St. Andelain; 03.86.39.11.37; alexis.jeannot@wanadoo.fr

The Jeannot family has been making wine in the Pouilly area for over 200 years. Today run by father Bertrand and son Alexis, both graduates of the Lycée Viticole de Beaune, the domaine consists of 13.25 hectares in St. Andelain, roughly 60% of which consists of flinty clay, with some Kimmeridgian marl and *calcaires de Villiers.*

Before Alexis's return to the property, the domaine sold most of its wine to négociants. Today, the emphasis is on estate bottling. The Jeannot's now practice sustainable farming. Harvesting is by machine, with yields averaging 65 hl/ha. The grapes ferment in temperature controlled tanks and age on their lees until bottling.

The Jeannot's make one cuvée each of Pouilly-sur-Loire and Pouilly-Fumé, though I sensed that there might be additional bottlings of the latter in the near future.

The Pouilly-sur-Loire, based on 60 year-old vines on flinty-clay soils, is sturdy, full, vinous, and well-made.

The 2009 Pouilly-Fumé, tasted in 2010, mixed notes of fig, gooseberry, slightly underripe peach and minerals. It wasn't an elegant Pouilly but it was a good and flavorful one. Tasted at the same time, the 2007 was less explosive, more discreet and verged on elegant, with a delicious weave of minerals, flint and citrus zest. The pungent and tangy 2006 was less refined. It was intrepid, however, so it would serve very nicely in a rough and tumble bistro. A sixth sense tells me to watch this house.

✌ Domaine Guy Saget
La Castille 58150 Pouilly-sur-Loire; 03 86 39 57 75; guy.saget@wanadoo.fr www.guy-saget.com

One of the top eight producers of Loire Valley wine, the grower-negociant house Domaine Guy Saget controls some 360 hectares from Pouilly-sur-Loire to Anjou. In addition to its 17 hectares in Pouilly, Guy Saget's properties include two in Sancerre – Domaine de la Perrière, purchased in 1996, and Domaine Balland-Chapuis, purchased in 1998. Domaine d'Artois, in Touraine, was acquired in 1988; and Domaine Chupin and Château de la Mulonnière, both in Anjou, in 1989 and 2003 respectively. Its negociant activities span from Quincy and Menetou-Salon to Saumur-Champigny. Additionally, Guy Saget has purchased two hotels in Sancerre, including the aptly named Hotel Le Panoramic.

There's something fitting about the union of hostelry and winemaking as I find that Guy Saget's wines, always competently made, predictable and available in sufficient quality, are ideal for chain hotels.

The best generally come from Saget's home base, Pouilly, where the family traces its vinous roots back nine generations. Today it produces four cuvées of Pouilly-Fumé in state-of-the-art cellars, built in 2001, under the direction of enologist Bruno Mineur.

Tasted in 2010, the basic 2008 Pouilly, much more appealing than Saget's Sancerre of the same year, was mineral with accents of lime and salt. A bit shallow but pleasant. The 2001, tasted in 2005, was a pungent, meaty Pouilly with flavors of grapefruit and grass. A bit coarse but food would help. The 2003 "Les Logerès" had pleasant notes of grapefruit and minerals. It was outshone by the 2002 "Prestige" bottling, a more discreet Pouilly with nicely balanced, well integrated flavors of fig and mineral.

Recommended

Domaine Hervé Seguin

Le Bouchot 58150 Pouilly-sur-Loire;03.86.39.10.75; www.domaine-seguin.com; herve.seguin@wanadoo.fr

Domaine Seguin's 16 hectares of vines are spread throughout the Pouilly appellation, giving them a mix of the major soil types – Kimmeridgian marl, compact limestone and flinty clay. Grapes are machine harvested and ferment in thermoregulated tanks.

The basic 2006 bottling, tasted in summer 2010, was fresh and textured, well balanced, with appealing flavors of lime and verbena. The "Cuvée Prestige" corresponds to a late harvest of 30 year-old vines. Curiously, the 2005 seemed less ripe than the entry level 2006. It was quite tart but concomitantly fresh, with flavors of grapefruit, some developing Chenin-like flavors (the result of aging, I'm assuming), and an adequate sense of place. I have not tasted "La Barboulotte," a 3000-bottle cuvée made from 60 year old vines and aged in oak.

Highly Recommended

Domaine Tinel Blondelet

58 avenue de la Tuilerie 58150 Pouilly-sur-Loire; 03.86.39.13.83; tinel-blondelet@wanadoo.fr; tinel-blondelet.fr

Annick Tinel represents the sixth generation to work family's vines. In this case, the land passed through Annick's mother's (the Blondelet) side of the family, as did those of Masson-Blondelet. Tinel-Blondelet follows the principles of sustainable farming on his 14.5 hectares of vines (mostly in

Pouilly but some in Sancerre). Grapes are machine harvested and vinification is conventional, with fermentation taking place in thermoregulated
stainless steel tanks. The wines stay on their fine lees until bottling, with
regular *batonnage*. There is one Pouilly-sur-Loire and several cuvées of
Pouilly-Fumé, of which "l'Arrêt Buffatte," named after the three hectare
parcel on which the grapes grow, is the signature bottling. The vineyard
site, on a southwest-facing hillside overlooking the Loire, lies on the
Roman Road and was once a rest stop for carriages. The 2006, tasted in
the summer of 2010, exhibited a thread of sur lie bubbles. It was relatively
full and fresh with subtle vegetal notes mixed with lime and verbena. A
lovely meal wine.

&. Excellent

&. Château de Tracy

58150 Tracy-sur-Loire;03.86.26.15.12; 06.16.35.18.98;
tracy@wanadoo.fr; château-de-tracy.com.

Enormous progress has been made at this historic château. But first, a bit
of that history, a saga rocked by revolutions and peopled by soldiers,
philosophers, and figures as iconic as Thomas Jefferson and Isaac Newton.

Briefly: In the 15th century, members of the noble Scottish Stutt family
came to France to aid the future king Charles VII during the Hundred Years
War. As a reward, the Stutts were nationalized, their name Gallicized to
d'Estutt and they were given the *seigneurie* d'Assay. In the late 16th century
a Stutt descendant married Françoise de Bar, whose dowry included the
Lordship of Tracy where grape growing had been documented as early as
the 14th century.

Today, the Château de Tracy is an exquisite, rambling castle in the hollow of a beautiful park. A diehard Janeite, I could see any one of a number
of Jane Austen's heroines at home here. Its 31 hectares of vines on hillsides
overlooking the Loire extend from Tracy to the plateau of the Champs de
Cri. They are supervised by Henry d'Estutt d'Assay who, over the past fifteen years, has essentially steered the domaine in a new direction.

Increasingly eco-friendly, the domaine's vines are farmed according to
the principles of sustainable agriculture. Chemical treatments are kept to
a strict minimum. Soils – a mix of flinty clay, Kimmeridgian marl and Portlandian limestone — are plowed, and yields are kept to an average of 50
hl/ha. With healthier, riper grapes, the domaine has been able to avoid
chaptalizing in most years, adding small amounts of sugar only in 2000,
2001 and 2004.

There are four cuvées, all harvested by hand and hand-sorted twice.

The domaine bottling comes from flint-on-Kimmeridgian marl slopes near the Loire. The most ambitious cuvée is "HD", or "Haute Densité", which comes from the *terres blanches* soils of the plateau of Champs de Cri. The vine density here is rare: 17,000 vine plants per hectare, easily 10,000 vine plants more than the normal Pouilly vineyard. Only two bunches are left per plant, to arrive at yields of around 30 hl/ha. Once harvested, the grapes undergo skin contact followed by a slow pressing. The wine is never chaptalized. Fifteen per cent ferments in barrel, the rest in tank, with a regular stirring up of the lees. Painstaking to make, and not cheap to buy, with a suggested retail price of $100. On the thriftier side, there's the cuvée "Mademoiselle de T." Essentially a young vines bottling from southwest facing slopes near the Loire, it is often called the "second" wine of Tracy. In 2008 the domaine introduced a new bottling "101 Rangs" which, when decoded, stands for 101 year old vines on silex soils. Vinified in demi-muids and in stainless steel tanks, the wine had the vivid gooseberry flavors and piercing acidity typical of so many 2008s.

As with many Loire domaines, I've drunk wines from the Château de Tracy regularly over the past twenty-plus years, most recently at the Salon des Vins de Loire in late January 2011. The 2009 domaine bottling, 14% alcohol, with yields of 45 hl/ha, was perfumed, full and creamy. There was a whiff of gooseberry and a bit of heat in the finish but it was hard to imagine who wouldn't like it. (Only the juice of the first press is used. The rest goes into "Mademoiselle T" or is sold to négociants.)

Because of hail damage, Tracy made only two 500 litre barrels (10 hl/ha) of "Haute Densité" in 2008. (The barrels were new but their force softened by having been used to ferment another wine for a week.) The wine was nicely ripe, quite creamy, and the oak, though present, was well integrated.

Here are some additional tasting memories.

One of the many reasons I enjoy entertaining is the process of selecting wines that will not only marry well with the food being served but with the guests I've invited. Thus it was that I selected wines from the Château de Tracy for two different events.

I always taste alone and take my notes before the guests arrive. When they are "normal" people, I simply serve the wines; when they are winemakers, I often serve the wines blind. This was the case on the following two occasions.

The first was a birthday lunch I threw for myself in 2008. The invitees: Guy and Annie Bossard (Domaine de L'Ecu in Muscadet); Henry and Marie-José Marionnet from the eponymous domaine in Sologne; and Jean-François and Martine Dubreuil. (Jean-François is the caviste who figures in the Wines of Memory and Sentiment essay in "A Wine & Food Guide to the Loire".)

I must have served at least a half-dozen dry whites as an aperitif, all blind. Two came from Tracy. The first was the 2005 domaine bottling, a fresh, tangy, and relatively rich white with juicy, grapey flavors and that hint of Concord-esque foxiness I often get in Pouillys, and my vigneron-caviste guests had no trouble placing this in that appellation.

Then came the 2005 HD. Extremely mineral, with notes of lime and grapefruit, the wine was dense and tight, nearly unctuous, and very racy. It had the same family traits as the domaine bottling but was much more powerful. Marionnet was trying to put the name on a floral note he detected which I took to be foxiness similar to – though much less marked than – the 2005 Domaine. Everyone found the wines elegant, though I was surprised to hear some describe them as "light." Everything's relative and these, particularly the "HD", are fairly potent Pouillys.

On another occasion, I'd invited two Angevin winemaking couples, Urterroirists Claude and Joëlle Papin (Château Pierre-Bise) and Vincent and Catherine Ogereau, as well as Philippe and Claude Alliet from Chinon. The first wine was a Cour-Cheverny. The second was the 2004 HD.

Tasting before the dinner, I found the wine somewhat evolved and oxidized. It was creamy and pungently varietal with notes of gooseberry and cat's pee. Densely textured but, to my mind, not phenolically ripe.

Claude Papin attacked the subject with questions characteristic of his highly personalized, much meditated philosophy of terroir, starting with, "Is the vineyard well ventilated?"

To this and to his subsequent questions, I said, 'You'll understand when you know what it is, Claude."

Although others noted the oxidation, everyone admired the structure of the wine. Of course, this led to discussion of vine density *chez mes invités* which usually came out to around 5000 vine plants a hectare. And there were open-ended questions and some theorizing about how just much vine density is desirable, and the effect that planting this dense might have on ripening. Few seemed as bothered as I by the loud green Sauvignon flavors, though I could feel Claude cogitating at the end of the table. The theory he came out with was that the vine density had prevented the grapes from reaching phenolic maturity but that the vines, forced to compete with each other, dug deeper into the earth, thus accentuating the expression of terroir. It was this that accounted for the wine's rather regal structure and imposing presence. Worth exploring. (The domaine did not bottle a 2009 "HD".)

And now for some random notes on the "Mademoiselle de T" and some older vintages of the domaine bottling: The 2006 "Mademoiselle de T", tasted in the summer of 2010, was fresh and relatively rich (13.5), with some herbaceous flavors but also nice, evolving herbal tea and quinine notes. A flavorful meal Pouilly. The 2005, like many Pouillys of that vintage, was surprisingly acidic with strong cat's pee flavors – a kind of throwback to the caricature of Pouilly-Sancerre that many consumers love. Question: did they pick early to keep the alcohol – which is listed as 13 degrees – under 14? Or was it the effect of drought? Still, it's a vibrant, sprightly wine.

Tasted in 2005, the 2003 domaine bottling, plump, with flavors of lime, minerals and banana was, thanks to the vintage, quite ripe. To its great credit, it wasn't heavy. Rather it was limpid and truly lovely. The 2002 had an attractive mineral-lime nose. It was slightly rustic but very true, and made for nice, punchy drinking.

Highly Recommended

Domaine Sebastien Treuillet
Fonteille 58150 Tracy-sur-Loire; 03.86.26.17.06; 06.78.11.96; domainetreuillet@orange.fr

In 1991, Treuillet began planting 4 hectares of Sauvignon Blanc and .35 hectares of Chasselas on the Portlandian and Kimmeridgian soils of the village of Fontenilles in the commune of Tracy. His first vintage was 1995. Treuillet practices sustainable farming, yields are sensible yields (60 hl/ha), and he harvests by machine. Nothing extraordinary. But you don't need to make a revolution to make good wine. I've only sampled three Pouilly-Fumés from Treuillet, the 2006, 2009 and the 2010. Tasted in the summer of 2010, the 2006 was ripe, textured and nicely evolved, with flavors of pear and verbena and some true depth. The 2009, tasted in October 2010, was a decisive, well-structured Pouilly, with lively flavors of grapefruit, tropical fruit, a whiff of currant buds, on a foundation of minerals. A very nice meal Pouilly. The 2010, tasted in January 2011 – a month after bottling – recalled 2008 in its balance of revivifing acidity, gooseberry flavors and ample mouthfeel. In 1998 Treuillet obtained 1.5 hectares in the Coteaux du Giennois. Located in the commune of Cosne, these vineyards are chiefly planted to Pinot Noir with 20 per cent Gamay.

Chapter Four
Menetou-Salon

Status: AOC 1959.

Types of Wine: White, red and rosé.

Grapes: Sauvignon Blanc for whites; Pinot Noir for reds and rosés.

Zone: The vineyard area, an extension of Sancerre, spreads over 10 villages, practically to the outskirts of Bourges, covering 466 hectares (1,151 acres) out of a potential of 1090. Over 300 hectares are planted to Sauvignon Blanc; the rest to Pinot Noir. The most important villages are Menetou-Salon and Morogues. The latter, alone, has the right to put its name on the label. The other villages are Aubinges, Parassy, Pigny, Quantilly, Saint-Céols, Soulangis, Vignoux-sous-les-Aix and Humbligny.

Production: For 2010: 26,364 overall; 17,046 hl white hl; 8,345 hlred and 973 hl rosé.

Soils: Chiefly sedimentary clay-limestone soils, Kimmeridgian marl, similar to those of Sancerre.

When to Drink: All but top cuvées, by their 6th birthday.

Price: $ to $$ ($)

Menetou Salon is a southwest extension of the vineyards of Sancerre. Its vines spread along a band of hillsides 200 to 300 meters high from Humbligny to the outskirts of the ancient cathedral city of Bourges. The Appellation takes its name from its most viticulturally-oriented commune, a provincial village with a large, leafy square lined with cafés (including a favorite, Cheu l'Zib) and a church. (A bit further on is Menetou's sumptuous château which once belonged to Jacques Coeur, finance minster under Charles XII.)

Documents show that Menetou-Salon was producing wine as early as 1063; its wines were served at the table of Jacques Coeur in the 15th century.

Its growers *syndicat* dates from 1890. More recently, the appellation began developing in the 1970s and continues to progress from vintage to vintage.

Most of the vines are planted on slopes running along a narrow five-kilometer band for some 25 kilometers between Bourges and Humbligny. The soils here are, essentially, similar to those of Sancerre and Chablis. Characterized by layers of pure, compact limestone and the more tender, clay-rich marl, they abound with oyster shells. Locals call Menetou's soils "oreilles de poules" (hens' ears).

Menetou Sauvignons, generally vinified at low temperatures in all types of tanks, are brisk and sprightly, often floral and/or herbaceous, with firm flavors of grapefruit and minerals. Special cuvées may ferment or age in barrel. Most of the reds vat for a week to ten days. They may or may not age in barrel before bottling. And with the progress that has been made within the past 15 years, many are fully the equals of the wines from neighboring Sancerre.

Not surprising then that many Sancerrois have bought and continue to buy vineyards — or grapes — here. And young vignerons from other regions have set up wineries. Additionally the ensemble of the appellation is taking steps to improve quality — in vines (notably with lower yields and a move toward sustainable viticulture), in cellars, and in hospitality. (At least one domaine – L'Ermitage – has an excellent B&B.)

In *A Wine and Food Guide to the Loire* I reviewed only two growers – Clément/Chatenoy and Pellé. It speaks to the great progress that has been made in the appellation that I've chosen to review twelve producers in this edition. I also said that, as Menetou Salon had everything going for it, it deserved to be better known and, given the popularity of both Sauvignon Blanc and Pinot Noir, it surely would be. It has undeniably become better known, the quality of the wines has progressed dramatically, but, as exports now account for only 20% of volume, and with ample acreage as yet unexploited, it has plenty of room to grow.

Producers

There are 70 growers and 6 grower-négociants.

Outstanding

Domaine de Chatenoy/Clément   Domaine Henry Pellé

Excellent

Domaine Philippe Gilbert
La Tour St. Martin/Albane & Bertrand Minchin

To follow

Domaine de l'Ermitage/ Géraud and Laurence de la Farge

Highly recommended

Henri Bourgeois/Le Prieuré des Aublats
Domaine Bernard Fleuriet & Fils

Recommended

Chavet & Fils Eric Louis   Prieuré de St. Céols

By the Glass

Jean-Max Roger   Domaine Jean Teiller

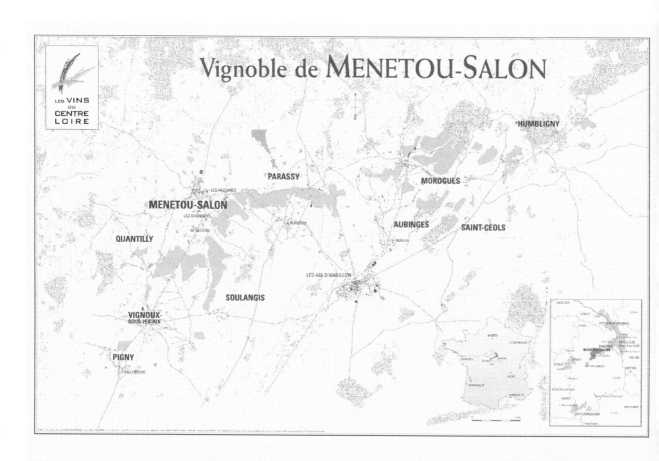

Vignoble de MENETOU-SALON

MENETOU - SALON

PAYS FORT	ZONE VITICOLE	CHAMPAGNE BERRICHONNE
Front de CUESTA de l'argile à silex (côte du Pays Fort)	en une côte simple : Menetou Parassy dédoublée : Morogues	

Luvisols limoneux sur argile à silex	Brunisols sableuses + argileux	Calcosols sur calcaires et marnes	Calcosols sur calcaires

La Borne   Le Colin   vers Rians

N   S

400 m
300 m
200 m

500 m

Formation argileuse à silex	Portlandien calcaires
Cenomanien sables et gaize	Kimméridgien marnes de St Doulchard
Albien sables et argiles	Kimméridgien calcaires de Buzançais
Barrémien argiles, sables et grès	Oxfordien supérieur calcaires lité
	Oxfordien supérieur calcaires crayeux de Bourges

ﾞ✤ﾞ Recommended

ﾞ✤ﾞ Henri Bourgeois

(See Sancerre)

From purchased grapes, this excellent house produces a high-strung Menetou *blanc* "Le Prieuré des Aublats."

ﾞ✤ﾞ outstanding

ﾞ✤ﾞ Domaine de Chatenoy/ Isabelle & Pierre Clément

18510 Menetou-Salon; 02.48.66.68.70; domainedechatenoy.com

Pierre Clément, who earned a degree in enology from the Lycée de Beaune, joined his father Bernard at the domaine in 1985, representing the 15th generation of Cléments to work the vines in Menetou-Salon. At the time, the domaine consisted of about 12 hectares; today, the Cléments own 60, two-thirds of which are planted to Sauvignon Blanc, one third to Pinot Noir.

From the 1990, when I first visited the property, to today, my tasting notes have repeatedly contained the phrase, "Not one false step." The Cléments turn out ambassadorial Menetous with admirable regularity.

The Cléments practice sustainable farming which, in their case, means (in addition to the usual), hiring twenty people to work in the vineyards from April to July to effectively carry out a second pruning of the vines in order to keep only the "most interesting" shoots. The basic cuvée of white is machine harvested; the rest of the grapes are harvested by hand. All ferment with indigenous yeasts. With the exception of the Cuvée Pierre Alexandre, all ferment in thermoregulated stainless steel tanks and all whites age on their lees before bottling.

There are three cuvées of white Menetou. The following wines were tasted in 2009. The basic 2006, one third of which undergoes skin contact, was sprightly, fresh and pungent, with a fine mineral core, a textbook Menetou. The Dame de Chatenoy is a hand-harvested selection of late harvested grapes, fermented and aged like the basic bottling. The 2005, with 13.5 degrees alcohol, was mellow and fresh. The oak was well integrated into this ripe, rather elegant wine with grace notes of lemon zest and grapefruit. The Cuvée Pierre Alexander is a selection of overripe grapes, fermented and aged in oak barrels, half of which are new. The unctuous 2005 seemed dominated by oak, allowing only glimpses of very ripe fruit and minerals. Still, it's an undeniably impressive wine.

Tart and highstrung, the 2006 rosé, a direct press of the harvest, drank like a lightly tannic white. It would have been a fine partner for dishes made with exotic spices. The basic Menetou *rouge* has a white label. The grapes are hand harvested, two thirds are destemmed and the wine ferments in tank for 10 to 12 days with regular punching down. The 2006 had abundant upfront fruit. It was suave and smooth, lightly tannic, with an appetizing note of bitterness. Delicious.

The grapes for the Menetou rouge Black Label are not destemmed; the grapes ferment in tank for fifteen or twenty days with regular punching down, before aging in oak barrels, a third of which are new. I watched the 2005 evolve over the course of three days. As it opened, its fruit, somewhat skeletal (in the nicest sense) to start, fleshed out and revealed juicy flavors of dark cherry and blueberry. The wine had aged in barrel but the oak here was a support, not a crutch, an accent, not a mask. And the wine went very well with spinach-and-ricotta-stuffed tortellini.

&. Recommended

&. Domaine Chavet & Fils: Recommended
Route de Bourges, 18510 Menetou-Salon; 02.48.64.80.87;
www.chavet-vins.com

Documents show that the Chavet family has been growing grapes and making wine on the classic soils of Menetou-Salon since the 17th century. Today, with 23 hectares, the family also purchases grapes *sur pied*. Since 2005, the estate has qualified for two "labels" indicating that they practice sustainable farming, Agriculture Raisonnée, and QualiTerre, and their own label states "*vignerons par natur*". Grapes are machine harvested and ferment in temperature controlled tanks. There are two levels of wine – the basic domaine bottling for early drinking, and the Cuvée Exception which can age for several years. The following wines were tasted in 2009 and 2010.

Pungent and squeaky clean, the 2006 Menetou *blanc*, with its tangy grapefruit flavors, would make a good bistro Sauvignon Blanc. The 2008, lively, structured and ample, was a mouthful of lemon, grapefruit and verbena. The Cuvée Exception *blanc* is harvested roughly 10 days after the grapes for the normal cuvée. The wine ages on its fine lees for at least 10 months, 25% of it in oak barrels. The 2006, clearly richer and riper than the domaine bottling, also had more character. Light oak and vanilla flavors interwoven with good fruit made for a stylish, suave white.

The 2008 rosé seemed ever so slightly off-dry but pleasant in every respect – fresh and light despite the 13% alcohol. The 2006 Menetou red was rather bitter. The 2005 Cuvée Exception, which ages in oak barriques for a year, started off quite astringent; with aeration, it softened up but not enough. The finish was still drying, slightly bitter, and the flavors were dominated by oak and St. Nectaire-like cheesiness. The 2006 Cuvée Exception rouge, light but firm, with direct varietal flavors and light tannins, was much more pleasant – an easy red that was smooth and specific.

Domaine de l'Ermitage/ Géraud and Laurence de la Farge:
18500 Berry-Bouy, 02.48.26.87.46; www.domaine-ermitage.com; domaine-ermitage@wanadoo.fr.

An idealistic young couple, Laurence and Géraud de la Farge, debuted in 2003 with nine hectares of vines which were planted in 1981. Harvest is by hand; fermentation takes place in temperature-controlled stainless steel tanks. The white grapes undergo several hours of skin contact; a percentage of the red wine ages in oak.

Their wines are works in progress but very promising. The high-strung 2008 *blanc* was a clear reflection of the vintage; the 2008 red was pure and delicate, with light mineral notes. The 2007 red was dominated by oak. Nice oak but oak all the same. The De la Farges also cultivate cereal crops and have an excellent B&B.

Domaine Bernard Fleuriet & Fils
(See Sancerre)

While most of their holdings are in Sancerre, the Fleuriets turn out an excellent Menetou *blanc*. The 2006 La Vigne au Paul had an icy crispness making it downright bouncy, an edge of citrus zest, and a fine mineral finish. The French are very fond of avocado and grapefruit salads. I love each of those foods separately, but together? Not so much. But pair them with this wine and I might be won over. The domaine's Menetou *rouge* needs work, as evidenced by a thin but pleasant 2006.

Domaine Philippe Gilbert
18510 Menetou-Salon; 02.48.66.65.90; www.domainephilippegilbert.fr.

Philippe Gilbert took over his family's 27 -hectare domaine in 1998. Working in close association with enologist Jean-Philippe Louis, he has turned this erstwhile ho-hum estate into one of the appellation's leading lights. In 2005 the team converted the vineyards to biodynamic farming; the soils – essentially compact limestone on Kimmeridgian marl – are hoed mechanically; vines are cluster-thinned and deleafed. All wines age on their fine lees and are filtered only when deemed necessary. It is evident from tasting that improvements in vinification have kept pace with work in the vineyards.

Gilbert produces two cuvées of white and red and occasionally one cuvée of rosé. The cuvée "Domaine" is meant to be drunk on the fruit – a fresh, supple, accessible wine. Les Renardières is the domaine's top-of-the-line cuvée in red and white. It comes from the oldest vines, yields are low, and the grapes are harvested by hand and then hand sorted. Both age in 225 or 400 litre barrels made of oak from the Tronçais and Nevers forests. Currently this cuvée is bottled only in magnum. Both the white and the red should be carafed before drinking.

Tasted in 2010, the 2009 generic Menetou *blanc* was ripe and rather plump. When first sampled, several months after the harvest, the 2008 Menetou was as gas-y as a cremant but quite appealing, like a vinous ginger ale. The 2007, tasted at the same time, was pure, ripe and well made. A year later the 2007 had blossomed into a white with tangy flavors of citronelle, lemon zest and minerals. On day two, it came across more "varietal" with notes of gooseberry. It was surprisingly delicious with a sandwich of smoked salmon, fresh dill and sweet butter, as well as with tzaziki mixed with red pepper, red onion, garlic and mint. A crisp, invigorating 2006 mixed flavors of apple, grapefruit and minerals, all expressed with admirable clarity. Good work here.

The 2008 Les Renardières *blanc*, tasted in November 2010, was rich and textured, a well upholstered white with good balance and adept acid management. An excellent bistro white. The 2007, tasted in late 2008, was still in barrel. A wine of real freshness and depth, it was very promising. Tasted again, after the wine had been bottled (having spent 12 months in barriques), the attack was elegant. Oak was there but so was minerality. The acidity was very refined and the flavors were an appetizing mix of grapefruit, citrus zests, stone, and an edge of salinity. The Gilberts recommended carafing the 2005, a wise idea: the wine was textured but so oaky that I only got glimpses of the vibrant, juicy fruit underneath. Still, a very commendable wine.

The fresh, mineral 2009 Menetou *rouge,* tasted in November 2010, seemed lighter than its 14% alcohol. The 2008, tasted several months after the harvest, was light and tart but truly charming; the 2007 was slightly more tannic, very pure, an excellent wine bar red, all the more admirable given the difficult conditions of the 2007 growing season. Tasted several months later, the wine came across dry but tender, honest and well-structured, with sweet strawberry grace notes. The 2006 had charming upfront fruit. Smooth, focused and slightly saline, it was an ingratiating medium-bodied Pinot Noir.

The 2008 Les Renardières *rouge*, tasted in November 2010, was lean, precise, and pure, a lovely blend of cherries and black tea. The 2006, relatively light in both color and saturation, had a deep cherry nose with notes of eau de vie. Firm and fleshy, it was a mouth-filling wine that was simultaneously subtle but firm, and gently seductive. The 2005, darker and more deeply saturated, was slightly saline, its oak well balanced by plush, ripe fruit.

  Recommended

❀ Eric Louis
(See Sancerre)

Principally a producer of Sancerre, this family winery makes a brisk, appetizing Menetou *blanc*. The 2008, with flavors of lime, creamed corn, black currant buds, and the salinity of Badoit, was an appetizing bistro white.

  Outstanding

❀ Domaine Henry Pellé
18220 Morogues; 02.48.64.42.48; www.henry-pelle.com

The first Menetou domaine I ever visited was Henry Pellé. That was in 1990. Wry and gregarious, Pellé told me that his parents, farm workers, had wanted him to be a teacher. "I remember thinking," he said, "Thirty kids everyday for the rest of my life? Not me!" So, "to the great despair" of his parents he returned to the land and became one of the leading winemakers of his appellation.

In 1990 Pellé, nearing retirement, was working with his son Eric, a Lycée de Beaune graduate, who would take over the domaine. Eric died in a car accident. His wife, Anne Pellé, subsequently hired Julien Zernott to take over the winemaking. Talented and dedicated, Zernott turned out excellent wines: the whites continued to be every bit as good as they had been under Henry, and the reds improved dramatically. Additional cuvées filled out the range, which came to include a red and white in Sancerre and a white in Pouilly. In 2009 Zernott left to work full-time at his own vineyard in the Languedoc, Pas d'Escalette, turning the reins over to Eric and Anne's 25 year old son, Paul-Henry Pellé.

Today the domaine consists of 40 hectares, chiefly on soils composed of Kimmeridgian marl in Menetou (35) and Sancerre (5) in the commune of Montigny. Two thirds are planted to Sauvignon Blanc, one third to Pinot Noir. Pellé also buys the equivalent of ten hectares of grapes for his basic bottlings but notes that he tends the vineyards.

The Pellé's practice sustainable farming, though Paul-Henry points out that viticulture is essentially organic but he wants to leave himself the leeway to use unauthorized treatments if the weather turns "dramatic". Harvest is by machine for whites, and by hand for reds, though the domaine will harvest their entire crop by hand by 2015.

In Menetou, there are four cuvées of white, all of which depend on indigenous yeasts and age on their lees until bottling: domaine (one-third from purchased grapes); Morogues (an assemblage of six *clos* within the village of Morogues). Next is "Clos de Ratier", from a 5 hectare parcel on steep, south-west facing slopes whose Kimmeridgian marl soils contain an abundance of fossilized oyster shells. This wine ferments in 400 litre barrels of four to five wines, and then ages on its lees, either in tank or barrel, for ten months. Finally, there is "Blanchais", from old vines – planted in the 1960s with a *selection massalle* – in a *clos* on a fine south-east facing slope with soils similar to those of Ratier mixed with silex. There is also a rosé and four cuvées of red, all of which are cold soaked, vat for 8 days to a month, and are punched down and pumped over once or twice daily during fermentation. The domaine bottling is made from purchased grapes; Morogues, from Pellé's vines in the village; "Le Cris", from grapes planted in the 1960s on a ten hectare plot with Kimmeridgian and Portlandian soils. The grapes ferment in tronconic oak vats and age in barriques. And, finally, "Z Coeur de Cris" (made only in certain years, eg 2000 and 2004), from a selection of grapes grown directly on Kimmeridgian bedrock.

I tasted the following wines at the Salon des Vins de Loire in late January 2011 and I'll describe them in the order in which Paul-Henry presented them. The 2010s had been assembled and filtered for bottling. First came Pellé's sole bottling of Menetou-Salon from vines not located in the commune of Morogues, called "Les Bornes Blanc". The 2010 was nicely varietal, tangy, though a bit hot. A very good entry-level wine. The 2010 "Morogues", from stonier soils, was completely different. Not at all varietal, it was somewhat floral, with heady aromas of white-fleshed peaches and grapefruit, and a long mineral, citrus finish. A 2008 "Morogues", served from magnum, seemed in its adolescence, with its aromas of creamed corn, marrowy sur lie texture, good depth, and its 2008 acidity well cushioned. It had a firm, mineral, lemon zest finish.

A 2008 Morogues "Clos de Ratier", like the Morogues, had aromas of creamed corn. On the palate, it was racy, deep, extremely mineral, with flavors of quinine and grapefruit. Truly terroir-driven. The 2008 "Les Blanchais", served from magnum, was regal, fresh and mineral, its acidity beautifully integrated. The finish was long and chalky. Excellent.

Next came two whites from 2007, both served from magnum. The first, the "Clos de Ratier" bottling, was ethereal and elegant, a pedigreed wine

with lacy citrus zest and mineral flavors. The second was "Les Blanchais".
This terroir-driven wine took me on a quick trip to Chablis. Fine and elegant, all depth and minerality, lightened by citrus zest. PMG.

A series of 2009s followed, all at or above 14% alcohol. The "Morogues"
bottling was swaddled in baby fat. Worth following. Les Ratiers was more
tender, with seductive flavors of herbal tea. "Les Blanchais" feared no vintage extremes. Textured and deep, it was a resolute presence, with a strong
undercurrent of quinine and herbal tea.

Next, the 2010 rosé, a tank sample, was good, fresh and alluring. Then
the 2008 Menetou red "Les Cris" which was a bit closed and tart and needed
time or simply aeration.

Here's a sampling of tasting notes from earlier vintages – when Paul-
Henry was working with Julien Zernott: a 2005 Menetou blanc from purchased grape was full and well made with flavors of grapefruit and freshly
cut grass; the "Morogues" bottling, tasted from tank, was truly lovely, with
great minerality; ditto for the "Clos de Ratier" which was a pure delight;
the 2004 was creamy, full, very appetizing, very mineral, and very specific;
the "Blanchais" *blanc* tends to be plumper and more tender, and was true
to form in both 2005 and 2004.

The 2004 "Les Cris" *rouge*, when tasted in early 2006, was tight, juicy and
vibrant; the 2002, lightly oaky and full of character, seemed to have a direct
link to Pinot Noirs from Irancy. And the 2004 "Z Coeur de Cris", in early
2006, was silky, lightly oaky and impressively elegant.

Recommended

✿ Prieuré de St-Céols/Pierre et Christine Jacolin
Le Prieuré, 18220 Saint-Céols; 02.48.64.40.75; sarl-jacolin@cege-
tel.net; www.menetou-salon-jacolin.com

Pierre Jacolin has 10.6 acres of vines and cultivates a assortment of red fruit
from which he makes his own liqueurs. Grapes are machine harvested and
ferment in temperature controlled stainless steel tanks.

The 2006 Menetou *blanc* was a bit rough-hewn but not without character. It came across like an old-fashioned white treated to some technological
advances. The 2006 red, the grapes of which had been cold soaked for 8 to
10 days, was tannic and astringent, and would have benefited from being
lightly chilled and served with young goat cheese. I have not tasted the oak-
aged Cuvée des Bénédictins.

🍷 Jean-Max Roger
(See Sancerre)

🍷 By the Glass

This conscientious grower-negociant bottles a clear, bitingly tart Menetou *blanc* "Le Petit Clos;" and a light, lean, rather astringent rouge "Le Charnay."

🍷 Domaine Jean Teiller
13 route de la Gare, 18510 Menetou-Salon; 02.48.64.80.71; domaine-teiller@wanadoo.fr; domaine-teiller.fr

🍷 By the Glass

This 17-hectare domaine is now run by two generations of Teillers, Jean-Jacques and his wife Monique assisted by their daughter Patricia and her husband Olivier Lumeau. Grapes are machine harvested and ferment in tank. Brisk and sprightly, the 2006 Menetou *blanc*, with appealing notes of lemon zests, was a lively bistro white. The 2006 rosé was somewhat dull, and the red, rather lean and mean. Stick with the white.

🍷 La Tour St. Martin/Albane & Bertrand Minchin
St. Martin, 18340 Crosses; 02.48.25.02.95; tour.saint.martin@wanadoo.fr

🍷 Excellent

In 1987, Bernard and Albane Minchin took over his family's 16 hectares of vines on the compact limestone over Kimmeridgian marl slopes of Morogues. A gregarious and dynamic couple, they first adopted the principles of sustainable farming and are now in the process of converting the vineyards to organic viticulture. My sense is that they are still refining their style but they are clearly a welcome addition to the appellation. And in 2004 they added Valençay to their portfolio with the purchase of Claux Delorme.

Plump and generous, the 2003 Menetou Morogues *blanc* successfully translated the extreme heat of the vintage into a broad Sauvignon Blanc with New World overtones and exotic fruit flavors. The 2006 was a clear reflection of Menetou's proximity to Sancerre. With light gooseberry and lively grapefruit and mineral flavors, it was a well-made white, perfect for an upscale bistro. The 2009 was ripe and floral, with scents of white fleshed peaches and clèmentine. It might have a gram or two of residual sugar. Serve nicely chilled.

Fermented and aged in new and newish barrels (there's a four-year rotation), the Cuvée Honorine is sometimes too much of a good thing. That was my reaction to the 2003 when the wine came across as what the French call a "*bête de concours,*" – essentially, a wine made to win tasting competitions. I'm sure that wasn't the case. It's just that the vintage and oak combined to make a full-blown, rather overpowering wine. The 2006 was fresher and more appealing but it lacked the bounce of the Morogues cuvée, and the oak masked what I'm sure was lovely fruit. Still, I admired the ambitions the Minchin's had for the wine. The 2008 "Honorine", with 13% alcohol, some CO_2, aromas of creamed corn and oak, had 2008's spirited acidity. To its great credit, it was also aromatically ripe. The wine seemed somewhat disjointed when I served it at Thanksgiving 2010 but one of my guests, a wonderful wine journalist, loved it.

Similarly ambitious is the deluxe red cuvée "Céléstin." After having been hand harvested in small cases, the grapes are stemmed, sorted, and undergo a week of cold soaking before fermenting for a month, with regular punching down and pumping over. One-third of the wine ages in large wood vats and demi-muids; two-thirds in barriques. The wine is bottled without being fined or filtered.

The 2006 was a suave red with attractive fruit but, even with aeration, I found it too oaky, and preferred the "simpler" 2006 Morogues *rouge*, which was a firm, stony, medium-bodied Pinot Noir. Fragrant, almost floral, it was fresh and clear. Some may have found it too light but I loved it.

Chapter Five
Quincy

Status: AOC (1936)

Grapes: Sauvignon Blanc.

Zone: northwest of Bourges and southeast of Vierzon, on the banks of the Cher, within the communes of Quincy and Brinay.

Volume: As of 2010, 255 hectares (630 acres) cultivated out of a potential of 1000 classified.

Production: In 2010, 15,915 hl.

Soils: Chiefly sand, gravel, and silt on clay, some chalk with outcroppings of lacustrine sand and limestone.

When to Drink: Most should be drunk within five years of the harvest.

Price: $ to $$ (Currently 80% is sold in France.)

The second viticultural region in France to receive AOC status – the first was Châteauneuf-du-Pape-, Quincy is one of the oldest vineyards of the *Région Centre*. Its vineyards occupy a long plateau bordered by woods above the left bank of the Cher. Documents show that vines were cultivated here as early as 1120; in the 14th century, it was the Cîteaux monks who pruned and hoed and harvested the grapes; and its wines were called "the wine of Bourges".

Many consider Quincy to be the cradle of Sauvignon Blanc: the grape is said to have been brought here from the Abbaye des Femmes de Beauvoir by Cistercian monks. And the Quincy appellation applies only to white wines made from Sauvignon, which, on Quincy's hot, light soils, ripens a full week earlier than it does in Sancerre, easily reaching a potential of 13 degrees alcohol, even 15. Acids are generally — and naturally — low, making Quincy the creamiest, and softest, of the Cher's Sauvignons.

Quincy's vineyards almost disappeared after World War II, however, as its young population moved to Paris, Bourges, and Vierzon, and as old vignerons retired with no successors. Quincy became a village of roofers.

In the 1980s, it began to waken from its long slumber. Newcomers arrived; vines were planted and, by the mid-90s, the local *syndicat* predicted that the appellation would soon have 200 hectares in production.

Today, Quincy has 255 hectares in production and its volume has nearly tripled, ranging from 11, 700 to nearly 16,000 hls a year. Above all, the quality of the wines is leap years ahead of what it was in the 80s and early 90s.

Old texts and old-timers talk about the elegance of Quincy Sauvignon which often had residual sugar. But, tasting the wines during my first visit to the region in 1990, it was hard for me to understand why Quincy won such early AOC recognition, or why it was considered one of the Loire's most elegant wines.

At the time, growers argued that tastes had changed. Consumers wanted fresher, livelier, and dryer whites. The Quincy vignerons obliged by picking grapes greener, and then chaptalizing to mask the lack of ripeness and to raise the finished wine's alcohol level. And the wines I tasted back in 1990 seemed caught between two worlds; the alcoholic, unaromatic, rustic, and perhaps slightly oxidized wines of grandfather, and the high-tech, squeaky clean, audaciously fruity style favored in the late 20th century – a style of wine more likely to be found in nearby appellations such as Reuilly. Most of the Quincys I tasted back then were straw yellow; their aromas blandly vinous, with banana and muscat notes; their structure, rather soft. This unfocused style was not surprising given Quincy's late reawakening and hit-or-miss vinifications. Progress seemed stalled by widespread, though not unendearing, amateurism.

Times, I am delighted to say, have changed once again. Quincy has taken giant steps forward. The wines, in general, offer the freshness today's consumer wants; they are usually 13 degrees alcohol or more, and have a gram or two of residual sugar. Now, however, the alcohol comes from riper fruit as growers pick later; and the flavors of the wine are more complex and pure. Sur lie aging, now generally practiced, gives the wines a satisfying, marrowy texture.

When analyzing this evolution, I think of Jacques Sallé and his Silice de Quincy. Sallé, a wine journalist, began making wine in Quincy in the late 90s. They were organic, they were hand-crafted, beautifully made, creamy, elegant, mineral, with picture-perfect Loire balance. If Sallé were still making wine, he'd be classed "Outstanding." Sad to say, Sallé was forced to give up winemaking due to a degenerative illness. As he told me when I spoke to him in April 2009, his health problems prevented him from doing the hard physical work needed to make wine, and he was not making enough money to hire anyone. So he was selling off what remained of his stock.

I write this as something of a tribute because I do think he set the example for today's crop of exciting producers, many of them newcomers to winemaking.

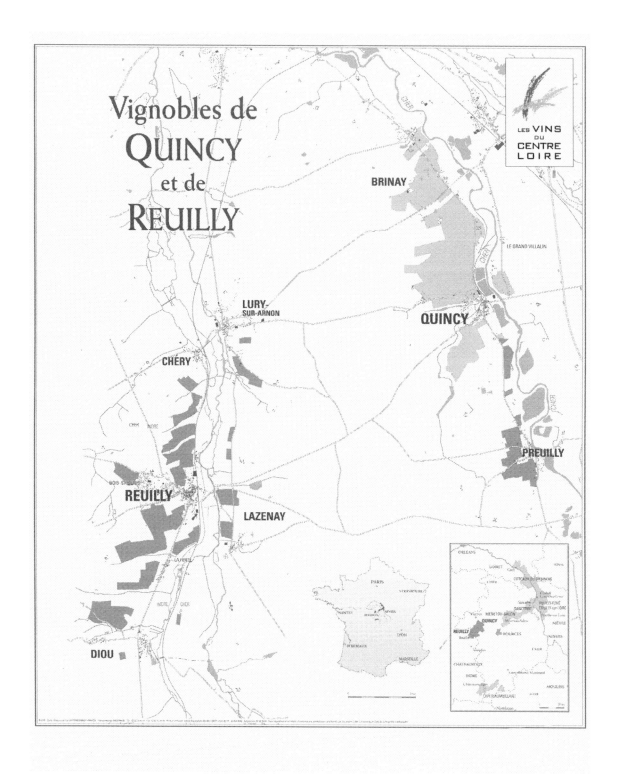

Vignobles de
QUINCY
et de
REUILLY

BRINAY

LE GRAND VILLALIN

LURY-
SUR-ARNON

QUINCY

CHÉRY

PREUILLY

REUILLY

LAZENAY

DIOU

LES VINS DU CENTRE LOIRE

QUINCY

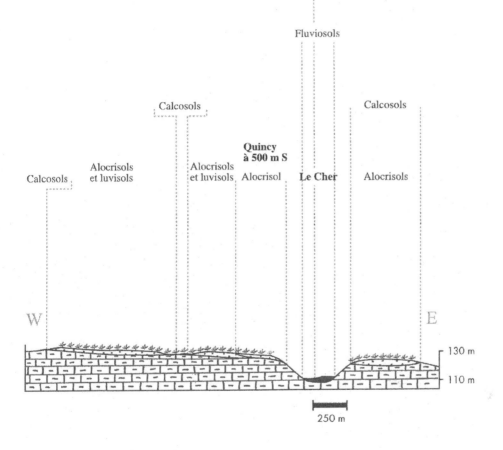

INTERFLUVE
CHER-ARNON

INTERFLUVE
CHER-YEVRE

Fluviosols

Calcosols

Calcosols

Calcosols

Alocrisols
et luvisols

Alocrisols
et luvisols

Quincy
à 500 m S

Alocrisol

Le Cher

Alocrisols

Calcosols

W

E

130 m

110 m

250 m

Alluvions subactuelles

Alluvions anciennes
sables graves et argiles

Alluvions anciennes
sables, graves et argiles

Alluvions anciennes non différenciées
argiles, sables et graves

Calcaires et argiles
lacustres du Berry

🐝 Producers

There are 25 winemakers and one cooperative. Additionally, a number of producers from Sancerre offer a Quincy. Joseph Mellot's Quincy's are reviewed here under the domaine Pierre Duret listing but many, among them Henri Bourgeois, are not. I recommend reading their profiles in the Sancerre section. Gérard Bigonneau and Valery Renaudat, producers in Reuilly (see reviews), also make Quincy, and a number of Quincy's producers make wine in Reuilly, as well as reds and rosés from Pinot Noir and Gamay and local obscurities such as Genouillet. Made in the zone of the Quincy appellation, these are sold as Vin de Pays du Cher et de l'Arnon.

🐝 Excellent

Domaine du Tremblay/ Tatin-Wilk   🐝   Domaine Trotereau/Pierre Ragon

🐝 To follow

Domaine du Grand Rosierès/Jacques Siret   🐝   Adele Rouzé   🐝
Domaine Vincent Siret-Courtaud

🐝 Highly recommended

Domaine des Ballandors/Tatin-Wilk   🐝   Domaine de Chevilly/ Yves & Antoine Lestourgie   🐝   Domaine Pierre Duret   🐝   Domaine Lecomte   🐝   Domaine Mardon   🐝   Domaine de Villalin

🐝 Recommended

Le Clos de la Victoire/Domaine Jean-Michel Sorbe   🐝
Domaine Philippe Portier   🐝   Jacques Rouzé

❧ Domaine des Ballandors/Jean Tatin & Chantal Wilk

18120 Brinay; 02 48 75 20 09; chantalwilk@hotmail.com;
domaines-tatin.com

The Domaines des Ballandors and du Tremblay (see below) are almost
inextricably linked. Both, in addition to Les Demoiselles Tatin in Reuilly,
are owned by Chantal Wilk and her husband Jean Tatin, two former agricultural engineers who created their domaines nearly twenty years ago. All
the wines are made in cellars in Brinay.

Ballandor consists of nearly 9 hectares of vines on three distinct parcels,
with the varying soil types characteristic of the appellation, and ages of
vines ranging from those recently planted to those over 40 years old. Viticulture follows the eco-friendly guidelines of *lutte raisonnée;* the grapes are
harvested by machine before being lightly pressed and undergoing a long,
cool fermentation in stainless steel tanks. The wines age on their fine lees
before being fined and filtered. There is a single cuvée and it is reliably very
good. The 2008, full and textured, fairly exploded with the stunning acidity
typical of 2008, and satisfied with flavors of lime and citronelle. A fine
choice for an upscale bistro or a Michelin-One-star. Bright and fragrant,
the 2006 was a wee bit herbaceous and nicely stony. A good, down-home
bistro white.

❧ Domaine de Chevilly/ Yves & Antoine Lestourgie

52 route de Chevilly, 18120 Méreau t/f: 02.48.52.80.45;
M:06.62.82.52.69; domaine.de.chevilly@orange.fr

Yves and Antoine Lestourgie created their domaine in 1994 with a mere 1.5
hectares. Today they have nine. And the results are admirable. Their 2008
truly embodied the unique structure of that vintage. With 13.3 alcohol and
4.9 g/l acid, it was full and invigoratingly fresh without being shrill: creami-
ness enveloped the angularity. Good ripeness, attractive minerality, zippy
citrus zest notes, in all, a good bistro white. The 2007 Cuvée Zoé, from a
parcel with chalky-clay soils, was more fine-boned and elegant, with similar,
though more urbane, flavors to the 2008.

🐝 Le Clos de la Victoire/ Domaine Jean-Michel Sorbe

Le Buisson Long, Route de Quincy, 18120 Brinay; 02.48.51.30.17;
jeanmichelsorbe.com

In 1997 the grower-negociant house Joseph Mellot took over the running
of this 14 hectare domaine from Jean-Michel Sorbe. Viticulture and vinification are identical to those practiced at other properties being directed by
the Mellot firm (see Domaine Pierre Duret/Quincy) and the results are similar without inevitably being equal. The wine I tasted was the 2005 which
won a silver medal in the Paris agricultural fair. It was crisp and clean, with
clear varietal flavors, as well as a hint of hard candy which, I hope, will disappear as the wine ages.

🐝 Domaine Pierre Duret

Le Buisson Long- Route de Quincy - 18120 Brinay; 0248 513 017;
lesentierduvin.com

In 1994, the grower-negociant house Joseph Mellot assumed the direction
of this 12.5 hectare property on the sandy, gravelly terraces bordering the
Cher. The average age of the vines is 25 years; yields are moderate, roughly
60 hl/ha; the grapes are machine harvested, destemmed, and pressed lightly
before fermenting in tank. The wines age on their fine lees and are lightly
filtered before bottling. Nothing original, here, but they are obviously doing
something right. I have only tasted the 2006, and it presented a very positive image of technically proficient commercial winemaking. The wine was
super fresh, crystalline, with good grip and focus, a satisfying sur-lie mouthfeel, and flavors of grapefruit, gooseberry and minerals.

🐝 Domaine du Grand Rosières/Jacques Siret

Le Grand Rosière 18400 Lunery; 02 48 68 90 34;
jacquessiret@wanadoo.fr

In 1995, after having spent years raising cereal crops and poultry, Jacques
Siret was able to buy himself 1.5 hectares of vineyard land in Quincy. Today
he farms 5 hectares of vines – from 5 to 35 years old – on the gravelly, clay-
flint terraces of the Cher and shares a cellar with his son, Vincent Siret-
Courtaud who produces wines under his own label (see below). I've tasted
only one of Jacques Siret's wines, the 2008. Full and ripe, it came across as
ever-so-slightly sweet which I think was more a function of its 13.5 degrees
alcohol than the presence of more than a degree of residual sugar. I partic-

ularly admired its purity – bordering on the crystalline – and its fine thread of minerals.

Domaine Lecomte

105 rue St Exupéry 18520 AVORD; 02 48 69 27 14; quincy.lecomte@wanadoo.fr

Bruno Lecomte created his 7-hectare domaine in 1995 which he farms following the supple guidelines of *lutte raisonnée*. Vinification is "modern-traditional" – tank, low temperatures, some sur lie aging, filtration etc – and the sole wine I've tasted was very good. This was the 2008. Lightly grassy, with flavors of creamed corn, it was mineral, faintly but pleasantly vegetal, and fresh as a cascade with wonderfully full and marrowy sur lie texture. He has recently extended his reach to Châteaumeillant, and his son, who worked with Drouhin USA, has joined him on the domaine. A property to watch.

Domaine Mardon

40 rte de Reuilly, 18120 Quincy; 02.48.51.31.60; domaine-mardon.com

Twenty years ago, Mardon's was one of the only Quincys I'd have considered buying. It's tangible proof of the evolution in quality in this appellation that, while I still love drinking wines from this fifteen hectare, eco-friendly domaine, it has been joined by an ever increasing cohort of what I like to call a "team of rivals."

Helene, who took over the domaine in 2003, represents the fifth generation. Her father, Pierre, died in a car accident in 1989, after which it was run – with admirable success – by Pierre's widow and by his brother Jean, a former roofer.

Viticulture follows the loose principles of *lutte raisonnée* and Helene has an experimental plot which she farms organically. Yields are moderate (50 to 62 hl/ha), the grapes are harvested by machine, ferment in temperature controlled tanks. and age on their fine lees for several months before bottling.

The domaine's signature wine is "Tradition", an assemblage of young and old vines on flinty-clayey soils. The 2010, which I tasted in January 2011, a month after it had been bottled, was fresh, nicely formed, pleasantly mellow, with flavors of gooseberry, minerals and citrus. I've had varied experiences with the 2009 in Paris restaurants: at the swank fish house, Garnier, near the Gare St. Lazare, the wine was ample, flavorful and totally satisfying; at Yoom, an upscale, neo-DimSum restaurant in my neighborhood, the wine was correct but not more. The 2006, however, when tasted in 2009, was a fine, limpid Loire Sauvignon with flavors of lime, stone and minerals. It had good grip, marrowy texture, and could have been taken for a particularly frisky Sancerre.

An old vines bottling, called "St. Edme", after Helene's great, great, great-grandfather – the founder of the domaine – is a distinct step up. The 2008, tasted in January 2011, was lightly floral, with aromas of peach and fresh apricot. It was very mineral and slatey, with lipsmacking sur lie texture and refined acidity. The 2009, while still very young in early 2011, offered the depth, freshness, marrowy sur lie texture, and mineral-slate flavors of the 2008.

As of 2010, Helene Mardon added a new bottling called "Côte Nature" from an isolated parcel that is farmed organically. Forty-five percent ferments in demi-muids, another 45% in larger barrels, and 10% in tank. Indigenous yeasts are used. In January 2011 the wine was unfinished but Mardon had made a sample blend for the Salon des Vins de Loire. Intriguigingly lime-tinged it was ample and pungent. Very promising. Mardon also recently began making wine in Reuilly. (See entry.)

Recommended

Domaine Philippe Portier
Domaine de la Brosse 18120 Brinay; 02 48 51 04 47; philippe.portier@wanadoo.fr; philippe-portier.com

Philippe Portier took over this established family domaine in 1990. His 18 hectares of vines, which grow on gravel- on-clay soils, are farmed following many of the precepts of *lutte raisonnée*. The grapes are machine harvested, ferment in tank, and age on their fine lees until filtration and bottling. They tend to be a bit rough-hewn. The 2008, with light citronelle notes and 2 grams residual sugar, was a good white for an animated brasserie, and much better than the rustic, somewhat unbalanced 2006 which, nevertheless, had a funky appeal that would suit a rough-and-tumble wine bar like Le Baron Rouge in Paris.

To Follow

Adele Rouzé
18120 Quincy, 02.48.51.35.61; arouzé@terre-net.fr

Young Adele Rouzé, who has earned a degree in viticulture from Bordeaux, has a tiny (2 hectare) property with gravelly-flinty soils, and works with her father, Jacques Rouzé, though she produces wine under her own label. Winemaking is fairly traditional in the contemporary "technically correct" sense – *lutte raisonnée,* machine harvest, low temperature fermentation in stainless steel tanks, aging the wine on its lees – but the results are good, and one feels she'll evolve further. (Thus, the "To Follow" rating.) The high-strung 2006 had mouthwatering flavors of granny smith apples, quince, citrus fruit and a core of minerals and stone. The floral, sassy 2008 mixed a saline note with toothsome flavors of grapefruit and lemon zests, white-fleshed peaches and stone.

ᣂ Jacques Rouzé

ᣂ Recommended

18120 Quincy; 02.48.51.35.61; rouzé@terre-net.fr

Rouzé represents what I'd call "modern traditional." He farms his vines in Reuilly with a nod towards ecology, harvests by machine, and ferments the wines in his new (as of 2007) cellars in temperature controlled stainless steel tanks. A reliably good producer his 2006 was fresh, ripe, and stony, with firm flavors of grapefruit and minerals. He makes numerous other cuvées, but, alas, I have not been able to taste them. For an explanation, see the Jacques Rouzé entry in Reuilly.

ᣂ Domaine Vincent Siret-Courtaud

ᣂ To Follow

Le Grand Rosières 18400 Lunery; 02.48.68.92.18; 06 63 51 71 18; vincesiret@hotmail.com

One of the newest comers to the appellation, Vincent Siret-Courtaud, the son of Jacques Siret, is a young enologist who worked in St. Emilion and in Gaillac before returning home and creating his own domaine. He purchased 10 hectares of vineyard land in 2006, of which eight are currently in production. Ranging from five to 60 years old, the vines grow on the sand and gravel of the terraces of the Cher. Yields are kept relatively low, 40 hl/ha. The wine ferments in temperature controlled tanks at 17 degrees and ages on its fine lees before filtration and bottling. His 2008 was quite convincing. An exuberant nose – with lightly Muscat-y perfumes reminiscent of Alsace – it was full, ripe and slightly off-dry. (About 1.5 grams residual sugar.) With its abundant flavors of grapefruit, gooseberry, and minerals mixed with dominant notes of peach and apricot, the wine was so lush that it might have been cloying but for the 2008 acidity. Not a Sauvignon for a *crottin de Chavignol*, I'd serve this as an aperitif or with dishes normally paired with Loire Chenin or Alsace whites.

🐾 **Domaine du Tremblay/Jean Tatin and Chantal Wilk**
18120 Brinay; 02 48 75 20 09; jeantatin@wanadoo.fr

Like his wife, Chantal Wilk (see Ballandors, above), Jean Tatin was a Paris-based agronomist for some twenty years before returning to his native Berry to make wine. He took over the family farm, the Domaine du Tremblay, and now cultivates some ten hectares of vines both in Quincy and in Brinay.

Sounds simple but the set-up is less straightforward than it seems. Tatin sought partners to develop his vineyards which occupy six different parcels. He created one "society" to cultivate the 1.40 hectare "Les Rimonets" vineyard in Quincy in association with the well-established porcelain maker Philippe Deshoulières who bought the property and has since sold his share; he created the *Groupement Foncier Viticole de Quincy* for the 1.30 hectare "Les Coudereaux" and the 1.25 hectare lieu-dit "Gatebourse," both in Quincy, in which the forty members of the *Groupement* receive wine in remuneration for their investment. The remaining vineyard plots seem to belong to Tatin. Among these are:"Les Nouzats,"a 1.10 plot on the red sands of Brinay, which was planted mostly in the 1950s, the remainder in the 80s; Chamoux, 1 ha of vines planted in the '60s on soils of lacustrine chalk; and Buisson Pouilleux, a 1.40 ha plot of vines planted in 2001 on sandy soils above subsoils of lacastrine clay.

The vines are farmed following the concepts of *lutte raisonnée* and yields are kept under control by pruning, debudding and, if necessary, cluster thinning in July. Grapes are harvested by machine, are pressed slowly and, with the exception of Cuvée Sucullus, undergo a slow fermentation in temperature-controlled tanks.

The highstrung 2006 won a Gold Medal at the big Paris wine competition held at the Salon d'Agriculture. Well-made and self-assured, it was full, fresh, and focused, with flavors of grapefruit zest, minerals, and cassis buds. It would be a perfect bistro Sauvignon Blanc. The tangy 2008, bursting with grapefruit, gooseberry, and mango flavors, was crisp yet full, with zesty 2008 structure.

The domaine makes two additional cuvées of Quincy, my favorite being the racy "Vieilles Vignes", from 30 to 50 year old vines from the "Gate-bourse," "Nouzats", "Chamoux" and Coudereux" vineyards. The chiseled 2006 had a fine mineral core surrounded by beautifully etched grapefruit and gooseberry flavors. While tasting, it was very hard not to swallow. The 2008 "Vieilles Vignes", though slightly less alcoholic than the traditional cuvée, seemed fuller; the sur lie texture more marrowy, the flavors riper –

more in the mineral, grapefruit and lime zest range. What the French call *gourmand,* the wine would be at home on any table.

Sucellus, a gaulois god traditionally pictured with a barrique at his feet, gives his name to a cuvée of old vines fermented in oak from the Berry. Its grapes come from old vines in "Gatebourse," 35-year old vines in "Chamoux," as well as vines from "Nouzats". The 2004, tasted in 2009, was too oaky for me, but impressive nonetheless – flavorful, stylish, ambitious. and full of sap. The Tatin-Wilks have also developed a domaine in Reuilly. (See entry.)

🐌 Domaine Trotereau/ Pierre Ragon

18120 Quincy, 02.48.51.3223; p-ragon@hotmail.fr

I wrote my first impressions of this domaine's wines in the pleasant haze of the memory of a meal I'd eaten the night before. The time was January 2010. The meal: *boudin blanc* made by one of my neighbors in Touraine who had been the village *boucher-charcutier* before his retirement. I served the boudin with potatoes mashed with sweet butter and *crème fraiche* and drank what remained of a bottle of 2007 Quincy from Domaine Trotereau.

What should be evident from the fact that I had polished off the entire bottle myself is that I really liked the wine. It easily fell into my PMG category.

When I opened the bottle, the day before, the wine greeted me with notes of menthol and pine and a light whiff that seemed to belong in the Muscat family. Full and creamy, it made me think of descriptions of historic Quincys – the kind of Quincys that might explain why this was the second of all French regions to win *Appellation Controlée* status. Its slight oxidation came across as a nuance. It was beautifully ripe, mineral, pellucid, almost off dry, with full apple flavors and a cleansing citric finish. Chavignol came to mind and then, Eureka!, Cotat. This was the "Cotat " of Quincy, and for no apparent reason, the realization made me recall my first successful food & wine pairing with this particular wine: a raw endive and well-aged Comte salad with a mayonnaise-based dressing. What a bridge of flavor!

Pierre Ragon, Trotereau's owner, is the last in line of a domaine created in 1700. He took over in 1973 and could, arguably, make wine even better than he already does – in the sense that he could make more "sophisticated" or "technically" perfect wine. But, from me to you, I wouldn't hesitate to order a Trotereau Quincy anytime, anywhere – even though I might not recommend it to those who prefer a more polished, midtown wine.

Ragon is somewhat old school and has no reason to change. He has 13 hectares of vines, three of them vines planted over 80 years ago, the remainder planted since 1985. He prunes hard to keep yields low, and is generally eco-friendly. The majority of the grapes are machine harvested and ferment in enamel-lined steel tanks. They spend a good four to six months on their lees before bottling.

The 2006, even more alcoholic (13.5) than the 2007, was slightly less phenolically ripe. Still it was full and tangy and quite mineral, with the same level of oxidation as the 2007. I finished the bottle as I did the 2006 Vieilles Vignes. With notes of honey, lime, verbena, tea, and steel, this was a rich, full, gorgeously pellucid Quincy. I could not help but think "Cotat".

The "normal" 2008 was highstrung and ample, a characterful wine with flavors of quinine and herbal tea and a lipsmackingly long finish. The 2009 opened with flavors of gooseberry, *pipi de chat*, grapefruit, minerals and stone. Its bright acidity lightened the weight of the wine's 14% alcohol and masked any sense of sweetness. With aeration, the wine's nuances, its herbal tea aspects emerged, as well as flavors of melon, peach and an appetizing bitterness. Not a simple wine. I'd love to open a bottle right now.

&. Highly Recommended

&. Domaine de Villalin/ Maryline & Jean-Jacques Smith
Le Grand Villalin 18120 Quincy; 02.48.51.34.98;
v.quincy@wanadoo.fr; domaine-de-villalin.com

Five generations of vigneron (from Maryline's side of the family) have farmed this eco-serious, 8-hectare domaine located for the most part on an ancient alluvial terrace on the "other side" of the Cher from most of the appellation's vineyards. The current generation, which took over in '99, wanted to return to the methods practiced by Maryline's grandfather: They have resumed harvesting by hand, essentially farm organically (though without the accreditation), and use wild yeasts. The Smiths don't like oak. Wine is made in thermoregulated tanks. And they are spunky and intense. The 2009, tasted in January 2011, was ripe, fragrant, fresh, and ample. Smith finds it "atypical" and denser than usual. The tangy 2008, tasted in 2010, surged with gooseberry and cat's pee aromas. It would not pass unnoticed. The 2006, textured, full and ripe, had good weight and tension and an engaging weave of mineral, stone, and grapefruit flavors. The 2008 cuvée "Les Grandes Vignes," as bracing as its little brother, was pure, punchy and vivid. Bring on da noise, bring on da funk, this wine can take it. The 2009 was savory, somewhat brothy, and went down very easily. A comfort Quincy. Another cuvée, called "Anastasie", is neither fined nor filtered. Regrettably, I've never tasted it. (The Smiths didn't feel the 2009 was ready to bring to the 2011 Salon des Vins de Loire.) The domaine also produces a red from Pinot Noir and a rosé from Pinot Gris, both sold as Vin de Pays des Coteaux du Cher et de l'Arnon.

Chapter Six
Reuilly

Status: AOC: 1937 for the whites; '61 for reds and rosés.

Grapes: Sauvignon Blanc for whites, Pinot Gris for rosés or vin gris; and Pinot Noir for reds and rosés.

Zone: 204 hectares (504 acres) out of potential of 600 hectares, within six villages west of Bourges in the Indre (Reuilly, Diou) and the Cher (Lury-sur-Arnon, Chery, Lazenay and Preuilly) départements, on hills overlooking the Arnon, a tributary of the Cher.

Production: Volume in the 2010 vintage was 11,460 hls, of which 6,248 hl for Sauvignon Blanc, 3,068 hl for Pinot Noir, and 2,144 hl for Pinot Gris.

Soils: The best sites are gentle slopes with soils of Kimmeridgian marl, like Sancerre, though that soil type tapers to its end here; also, terraces of sandy, gravelly topsoils with clayey subsoils.

When to Drink: Most should be drunk by their fifth birthday.

Price: $ to $$

The monks of the St.-Denis Abbey may have been the first to cultivate grapes and make wine in Reuilly in the VIIth century. Midway between the vineyards of the Loir & Cher and those of Touraine, a mere 10 kilometers to the west of Quincy, Reuilly's wines once slaked the thirst of the citizens of Bourges and Vierzon, and graced the tables of French royalty. In an edict dated 1365 King Jean II "le Bon" fixed the dates of harvest, and the vineyards extended over 4000 hectares.

And although its whites were among the first to receive Appellation Controllée status (1937), Reuilly's vines nearly disappeared entirely having been devastated by phylloxera: in 1980 the surface planted to vine did not exceed 100 hectares.

It was in the 1980s, then, that Reuilly was reborn. Given the long period of desuetude, however, Reuilly should more accurately be considered a new wine region than one enjoying a renaissance.

The Reuilly appellation stretches over 7 villages in the Indre and Cher départements. Its vines grow on gentle slopes overlooking the Arnon and the Cher rivers, or on high plateaus. Its climate is relatively warm and dry; the soils, a mix of Kimmeridgian marl (as in Sancerre), and those composed largely of sand and gravel.

When I first visited the region, in the fall of 1990, Reuilly had roughly 130 hectares of vine in production; accounting for about 7000 hls of wine a year. At the most, a dozen growers made wine in commercial quantities. Today, with 204 hectares in production, an output of roughly 11,500 hls of wine a year, some 22 vignerons bottle their own wines, another ten sell to grower negociant houses, mostly located in Sancerre, and the vines, on the average, are less than 20 years old. Most producers cultivated cereal crops then and continue to do so today.

Yes, it's a young vineyard. And frankly, I thought Reuilly would evolve more quickly than it has. It is, after all, a satellite of Sancerre and, as such, a potential source of a lot of good, reasonably priced Sauvignon Blanc. Back in 1990, it seemed much more dynamic than its neighbor, Quincy. And its whites came in two basic styles: rustic, rather neutral, creamy, and alcoholic from older growers; from younger producers, fresher, more perfumed wines based on rigorous decantation of the juices, the use of aromatic yeasts, tank fermentation at low temperatures, and other techniques in the then contemporary handbook of vinification.

What I found nearly twenty years later was that, while Quincy has progressed by leaps and bounds, Reuilly is pretty much where it was when I first visited. But it seems to be on the verge of change.

At the time, Reuilly's dynamism was almost solely represented by the person of Claude Lafond, who was then the president of the growers' *syndicat* and the appellation's loyal ambassador. Most significantly, it was Lafond who essentially founded the Chai de Reuilly.

In 1992 Lafond and eight other vintners converted a building that had been the local cooperative cellar into a communal chai. Each vigneron made and sold his own wine, shared equipment, as well as the supervision of an enologist, currently Stéphane Vaillant. The nine growers – who account for more than half the production of Reuilly – are Lafond (who will leave the chai once his own cellars are built), Denis Jamain (Domaine de Reuilly), Bénédicte and Christian Dyckerhoff, Bernard Aujard, Pascal Desroches, Chantal and Michel Cordaillat, and Alain Mabillot.

The Chai was an excellent idea as well as a structure that was sorely needed at the time. Based on recent tastings, however, I feel that the wines of most of its members haven't advanced: they are still made like and taste like wines made in the mid-90s. Winemaking, in general, has evolved since then – notably by increased concentration on viticulture as well as by a growing sense that too much "wine making" is too much: better to harvest riper grapes and use technology as one of many supports to help express the uniqueness of fine grapes grown on good soils rather than expect it to be a magic wand, a silver bullet or universal panacea.

While a number of growers adhere to the loose scriptures of *lutte raisonnée,* none, at this time, farm organically. Less than 5% harvest by hand. Whites ferment in tank, at low temperatures, and most age on their fine lees for several months before bottling. The grapes for rosés, or vin *gris,* are either pressed directly or allowed to macerate for several hours, and are then fermented like the whites. Vatting time for reds is relatively short; some age in oak.

On the whole, these are very good bistro wines, great wines to discover locally, and to serve at casual meals at home. That's not bad at all, but evidently I believe Reuilly can be more than that. There's plenty of hope for the future, however: a new generation is coming of age, new energy – from neighboring appellations – is investing in vineyards here (cf Tatin-Wilk). Once known for its pink Pinot Gris, Reuilly could easily capture a chunk of a market thirsty for rosé by planting more of that increasingly popular grape, still leaving enough delimited land for additional plantings of Pinot Noir. And it might not be a bad idea to turn some of that Pinot Gris into a lightly sparkling wine, like a *crémant* or a *pétillant.*

All that said, it's to the credit of the vignerons of Reuilly that the progress they have made, though it hasn't gone far enough, has succeeded in revealing serious potential in its *terroir.* I wonder who will be the first vintner to fully express it.

🐾 Producers

There are 22 winemakers and one grower-négociant. Unless otherwise stated, the wines tasted here were from the 2006 vintage and were tasted in 2007, 2008, and 2009.

🐾 Outstanding

Domaine de Reuilly/Jamain

🐾 Excellent

Domaine Claude Lafond

🐾 To Follow

Domaine Chassiot 🐾 Domaine Mardon 🐾 Domaine Valéry Renaudat 🐾 Les Demoiselles Tatin/Tatin-Wilk

🐾 Highly Recommended

Domaine Gérard Bigonneau

🐾 Recommended

Les BerryCuriens 🐾 Domaine Henri Beurdin & Fils 🐾 François Charpentier/Domaine du Bourdonnat 🐾 Domaine Carroir du Gué/Benedicte & Christian Dyckerhoff 🐾 Domaine Gérard Cordier 🐾 Pascal Desroches 🐾 Alain Mabillot 🐾 Jacques Rouzé 🐾 Jean-Michel Sorbe 🐾 Jacques Vincent

🐾 By the Glass

Domaine de l'Artuis/René Ouvrat 🐾 Domaine Bernard Aujard 🐾 La Commanderie 🐾 Domaine Cordaillat 🐾 Guy Malbête 🐾 Gilles Pauvrehomme 🐾 Domaine de Seresnes/Jacques Renaudat 🐾 Domaine des Templiers

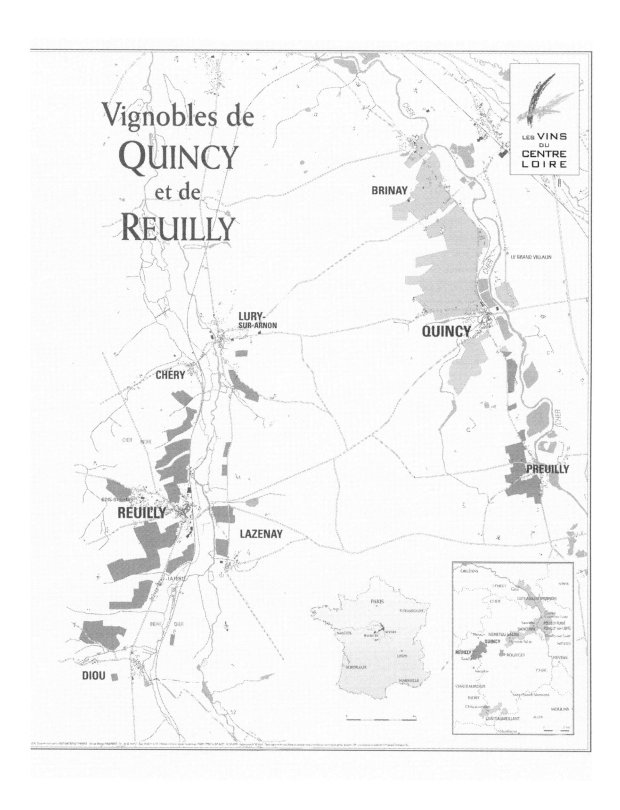

Vignobles de
QUINCY
et de
REUILLY

LES **VINS**
DU
CENTRE
LOIRE

BRINAY

LE GRAND VILLALIN

LURY-
SUR-ARNON

QUINCY

CHERY

PREUILLY

BOIS-ST-DENIS

REUILLY

LAZENAY

LA FERTE

DIOU

PARIS
STRASBOURG
NANTES
NEVERS
LYON
BORDEAUX
MARSEILLE

ORLÉANS
CÔTEAUX DU GIENNOIS
POUILLY-FUMÉ
SANCERRE
MENETOU-SALON
QUINCY
REUILLY
BOURGES
NEVERS
CHÂTEAUROUX
CHÂTEAUMEILLANT

REUILLY

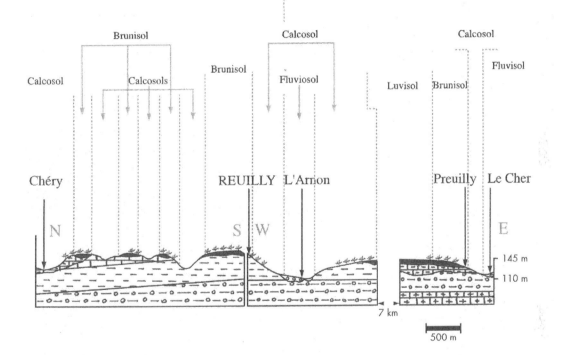

COTEAU RIVE GAUCHE
Arnon incisé par petits vallons

COTEAU
RIVE DROITE
ARNON

COTEAU
RIVE GAUCHE
CHER

Brunisol

Calcosol

Brunisol

Calcosol

Fluviosol

Calcosol

Calcosols

Brunisol

Luvisol

Brunisol

Fluvisol

Chéry

REUILLY   L'Arnon

Preuilly   Le Cher

N

S W

E

145 m

110 m

7 km

500 m

 Alluvions actuelles
et subactuelles des rivières

Portlandien
calcaires Bréchoïdes

 Alluvions anciennes
sables - argiles et graves

Kimméridgien supérieur
Marnes de St Doulchard

Alluvions anciennes
argiles - sables et graves rouge

Kimméridien inférieur
calcaires de Buzançais

Calcaires lacustres du Berry

Calcaires
de l'Oxfordien supérieur

By the Glass

Domaine de l'Artuis/René Ouvrat
36260 Reuilly; 02.54.49.27.95

Twenty years ago, the wines from this small family domaine were rough-hewn and woody. Today they are squeaky clean, commercial and standard. Relatively young vines, relatively high yields, so-so terroir (sand and clay) result in light, thin, cherry-accented reds; pale, vinous, lightly floral and delicately fruity *gris*; and, best of all, brisk, highstrung whites with a bit of co2 and light flavors of grapefruit, lemon and stone.

By the Glass

Domaine Bernard Aujard
18120 Lazenay; 02.48.51.73.69; domaineaujard@wanadoo.fr

This five-hectare family domaine has vines in Reuilly and in Lazenay, all on sunny hillsides with a variety of soils. Again, relatively young vines, relatively high yields, machine harvesting and tank fermentation — at the collective cellar — beget wines that are not without charm but could be a lot better. The white, which comes from chalky-clay soils, seemed somewhat confected but was tangy, fresh, and clean; the *gris*, similarly zingy, also seemed confected; the red was surprisingly tannic for such a light wine but was firm and rather appealing with rose and cherry-scented fruit.

Recommended

Les BerryCuriens
18120 Brinay; 02.48.51.30.17; www.jeanmichelsorbe.com

In 1995 a group of 28 proud Berrichons joined forces to form Les BerryCuriens. Under the direction of Jean-Michel Sorbe, the group makes wine in Quincy and Reuilly. Until 2008, when they got hold of vineyard land for Pinot Noir, the BerryCuriens produced a sole Reuilly, a hand-harvested *gris*, on the lieu-dit Les Chatillons. The appealingly textured 2006 had light flavors of apricot and grapefruit zest. A solid, clean, commercial rosé.

Recommended

Domaine Henri Beurdin & Fils
Le Carroir, 18120 Preuilly; 02.48.51.30.78;
domaine.beurdin@terre-net.fr

On their 16 hectare property, Henri and his son, Jean-louis Beurdin, make wine much like their confrères — machine harvest, cold fermentation in tanks – though the results are somewhat more seductive. His 2006 *rouge*, tasted on two occasions, elicited the same response: light in color and saturation, it drank like a rich rosé, and had attractive strawberry, cherry pit, and stone flavors. His 2008 "Le Pinot Noir," tasted in 2010, seemed a cross between a red and a rosé with its light color and saturation and charming flavors of plum and black tea. If you pay a bit of attention to his *gris*, which is made from Pinot Noir, and don't just knock it back, it, too, can charm. The 2006 seduced with its delicate rose petal, stone, and lemon zest flavors; the 2008, equally delicate, was very dry, very tart, and drank like a white. The 2006 white, though slightly confected seeming, had good mineral, stone, and citrus zest flavors. Well-chilled, it would be a good partner for shellfish. The 2007, tasted in 2010, was herbaceous, with additional flavors of lemon zests, slate, and minerals. More like a 2008 than a 2007 in its vigor, it was a good bistro Sauvignon Blanc. The 2008, however, was like the 2007, squared. It fit the model of the 2008 vintage even more than the 2007, which is as it should be. With vivid flavors of tropical fruit, gooseberry, cat pee, minerals, and slate, it was another pungent and effective bistro white. The "Bellevue" bottling is made from vines over twenty years old. The 2008 came across like a more discreet and nuanced brother of the previous wine, with notes of lime zests, slate, and gooseberry and an enticing marrowy texture which suggested aging *sur lie*.

✌ Domaine Gérard Bigonneau

Highly Recommended

18120 Brinay; 02.48.52.80.22; earl-bigonneau@orange.fr

Daughter Virginie, an enologist, works with father Gérard on this family domaine. Their new chai was completed in time for the 2006 harvest. The white from that year was tangy and mineral, with a texture that suggested some aging on its lees; the *gris*, the color of shrimp shells, was a taut palate cleanser that drank like a white; the fresh 2005 red, quite stony with a core of griotte cherry fruit, might not be a wine for everyone but I really liked it. The Bigonneaus also make Quincy.

✌ Domaine Carroir du Gué/Benedicte & Christian Dyckerhoff

Recommended

18290 Charost; 02.48.26,20.46; cri.dycker@libertysurf.fr; www.carroirdugue.fr.

The Dyckerhoffs have four hectares of vines as well as a well-stocked pond where, for a nominal fee, you can fish for trout. Members of the collective cellars, they produce mostly Sauvignon Blanc and it's not bad at all. The

2006 was fresh, stylish, with a whisper of co2, and very good flavors of grapefruit pulp and zest, bitter almond and minerals. This from 7 year old vines on sandy, gravelly soils!

🍇 Recommended

🍇 François Charpentier/ Domaine du Bourdonnat
12, rue Jean Jaurés, 36260 Reuilly, 02.54.49.28.74;
françois.charpentier4@wanadoo.fr

Since François Charpentier's son Géraud returned to the family domaine – after having worked in Australia and studied agronomy in Tours and Bordeaux – the wines seem greatly improved. The 2006 red, tasted in 2008, was a bit thin, sour and evolving quickly. The 2010 *gris*, tasted in 2011, was pungent, lightly vegetal and tart but a tasty food companion. It drank like a dry, fresh white. The 2010 red had light cherry, black tea and cherry pit flavors. An insinuating quiet red – if you paid attention. My radically different impressions of the 2006 white – at one tasting it was vivid and bracing; at another, confected seeming and tart – makes me wonder about my state of mind at one or both of those occasions (before going on to question other potentially contributory factors). The 2010 white, on the other hand, was solid, clean, fresh, ripe and tense with nice balance and attractive citrus flavors.

🍇 To Follow

🍇 Domaine Chassiot/Christian and Didier Chassiot
La Ferté, 36260 Reuilly;02.54.49.20.70.

Fifth generation vignerons, Christian and Didier Chassiot took over the family's 7.5 hectares in 1990. Although their work methods follow more-or-less the norm for Reuilly – notably machine harvesting, by-the-book vinification – they come across as forward- looking and ambitious. They seem to be moving in the direction of organic viticulture. They are not part of the collective cellars. They make wine in their own attractive, air-conditioned *chai*, producing about 50,000 bottles a year, most of which is sold at the cellar.

I've tasted their 2006s on several occasions. The white was fragrant, textured, and ripe, nicely tense, with flavors of peach and stone, a fine Sancerre satellite. The Pinot Gris was fresh, taut, and appetizing with notes of lemon and lemon peel. It nicely partnered sour dough bread covered with smoked salmon and a very strong, wasabi-mustard. Somewhat reduced when tasted, the red was plumy and well-balanced. I believe the Chassiot brothers will be part of the generation that moves Reuilly into the 21st century, pushing the appellation further toward realizing its potential.

🍇 La Commanderie/Jean-Michel Sorbe

18120 Brinay; 02.48.51.30.17; www.jeanmichelsorbe.com

Jean-Michel Sorbe directs this roughly 13-hectare property. I have long felt that, to paraphrase the old saw, the proof of the wine is in the tasting. A producer can claim dramatically low yields, tweezer-perfect viticulture, and harvesting with the tenderest of loving care. But it's what's in my glass that counts. So although La Commanderie describes model viticulture and vinification techniques, the wines I've sampled were mediocre at best. The 2004 white was tart and slightly earthy, with flavors of green pea. The 2005 was a solid commercial Sauvignon Blanc. The barrel-aged red, though fragrant, with light cherry flavors, was too oaky and its finish, dry as a bath towel, the wood having leached the wine of its charm and juiciness.

🍇 Domaine Cordaillat

18120 Mereau, 02.48.52.83.48; michel.cordaillat@wanadoo.fr

Members of Reuilly's collective cellar, Chantal and Michel Cordaillat created their domaine in 1995 with two hectares of vines. Today they have seven hectares, including a parcel of Sauvignon Blanc where the vines have an average age of nearly 60 years old – quite rare in this appellation. The '98 Reuilly *blanc* "Spéciale Centenaire de la St. Vincent de Mereau," tasted in September 2007, was surely the product of these vines. Grassy, textured, rich, lively, with flavors of celery and celery seed, it approached a Menetou-Salon in quality. A 2005 *blanc* "Les Sables", however, was considerably less interesting – hot, acid and unbalanced. The 2006 *blanc* was taut, pungent, and clean as a whistle, with flavors of minerals, cat pee and grapefruit – and so technical that it was clearly the work of a consulting enologist. The reds are a decidedly mixed bag: a relatively meaty 2002 had appetizing varietal flavors mixed with those of tea and oak. It was aggressive and somewhat off-putting but, curiously, not uninteresting. The 2006 red, which won a gold medal at the Paris fair, had a certain immediate, *primeur* charm and a smooth attack, but fell off quickly, revealing a hollow core. The Gris, however, though equally "commercial," was taut, fresh and vinous.

🍇 Domaine Gérard Cordier

La Ferté, 36260 Reuilly; 02.54.49.25.47; f: 02.54.49.29.34

Time was when Cordier bottled only his *gris* and sold a lot of it to La Mère Poulard in Mont St. Michel. That relationship ended when the legendary restaurant changed hands and, since that time, Cordier, one of the few local vintners to harvest by hand, has started bottling the full range of Reuilly. Fresh, tart and rustic, Cordier's white also has some oxidative notes, along with tangy flavors of grapefruit zest and minerals. A great choice for a funky wine bar and a half-dozen oysters. His pale coral *gris* is so rich it's almost viscous. Taut, dry, and fresh, it's a good terrace rosé. Cordier's red represents state-of-the-art-Reuilly circa 2009 – almost Gamay-like in its upfront charm, with clear cherry flavors and cool stoniness. Lightly chilled, it's what I'd like to drink with an omelette. Regrettably, Cordier is set to retire in 2011.

To Follow

Les Demoiselles Tatin/Jean Tatin and Chantal Wilk
Le Tremblay 18120 Brinay; 02 48 75 20 09; 06 08 60 55 66;
jeantatin@wanadoo.fr; www.domaines-tatin.com

Like a number of their Quincy confrères, the Tatin-Wilks have expanded their domaine to include two hectares in the Reuilly appellation. Most of the vines are young, planted in 2003. The first vintage was 2005. The domaine practices sustainable farming; red grapes are harvested by hand; the rest by machine.

Their white comes from the lieu-dit "Les Lignis," a slope with sandy-gravelly soils overlooking the Arnon. Its vines were planted in the 1950s by *séléction massalle.* The 2006 was super clean and palate cleansing, with vivid flavors of lemon peel, grapefruit, and stone. A very nice bistro white. Their appealing *gris* "les Lignis" comes from the same slope. The fragrant and nicely structured 2006, with its flavors of apricot, stone, and bitter almond, is a fine all-purpose rosé. The Tatin-Wilks even propose it as a partner for *tarte Tatin.* The 2008 was ethereal, delicate, mineral, and very pale. It bordered on elegant. You could finish an entire bottle without realizing it.

I've tasted the 2006 *rouge* "La Commanderie," made from young vines (selected from Pinot Noir plants in Burgundy) on gravel and clay soils, and aged in Tronçais oak, on two occasions. It was hopelessly reduced each time. The 2008, however, tasted in the spring of 2011, was a charming wine bar red, nicely ripe, with flavors of black cherries, licorice, and strawberry jam. I expect the reds will become more serious, more seductive and ever more delicious as those vines age.

🌿 Pascal Desroches

18120 Lazenay;02.48.51.71.60; desroches18120@orange.fr

In 1990 Pascal succeeded father on this seven-hectare domaine with roots going back to 1894. He's part of the collective cellars and, once again, the wines – all irreproachable but without distinction – have the whiff of a consulting enologist at work. The white is ripe and varietal, with notes of grapefruit, asparagus, and cat pee; the *gris* is taut and dry and given a lift by a thread of CO_2; the red, a bit thin, displays an attractive blend of strawberry and cherry fruit on stone. Not bad with fresh goat cheese.

🌿 Claude Lafond

Le Bois St. Denis, 36260 Reuilly; 02.54.49.22.17;
claude.lafond@wanadoo.fr; www.claudelafond.com

In a real sense Claude Lafond is the heart and soul of the Reuilly appellation. Its leading winemaker, he has been president of its growers *syndicat* and he instigated the creation of the Chai de Reuilly in the early '90s when such a structure was sorely needed.

Appreciating all he has done and continues to do for Reuilly makes it difficult to criticize him. But, though his wines are very good, they are underwhelming, stuck in the "make the wine in the cellar" 80s and 90s. I believe that he can do better and should do better – first and foremost by putting more emphasis on the raw material, on what happens in the vineyard.

There are signs of change. Lafond has recently started harvesting the grapes for certain cuvées by hand, for example. Youth may also bring a breath of fresh air: Lafond's daughter Nathalie has joined him in running the venture. And 2010 was the last vintage the Lafonds vinified with the Chai de Reuilly: they are building a new cellar next to the communal Chai that they expect to be ready to receive the 2011 harvest.

The domaine, itself, continues to grow. Created in the '60s by André Lafond – with 2.5 hectares — Claude succeeded his father at the end of the 70s. Today the domaine comprises 27 hectares on a variety of soils – chiefly sandy, gravelly clay though some plots have limestone subsoils — and Lafond buys additional grapes from local growers. He has also expanded his reach to Valençay and to the Coteaux de Menoux in the area of Argenton-sur-Creuse, south of Reuilly, where he and son Sylvain are reviving vineyards abandoned since phylloxera. Additonally, he created a joint venture with Gérard Chomette called Château Gaillard, and he has extended his line with both new cuvées of Reuilly as well as vins de Pays.

My favorite of Lafond's whites is his "Clos des Messieurs". The 2006, with pleasant lemon-lime zest aromas, was round yet fresh, mineral, and appetizing. In both texture and flavor it brought to mind the rock crystal sensation I find in deluxe vodkas, and its finish was long and bright. "La Raie", another Lafond white, presented a grassier version of 2006 along with satisfying texture and lively flavors of grapefruit; the 2003, tasted in September 2007, was ripe and a bit heavy – vintage *oblige*—, and the 1995, tasted at the same time, came across rough and raw but characterful. Lafond's basic white Reuilly is just that: a good basic white from a good producer. The 2005 lacked phenolic ripeness as have many of the 2005 whites; there was more than a whiff of cat's pee; but the wine was pleasantly varietal and a thread of co2 brought lift to a wine from a rich vintage.

I've tasted the apricot-scented 2006 Pinot Gris "La Grande Pièce" (*vin gris*) on several occasions. A bit hot, very clean, rich, and ripe, it's commercial, pleasant, and food friendly but it seems stylistically stuck in early '90s "technical" winemaking. Not bad, in other words, but it could be a lot more. The 2007, tasted in 2011, was vinous, with a note of marzipan. Steely, well-structured, with an appetizing bitterness, it was still very fresh, though I think it might have been even tastier if drunk two years earlier.

Les Grandes Vignes, Lafond's Reuilly *rouge,* is always a pleasure to drink, even when it seems an under-achiever. The 2005 was an accurate, light Pinot Noir, lightly hot but not aggressive, with attractive plum and tea flavors. Just fine for Sunday lunch in a country restaurant. The 2008, smooth, supple, with flavors of cherries and crushed berries, was a comfort red, and perfect for a comfort lunch of rotisserie chicken and salad on a chilly April (2011) Sunday.

Claude Lafond: Reuilly's ambassador emeritus: Domaine Claude Lafond: watch this spot for future developments.

❦ Recommended

❦ Alain Mabillot
36620 Sainte Lizaigne; 02 54 04 02 09;
alain.mabillot@wanadoo.fr

Before Alain Mabillot's Matthieu son returned to the family property in 2008 – after traveling, working, and tasting in the New World — this domaine's wines, like those of other members of Reuilly's collective cellars, were technically impeccable and pretty attractive. The 2006 white, though a bit catty, was vigorous, focused, and tangy. The 2006 *gris*, pink as a tutu, would be just the ticket with spicy food or as an aperitif on a sunny terrace.

The oak-aged 2005 red, from chalky soils, was nicely fresh and ripe with pleasant oak flavors blending in with the strong griotte cherry fruit. Sure, it could be more ambitious, but it was stylish and tasty.

Since Matthieu joined the domaine in 2008 the wines – with one exception – have gotten even better. The 2010 *gris* was dry, taut, and mineral. Nicely balanced, it drank like a blushing white. The 2010 *blanc*, with flavors of gooseberry and grapefruit, was crisp, tense, and solid. A good bistro white. "Le Mont Cocu" is a recent cuvée of white that comes from a parcel of the same name which, in this case, means "rounded slope" and not "cuckold." The 2009 was full, textured and substantial. My, but it was tasty! Make way for the new generation!

Well, the new generation, like all new generations, also learns from its mistakes. While the 2009 red was fresh and structured, it also had noticeable flavors of bandaid. The flavor of bandaids, when Pinot Noir is involved, says Brettanomyces to me. As more of the 2009 reds become available, I suspect Mabillot's won't be the only Bretty Pinot. Their barrel-aged cuvée of red, "La Ferté" was, well, dominated by oak flavors. But the wine I tasted was a barrel sample. Cool, clean fruit could be perceived under the veil of oak. Verdict: give La Ferté time and keep an eye on this domaine.

❧ Guy Malbête

By the Glass

Le Bois St Denis, 36260 Reuilly; 02 54 49 25 09;
earl.guymalbete@wanadoo.fr

Among many charming French expressions is "*c'est un ours mal léché*" of which the dictionary definition is "an uncouth person." I prefer the literal: 'a poorly licked bear' which I see as someone who can't quite be trusted in public (whose mother never cleaned him properly) and I suspect that's what Malbête's fellow vignerons mean when they say "he's a good professional *mais un ours mal léché*". Fifteen years ago I wrote that his were pleasant wine bar Reuillys across the board: Ripe sauvignons; rough, cherryish Pinot Noirs; vinous, hard, dry, Pinot Gris. After tasting his range of 2006s, I have no reason to alter that description.

❧ Domaine Mardon

To Follow

(See Quincy)

Since 2001 Helene Mardon has been making a bit of promising Reuilly rouge on one hectare of sandy, flinty-clay soils in the commune of Preuilly. Luc Tabordet, the son of a local vigneron, takes charge of the winemaking.

Harvest here is by hand, with yields averaging between 35 and 40 hl/ha. Grapes for the reds sometimes go through a cold soak, sometimes not. The wines ferment in fiberglass tanks, 30% ages in tank and the rest ages in Burgundy barrels of two to four wines. The 2008, tasted in 2010, was cool and clean. It had a bright, springy Pinot nose, inviting texture, and flavors of plum, cherry, black tea, and the take-no-prisoners acidity of the vintage. The 2009 needed more time to digest its oak but it offered charming aromas of griotte cherries and a soft, friendly attack.

By the Glass

Gilles Pauvrehomme
La Ferté, 36260 Reuilly; 02 54 49 22 07

The white is the best bet from this small domaine. The 2006 "Lot #1" is stony and mineral, with good grip and accents of grapefruit and grapefruit zests. Drink with Loire chevre.

Outstanding

Domaine de Reuilly/ Denis Jamain
Villa Camille – 20 route d'Issoudun, 36260 Reuilly, 02 38 66 16 74; 06 08 25 11 18; denis-jamain@wanadoo.fr

Denis Jamain created his domaine in 1988 and in 1996 was able to acquire land in the heart of the Reuilly appellation, on well-exposed, south-east facing slopes whose soils are predominantly Kimmeridgian marl, a mix of limestone and clay embedded with sea fossils. Today, he has 17 hectares, with 10 planted to Sauvignon Blanc, four to Pinot Noir and three to Pinot Gris.

One of the largest producers in the appellation. Jamain practices *lutte raisonée*. He was the first in the appellation to plant cover crops and is the first to convert part of his holdings to organic viticulture. He keeps yields low to moderate. While Jamain is part of the Chai de Reuilly, his wines always seem hand-crafted and personal. He attributes their individuality to his soils, to the fact that winemaking is his sole activity (he does not cultivate cereal crops), and his parcel-by parcel involvement in the winemaking process.

Jamain's very good basic white is "Les Pierres Plates" which takes its name from its appropriately named vineyard: *pierres plates* means flat stones. The 2008, tasted in 2010, offered discreet but persistent aromas and flavors of gooseberry and grapefruit. Vivid, relatively full and revivifying, it was easily as good as a first-rate Sancerre. The bracing 2006 had a delicately varietal nose with floral notes and pungent aromas of grapefruit zests. On the palate, it was clean and pure, all grapefruit zest and stone. Ditto for the tight, textured 2002.

"Anne de Varennes" is the name of Jamain's old vines cuvée. The vines aren't all that old in the scheme of things, averaging about 30 years. But yields are low, around 35 hl/ha, and harvest is by hand. The grapes undergo skin contact and malolactic fermentation. The wine ages *sur lie,* and is lightly filtered before bottling. Jamain does not make it every year.

While "Les Pierres Plates" can hold its own against most Sancerres, Anne de Varennes is better than all but the best. The 2006, weightier, richer, denser, and more mineral than "Pierres Plates", was stony, invigorating, and had a sinuous way of winding itself around your tongue. Seductive indeed.

The Pinot Gris, from 20 year old vines grown on silex and clay soils is generally the color of very pale onion skin or tea rose,and drinks like a white. The blossomy 2008 was dry but tender with an appetizing quinine-like bitterness and a very long finish. The lively 2006 might have been taken for a Sauvignon Blanc. It was tart, taut, and fresh with vivid citrus zest flavors. The 2003 was vinous, perfumed and firm. These are great all-purpose food wines.

Jamain harvests his Pinot Noir by hand. The grapes for the normal bottling undergo a prefermentation at low temperatures before fermenting and aging for ten months in stainless steel tanks, and another ten in bottle, before being released. The 2007, tasted in 2010, was a pleasuring wine that fleshed out with aeration. Lightly tannic, with pure griotte cherry flavors, it had admirable stuffing for such a light vintage. The 2006 seemed leaner than its 13 degrees alcohol. Smooth, taut, and lightly tannic, it was focused and fresh. A day after having been uncorked, the wine showed flavors of sour cherries and stone. It was not what anyone would call a "charming" wine; it was a true wine, and very tasty.

"Cuvée de la Comtesse" is Jamain's special red bottling, from a tri of very ripe grapes, aged for a year in oak barrels on a four year rotation. The wood comes from a forest Jamain inherited from his grandfather. Each year he selects a couple of 200 year-old oak trees to make the barrels his wines will age in. Not many people can say this. And perhaps this explains why the oak presence is so blessedly understated in his wines.

"Cuvée de la Comtesse" is not made every year. In 2008, Jamain was selling the 2004. A fascinating wine, with jewel-cut fruit, real elegance, and detailed minerality, the wine was so stony, it seemed to have no color at all. The opposite of a "fruit bomb," it was like stone juice mixed with the juice of sour griotte cherries. Sadly, most wine drinkers would pass right by this unique statement. I wish I could uncork a bottle right now.

&ã, To Follow

&ã, Domaine Valéry Renaudat

36260 Riou; 02.54.49.21.44;domainevaleryrenaudat@cegetel.net

Valéry Renaudat, the son of Jacques Renaudat, created his domaine in 1999 with 2.5 hectares. He was 25 years old and had studied viticulture and enology at Mâcon and worked in vineyards around France and in Oregon where he spent seven months. Today he has 12 hectares, 5 in Quincy and 7 in Reuilly. He seems very much caught between the "old" Reuilly (circa 1990) and the new, or rather, up-and-coming. I think he's serious and, with peer pressure that's more enlightened, he may develop into an excellent producer. For now, the wines are something of a mixed bag – though suitable for any wine bar.

Grapes for red wines, as well as those from old vines, are harvested by hand. The red grapes undergo a two-day cold prefermentation followed by an 8-day vatting. Part of the wine is aged in oak, 30% of which is new. The 2006 *rouge* "Les Lignis," from clay-chalk soils, had bizarre deviations of oak flavor; another bottle, while tart and lightly sour, came across better, with flavors of cherry, strawberry and stone and glimpses of a sense of place. Both the white and the *gris* ferment in tank at low temperatures and age sur lie until bottling. The former was pale and pungent; the *gris*, a delicate salmon, displayed attractive notes of rose, stone and lemon peel.

&ã, By the Glass

&ã, Domaine de Seresnes/Jacques Renaudat

Seresnes, 36260 Diou; 02 54 49 21 44; F: 02 54 49 30 42

I've tasted one wine here. It was 1999 red, came in a blue bottle, and, at seven years old when sampled, it proved a quirky wine, with oak flavors and a fair bit of sap, it would be fine in a local wine bar.

&ã, Recommended

&ã, Jacques Rouzé

Chemin des Vignes, 18120 Quincy; 02 48 51 35 61; rouzé@terre-net.fr; www.jacques-rouzé.com

I rely on the dictionary definition ("an uncouth person) of "*un ours mal léché*," when it comes Jacques Rouzé, the father of Adele Rouzé, and a vintner in his own right. A large, gruff man, he speaks to whom he wants, when he so desires. Period. The nerve center of his eco-friendly domaine is in Quincy where he has 13 hectares of vines and a new cellar, completed in 2007. In Reuilly, he has 2.5 hectares of vines, with the Sauvignon planted on flinty soils and the Pinots Gris and Noir on clay-limestone soils. The grapes are harvested mechanically, tank fermented at low temperatures, and age on their lees until bottling. I have tasted only one of his wines, the solid, lightly tannic, 2006 red, which had real texture and engaging flavors of strawberry, plum, black cherry and tea. I would have loved to have tasted more of his wines and learned more about his domaine(s). When I visited his stand at the Salon des Vins de Loire in 2009 with this in mind, however, Rouzé barked his answers at me in single syllables, exhibited a distinct disinclination to have me taste, and brushed off my request to have samples from both his domaine and daughter Adele's sent to me, with a wave of the hand, and a grunted "Oui, oui." No surprise that I never received any samples. Too bad. Rouzé makes numerous cuvées of Quincy such as "Vignes d'Antan" and "La Cinquantaine" which I'm sure are worth tasting.

Jean-Michel Sorbe   Recommended
SCEV Le Berrycuriens, 18120 Brinay; 02.48.51.30.17;
www.jeanmichelsorbe.com

Nothing if not a dynamo, Jean-Michel Sorbe seems the self-appointed ambassador of all things Reuilly and Quincy. A large, pushy guy, he talks loud and can take up an awful lot of space in a small tasting room. You can't avoid him.

He took over the family farm in 1973 and built it up to 11 hectares in Reuilly and 3 hectares in Quincy. He built new cellars, he was the moving force behind the BerryCuriens, vinified for Sancerre-based negociant Alexandre Mellot, and, most recently created a kind of tasting association *le Sentier du Vin.*

In 1999, when none of his children wanted to succeed him in the winery, he handed over the domaine to the Mellot firm though he is still a presence.

The most ambitious wine in this particular Sorbe line-up appears to be the "Cuvée Armand", a white made with all trendy techniques of the end of the 20th century: skin contact for 1/3 of the harvest, low temperature fermentation in new barrels made from oak from local forests, and bottling without filtration. It is not made every year which may explain why I've only tasted the 2003 vintage – on numerous occasions. It's ripe, and tasters can occasionally discern flavors of creamed corn and pineapple underneath the wall of oak. That said, I've served the wine to friends who drank it enthusiastically. It might be a crowd pleaser – and heaven knows there are oceans of lesser wines in the world — but I think real wine lovers will find it unconvincing.

Sorbe's 2006 Pinot Gris was more straightforward – taut, with flavors of grapefruit zest and stone. The 2006 red offered some pleasant cherry fruit but was overwhelmed by tannins as drying as overbrewed tea. The 2005 was only slightly less tannic and it seemed stripped. A '90, tasted in late 2007, smelled of low tide. I don't know what causes that odor but I'm sure it is a defect.

Looking back at notes I took on Sorbe's wines in the '90s were somewhat more positive: A '94 Reuilly blanc was crisp, clean and herbaceous. His barrel-fermented Sauvignon seemed a curious mix of the bland and the quirky. Flashes of pistachio and coffee mixed with oak and fruit enlivened an otherwise neutral '89. Sorbe's Pinot Noirs ranged from the tart, light '93 and '94, to the engaging '89, with pretty flavors of cherries and cherry pits.

By theGlass

Domaine des Templiers

L"Ormeteau, 36260 Reuilly; 02.54.49.23.25; fpoirier@terre-net.fr; www.domaine-des-templiers.com

Franck Poirier and Bernard Pousset have a young 3.3 hectare domaine with very young vines. Their 2006s – *blanc, gris* and *rouge* — were bland and watery.

Recommended

Jacques Vincent

18120 Lazenay; 02.48.51.73.55; jacques.vincent@wanadoo.fr; jacvin@aliceadsl.fr

Jacques Vincent has 9.5 hectares, 4 of which are planted to Pinot Gris. He's something of a Gris specialist and readily pulls out old vintages to show with the new. Thus, at a tasting in 2007, he started with a 2006 – an appealing pale apricot in color, fresh, and mineral and nicely insinuating with flavors of apricots and blossoms. Next came an oxidized, alcoholic 2003, as catty as a Sauvignon. A '98 was quite oxidized but very alive, with flavors of hay and wax; ditto for the '92, which was also developing flavors of truffles and forest underbrush. I thought both the '92 and the '98 might have been much better as *pétillants*. Vincent's whites are good wine bar quaffs – stony, slightly rustic, with flavors of grapefruit zest and creamed corn. The reds, which undergo a cold prefermentation, are stony and tannic. They drink like big, dark rosés and, frankly, the wines would shine in that context. Vincent is surely right to recommend that they be served at 14 degrees.

Chapter Seven
Coteaux du Giennois

Status: A.O.C. (since 1998)

Types of Wine Made: dry white, red and rosé

Grapes: Sauvignon Blanc, Pinot Noir and Gamay. (As of 1995, reds must be a blend of Pinot Noir and Gamay.)

Zone: 195 hectares (481 acres) on high arching slopes and plateaus overlooking the Loire, in 14 villages north of Pouilly, in the Nièvre and the Loiret départements, principally Gien and Cosne-sur-Loire on the right side of the river, and Bonny on the left. Other villages are Beaulieu, Briare, Ousson, Neuvy, St. Loup, Alligny, La Celle-sur-Loire, Myennes, Pougny and Saint Père.

Production: Volume: In 2010, 8,673 hl of which 4,682 hl are white; 2 912 hl are red; and 1,079 hl are rosé.

Soils: flint or limestone hillsides above the Loire as well as flinty soils to the west of the appellation, and limestone soils to the east of the Cosne fault.

When to Drink: Within four years of the harvest.

Price: $ to $$

The vineyards straddling both banks of the Loire from Sancerre and Pouilly, extending north to the pottery city of Gien, date back to the Gallo-Roman period. In 27 BC Emperor Augustus authorized the planting of vines in Cosne. In the 13th century wines from the region were served at the Royal court of Charles V in Paris, and when the Bishop of Auxerre built the castle of Cosne, he included vast wine cellars and extensive vineyards. In 1930, according to Pierre Galet, the region of Cosne had almost 2000 hectares under vine —which seems like a lot, given that phylloxera did not spare the Giennois.

When I first visited in 1990, the Coteaux du Giennois seemed a footnote to Loire wines. Since that time, however, it has evolved nicely, and now appears to be blossoming into a credible little appellation – the home of reasonably priced, characterful, user-friendly wines: brisk, zesty Sauvignon Blancs; taut, food-adaptable rosés; and juicy, supple reds.

Most of the appellation's vines, as well as its producers, are located around Cosne. Many years ago they applied, unsuccessfully, for their own appellation. The INAO also refused to include them in Pouilly, grouping them instead with the Giennois.

Most of the tastings described below took place in 2009.

ᕤ Producers

There are forty growers in the appellation and one cooperative. Note that a fair number of Sancerre and Pouilly producers also make Coteaux du Giennois: those not individually reviewed here include: Michel Bailly (See Pouilly), Joseph Balland-Chapuis (See Guy Saget Sancerre, Pouilly), Domaine Gitton (See Sancerre), Joseph Mellot (See Sancerre).

ᕤ Excellent

Domaine Quintin Frères

ᕤ To Follow

Domaine Mathieu Coste

ᕤ Highly Recommended

Domaine Emile Balland ᕤ Domaine Henri Bourgeois ᕤ
Domaine de l'Epineau/Emmanuel Charrier ᕤ
Domaine Poupat & Fils ᕤ Sebastien Treuillet ᕤ
Domaine de Villargeau/ Marc & François Thibault

ᕤ Recommended

Les Aupières/Caves de Pouilly sur Loire ᕤ
Domaine Catherine & Michel Langlois

ᕤ By the Glass

Domaine Hubert Veneau/ Domaine des Ormousseaux

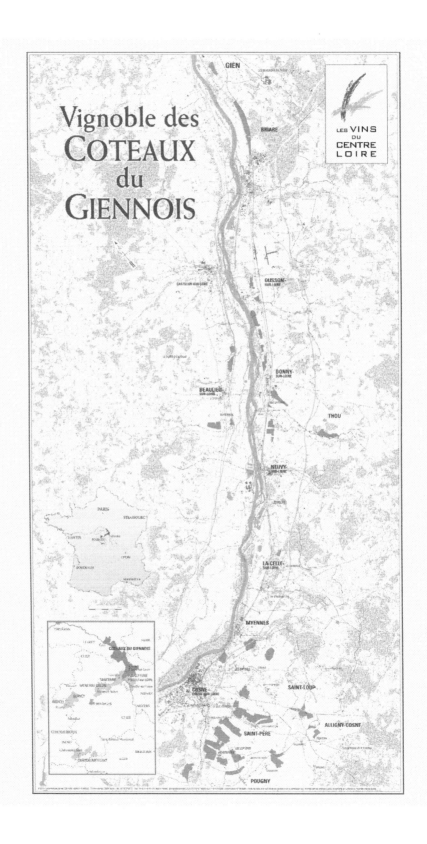

Vignoble des
COTEAUX
du
GIENNOIS

Coteaux du Giennois

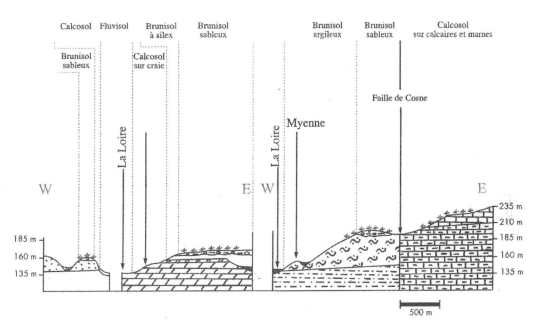

COTEAUX
RIVE GAUCHE

COTEAUX
RIVE DROITE
(aval de la zone)

COTEAUX
RIVE DROITE
DE LA LOIRE
(amont de la zone)

Calcosol   Fluvisol   Brunisol   Brunisol   Brunisol   Brunisol   Calcosol
                        à silex   sableux   argileux   sableux   sur calcaires et marnes

Brunisol   Calcosol
sableux   sur craie

Faille de Cosne

La Loire   La Loire   Myenne

W   E   W   E

235 m
210 m
185 m   185 m
160 m   160 m
135 m   135 m

500 m

Alluvions modernes.

Alluvions anciennes
argiles, sables, graviers et galets.

Calcaires et marnes
lacustres de Briare.

Céno-Turonien
silex et argile blanche.

Turonien
Craie ou calcaire.

Cénomanien
craie et marnes

Albien
sables fins, argiles de Myenne,
sables de la puisaye

Barrémien
argiles bariolées, sables et grés.

Portlandien
calcaire.

Kimmérigien
marnes et calcaires.

❧ Les Aupières/Cave de Pouilly sur Loire
(See Pouilly)

Textbook renditions of the appellation: a bracing 2008 *blanc* with intense gooseberry, *pipi de chat* flavors, a veritable 2008 wake-up call. Similarly true to its vintage, the 2007 red comes across like lightly infused black tea with notes of fig.

❧ Domaine Emile Balland
Route Nationale 7 - BP 9 45420 Bonny-sur-Loire; 03 86 39 26 51;06 83 46 81 76; emile.balland@orange.fr

The Balland family has been making wine in the Sancerrois since 1650. When I met Emile Balland's father, Joseph Balland-Chapuis, in 1990, he had extensive holdings in both Sancerre (18 hectares) and the Giennois. Problems of succession led to the sale of these properties to Guy Saget in 1998.

At the time, Emile Balland was finishing his studies, earning an engineering diploma in Angers and a degree in enology in Toulouse. In 1999 he was able to put together a small, 5 hectare domaine on his home turf – with one hectare in Sancerre, in the communes of Bué and Amigny, and four in the Giennois.

Most of his Giennois holdings –3.4 hectares – are in Bonny-sur-Loire and Beaulieu, which face each other across the river. Balland also has a parcel in Saint-Père, in the southern reaches of the appellation, bordering Pouilly. This vineyard, on silex rich soils, also has Balland's oldest vines, from 20 to 40 years old.

Balland's Giennois come in two basic styles: "Les Beaux Jours" is a bottling for red, white and rosé made from young vines and meant to be drunk 'on the fruit.' "Le Grand Chemin" – in red and white – comes from Balland's oldest vines on silex soils. The whites ferment in newish barrels (two to four years) and both age in oak.

A perfect example of the first style was the 2006 "Les Beaux Jours" *blanc* which was bottled in April 2008. Fragrant, crisp and bracing, it offered flavors of grapefruit against a backdrop of minerals. Ditto for the 2007 which was light as a whisper. The 2006 rosé was fresh, dry and rather neutral: a serviceable wine for all your beach or picnic needs. The 2006 red, served lightly chilled, was a pleasant, if somewhat earthy wine, with good structure and lively acidity.

Clearly more ambitious, the 2005 "Le Grand Chemin" *blanc* was oaky and tart. Balland does not destem the grapes and I wondered if that accounted for the tannins and a stemmy-woody note. There was a lot to admire here – with reservations. The 2005 "Le Grand Chemin" *rouge* was a fragrant, medium-bodied red. Fluid and user-friendly, it's a perfect summer red to serve lightly chilled, with casual outdoor meals.

In certain years Balland also makes a cuvée named after himself (or a previous Emile Balland). The pungent 2004 *blanc* mixed grapefruit flavors with cat pee. It wasn't perfect but it had good weight, focus, and concentration, and a nice blend of citrus zest and mineral flavors. It was a real wine, and very much in the Sancerre-Pouilly-Fumé family. In addition to Sancerre, Balland also makes wines at Domaine des Ratas in the Giennois. I have not tasted these.

Clearly a young man with a lot of good ideas, Balland's mastery of his craft does not seem quite up to his ambitions. When the two meet, Balland should easily qualify as Excellent or even Outstanding.

Domaine Henri Bourgeois
(See Sancerre)

Highly Recommended

This important grower-negociant buys must from such established growers as Domaine Hubert Veneau and Marc and François Thibault (Domaine de Villargeau), and does an impressive job with them. The 2004 "Terre de Fumé" was highstrung and feisty; the 2008 was equally brisk, nicely fragrant, and lightly chalky.

Domaine Mathieu Coste
3, rue des Bougiers, Villemoison 58200 Saint Pere; 06.45.26.10; domainebio.coste@orange.fr

To Follow

When I went to the Giennois in the fall of 1990, I fell in love with the wines of an eccentric vigneron named Alain Paulat. An early convert to organic viticulture, he made no white wine, only age-worthy Gamays and Pinot Noirs which he would release several years after the vintage date. (At that time you could make red varietals.) I was able to find his wines at a bistro near my apartment in Paris but, when time came to write this book, I wondered, What has happened to Alain Paulat?

There was bad news and there was good news: Paulat, as I had feared, had gone out of business; in August 2008 he sold his property to Matthieu Coste, a like-minded vigneron who, I was pleased to learn, has kept Paulat on as an employee.

Coste, a former manager at the Lycée Viticole de Beaune, also practices organic viticulture – his wines bear the Ecocert label – and is punctilious in his vineyard management, from his preparations of homeopathic treatments, to his harvesting by hand by successive passes through the vineyard, to his control of yields, starting with pruning hard in the beginning of January, at the Epiphany, the "date at which the sun rises on the horizon which causes the sap also to rise, thus avoiding infections by wounds caused by the pruning shears."

Natural yeasts, medicinal doses of sulfur at the time of bottling, and rare as well as limited use of chaptalization, are the basics of Coste's cellar practices. Only 20% of the grapes for his red wines are destemmed. Vatting lasts about 15 days, and the wines age for a minimum of two years in tank to permit natural decantation – which obviates the need for fining – followed by four to eight months in old barrels.

I don't know if this is always the case, but the two bottles of wine I sampled from Coste demonstrated the importance of Slow Tasting. I started with "Rebelle," his white, which was labeled Vin de Table. My guess, from its pale, almost translucent color, was that it was a 2010. The wine had texture and structure but absolutely no flavor. None. That was Day One. On Day Two, I could perceive some citrus notes and figured the problem was one of reduction. On Day Four, the real wine showed its face: it was pure, fresh, and mineral, somewhat meaty, well-balanced, with solid flavors of lemon and grapefruit. I liked it a lot.

I had pretty much the same experience with his 2008 Coteaux du Giennois *rouge* "MC." On Day One, it was smooth, mineral, and nicely structured, with nice acidity, a sense of slate and chalk, but only the merest suggestion of fruit. On Day Two it was even more mineral, and light tannins emerged. On Day Four, it said, "I am an austere, tart, tannic light red of character. You can drink me now or cellar me. I fear nothing." And on Day Five, the pretty morello cherry flavors appeared. On Day Eight, the wine was just as juicy as on Day Five but those tannins – surely from the stems of perfectly ripe grapes – had me thinking 'lean, cool, Cabernet Franc' rather than 'Gamay/Pinot blend.'

Highly Recommended

Domaine de l'Epineau/Emmanuel Charrier
Paillot 58150 Saint Martin sur Nohain; 03 86 22 57 15; earl.charrier@free.fr; www.domaine-charrier.com

A good, small family domaine making wine in both the Giennois and Pouilly.

Charrier's "Premices" *blanc* comes from young vines, ferments in tank at low temperatures, and ages on its lees for four to six months before bottling. The 2006, tasted in 2009, was still a frisky bistro white though, at three years old, its glory days were supposed to have been over. The red Premices is hand harvested, partially destemmed, and cold soaked for two or three days before fermentation in stainless steel tanks at 25 to 30 degrees. Charrier pumps over the punches down the fermenting mass daily for ten to twelve days before pressing lightly. Ten percent of the wine ages in barrel. The 2006 captivated with cool, lean fruit, light tannins, and lively acidity. Like all such reds it should be served slightly chilled and, in this case, drunk with pals, some charcuterie, and a nice, week-old goat cheese just beginning to develop blue splotches on its rind. Charrier has recently added another red, "Condates", to his line-up. I've not yet tasted it.

✒ Domaine Catherine & Michel Langlois

58200 Pougny; 03 86 28 06 52; catmi-langlois@orange.fr: www.domaine-langlois.fr

Recommended

The Langlois created their 17-hectare domaine in 1996. In addition to a range of bottlings from the Giennois appellation and a Pouilly-Fumé, they also produce Vin de Pays, including Mon Chardonnay, a sparkling rosé, "Cuvée Valentin", made from Pinot Noir and Chardonnay, "Douceur d'Automne", a sweet, late-harvest Sauvignon Blanc, and several crèmes de fruit.

Their barrel-aged "Le Champ Gallant", with a majority of Pinot Noir, is hand harvested. The smooth 2005, with flavors of oak and cherry, was by far the best of the samples I tasted from them. The basic red, "Champ de la Croix", consisted of 80% Pinot Noir. It had faint raspberry notes and was pleasant, but dilute. Fine to quaff while you're just hanging out. The 2005 white came across candied, alcoholic, and watery; while the rosé, pale, taut and faintly fragrant, would be pleasant to drink, well chilled, on a terrace by the sea.

✒ Domaine Poupat & Fils

Rivotte 45250 Briare; 02 38 31 39 76; domainepoupat@hotmail.fr; www.domaine-poupat.fr

Highly Recommended

Grandfather René Poupat was one of the founding fathers of the Giennois appellation who fought for, and won, VDQS status for the region's wines in 1954. Today Philippe Poupat, third generation, runs this family domaine of 9 hectares (6.5 planted to Gamay and Pinot Noir and 2.5 to Sauvignon

Blanc) on an alluvial terrace overlooking the Loire.

When I visited the domaine in 1990, I found the wines rather diluted and unconvincing. Tasting in 2009, I was delighted by the evolution in quality. The 2006 "Rivotte" *blanc* was pungent, crisp, and focused. Though I was bothered by a slight note of sugar, I admired the wine's minerality, its briskness and, above all, the evidence it afforded of overall progress within the appellation. It was light years better than anything I tasted *chez* Poupat or most of his confrères in 1990.

The Rivotte red is chiefly Pinot Noir. The 2006 was lean and cool, with pretty cherry fruit. Le Trocadero, principally Gamay with a bit of Pinot Noir, was deeper and had a bit more gravitas. With its dark cherry flavors, slight saltiness, and a bitter almond note, it would be an attractive choice in a wine bar.

🐝 Excellent

🐝 Domaine Quintin Frères
Villegeai 58200 Cosne sur Loire; 03 86 28 31 77;
quintin.françois@wanadoo.fr

François and Michel Quintin have been running this domaine since 1991, making wine in both Pouilly and in the Giennois. Most of the vines are young – around 15 years old – and winemaking is fairly traditional, though the brothers now practice sustainable farming. I haven't tasted all their cuvées but what I have tasted is delicious.

It would be so easy for restaurants to do right by their wine-loving customers by choosing a good, spirited, reasonably priced white to serve by the glass. Here's one suggestion: the Giennois *blanc* "Rive Droite" from this domaine. The 2010 was punchy and pungent with sprightly flavors of grapefruit and lemon zests. The 2009 was smooth, ample, and ripe, and so fresh you didn't feel the 14% alcohol. The 2008, also admirably ripe, had flavors of pear, creamed corn, grapefruit zests, and some floral high notes. Hard not to like. A 2006 white was equally winsome. So brisk, lively, and focused that, as with the 2009, you didn't feel the 13.5 degrees alcohol, just the fresh flavors of grapefruit, black currants buds, minerals and lime. So satisfying.

The 2006 Coteaux du Giennois rosé "Frénésie" was a yummy, supremely food friendly wine. I drank it with cèpe chips – small, cèpe-flavored, melba-toast-like chips that a friend had brought back from her native Latvia. Smooth, taut and focused, the wine had a lovely fluidity and went down all too easily. It had grace notes of strawberry but was dominated by flavors of stone and minerals. It wasn't surprising that the wine won a Gold medal in the Salon des Vins de Loire wine competition – as did the domaine's 2005 red blend of Pinot Noir and Gamay, which goes by the name "Terre des Violettes." Hand-harvested, the grapes were cold soaked before fermenting in tank. Another charmer, this was a supple red with flavors of blueberry, cassis and minerals. Both the 2009 and the 2010 Terre des Violettes were smooth, cherry accented charmers. Seductive quiet reds.

✺ Sebastien Treuillet

(See Pouilly)

✺ Highly Recommended

Treuillet rents 1.5 hectares of vines in the Giennois on which he makes a white and a red. I haven't tasted the former, but sampled the 2009 red in January 2011. A tank fermented blend of 20% Gamay and 80% Pinot Noir, it weighed in at 14.5% alcohol. Surprise. You didn't feel the alcohol at all. The wine was a total charmer, full of ripe cherry and black tea flavors. In France, they'd say it was a wine you could "*boire sans soif*" – drink without being thirsty. I say it was PMG.

✺ Domaine de Villargeau/ Marc & François Thibault

Villargeau 58150 Pougny; 03 86 28 23 24; 06 62 29 69 30;
domainedevillargeau@orange.fr

✺ Highly Recommended

On their 22 hectare domaine, Marc and François Thibault take a seriously eco-friendly approach to viticulture – vine density is 6,500 plants a hectare, pruning is severe, as is debudding, in order to give the grape clusters the maximum amount of aeration.

The domaine's white Giennois comes from grapes grown on the silex slopes of a parcel with southwestern exposure. It ferments in small stainless steel tanks and ages on its lees until bottling in the spring following the harvest. The 2006, 13.5 alcohol, was fragrant, ripe and floral, with flavors of white-fleshed peaches. Both mellow and fresh, it had nice focus and a suggestion of light tannins. The 2010 was crisp and bracing, a lively bistro Sauvignon.

For the rosé, red grapes macerate for one night before being pressed and vinified like the white. The 2006, with 13 degrees alcohol and a thread of CO_2, was taut but not skinny. Nicely structured, fresh, and strawberry-scented, it was an adaptable meal wine. The red "les Licôtes," from a southwest facing slope with clay-limestone soils, is pure Pinot Noir. It ages for ten months in barrels from four to six years old. The 2006, once carafed, was lean, cool, and supple, with pretty fruit and light tannins. A fine red for an informal meal as was the smooth, lightly oaky 2010.

❧ Domaine Hubert Veneau/ Domaine des Ormousseaux

The next generation has taken over the reins of this 36-hectare family domaine but not much has changed in the style of the wines. A 2006 *blanc*, with 13.5 degrees alcohol, tasted sweeter than its stated one gram of residual sugar would lead you to think. It was big, grassy and varietal, but also fresh, with good focus and grip, and flavors of string bean and green pea. I much preferred it to the 2005 red which, despite a candied nose, was somewhat vegetal, thin and sharp.

Chapter Eight
Châteaumeillant

Status: AOC (2010)

Types of Wine: Reds and rosés.

Grapes: Gamay (a minimum of 60% of the planting) and Pinot Noir. Pinot Gris is permitted for use in the rosés but is limited to 15% of the planting.

Zone: 90 hectares (222 acres) out of a potential 550 hectares within seven villages of which three – Châteaumeillant, Saint Maur and Vesdun — are in the Cher département and four – Champillet, Feusilles, Néret and Urciers — are in the Indre département.

Production: In 2010, 2,887 hl or which 2,118 were red, 769 rosé.

Soils: chiefly sand, clay and silt topsoils, mixed with pebbles, on a clay-flint base; subsoils are primarily micaschist, sandstone and gneiss.

When to Drink: within two to three years of the harvest.

Price: $

In the heart of Georges Sand country — a panorama of narrow rivers, fields given over to cereal crops, pasture lands for prized Charolais cattle, small, grey villages of stone cottages and of bourgeois villas once inhabited by this or that solicitor who somehow figured into Sand's life — are the low vine-covered plateaus producing Châteaumeillant.

We are halfway between the provincial towns of Montluçon and Châteauroux, and at the juncture of the Paris Basin and the Massif Central. In other words, we are truly at the center of France.

As a winemaking region, Châteaumeillant is on the cusp of the Loire and the Auvergne; its attenuated oceanic climate means that its seasons are less rude than those of St. Pourçain or the Côtes d'Auvergne, but they are far less mild than those of Anjou and Touraine. It shares some of the

flinty-clay soils of the Paris Basin, but these are mixed with those of volcanic origin, such as the gneiss, schist and micaschist more typical of the
Massif Central. But for its historic association with the Berry, Châteaumeillant could be grouped with the vineyards of the Auvergne with which –
arguably – it has more in common.

Winemaking here dates back at least to the 5th century. Grégoire de
Tours speaks of vines in the area in 582. Documents from the 12th century
show that the vine was cultivated more intensively during the Middle Ages,
a practice which continued until phylloxera and other maladies decimated
the vineyards. In 1869 the region counted 1200 hectares of vines.

In 1773 "le plant Lyonnais" was introduced into the region and, as of 1830
the grape, by then identified as Gamay, had spread throughout the growing
area, leading to the creation of its signature wine, a vin "gris" made by a
direct press of the Gamay grape. Pinot Noir entered the picture much later,
in the 1970s.

Winemaking continued throughout the 20th century, though most of it
was purchased and sold by négociants. A year after the cooperative was
established, Châteaumeillant attained the status of VDQS and wines of
higher quality began to be made. It was in the 1990s, however, that
Châteaumeillant, whose acreage had fallen to under 60 hectares, began to
stir. A handful of new growers restored abandoned vineyards and the
demand was made for Châteaumeillant to accede to AOC status.

Rosé, or *vin gris*, is still Châteaumeillant's signature wine. Made by a
direct press of the harvest, it is fresh, utterly dry, and food-friendly. Reds,
medium-bodied (rarely more than 12.5 alcohol), and easy-drinking, usually
ferment in tank, vatting for a week. Like the rosés, they benefit from chilling; most are made to be drunk immediately, though reds can age for up to
five years.

❧ Producers

There are eight growers — most of whom also raise Charolais beef — and one Cave Cooperative which accounts for more than half the production of Châteaumeillant. 98.5 percent of Châteaumeillant is sold in France. Unless otherwise specified all of the wines mentioned here were tasted in 2009 and 2010.

❧ Excellent

Domaine Geoffrenet-Morval

❧ To Follow

Domaine Lecomte ❧ Vincent Siret-Courtaud

❧ Highly Recommended

Domaine du Chaillot/Pierre Picot ❧ Domaine Lanoix

❧ Recommended

La Cave des Vins de Châteaumeillant ❧
Domaine des Tanneries/Raffinat

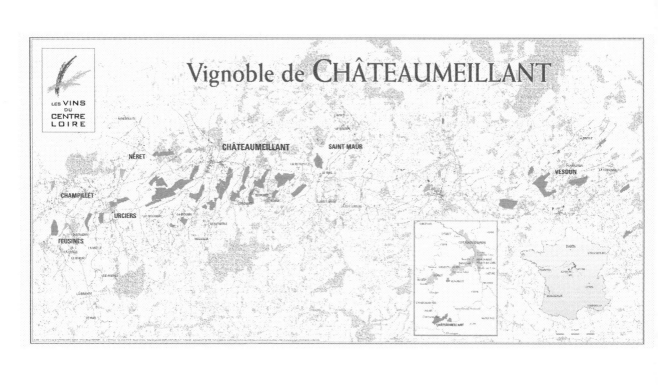

Vignoble de CHÂTEAUMEILLANT

CHÂTEAUMEILLANT

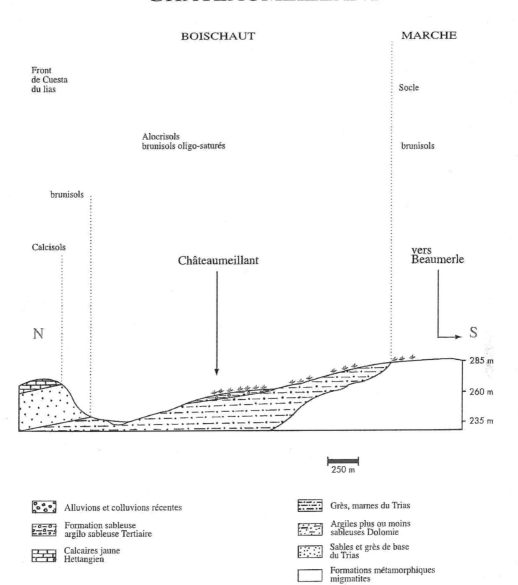

BOISCHAUT   MARCHE

Front
de Cuesta
du lias   Socle

Alocrisols
brunisols oligo-saturés   brunisols

brunisols

Calcisols

Châteaumeillant   vers
                                        Beaumerle

N   S

285 m

260 m

235 m

250 m

Alluvions et colluvions récentes   Grès, marnes du Trias

Formation sableuse   Argiles plus ou moins
argilo sableuse Tertiaire   sableuses Dolomie

Calcaires jaune   Sables et grès de base
Hettangien   du Trias

                                        Formations métamorphiques
                                        migmatites

ໄ& Recommended

ໄ& La Cave des Vins de Châteaumeillant
Route de Culan 18370 Châteaumeillant; 02 48 61 33 55;
www.châteaumeillant.com

Founded in 1964, the Cave produces well over half of Châteaumeillant's wines. It has twenty members, most of whom have other activities – raising Charolais beef, sheep and cereal crops, for example — and controls 58 hectares of vines. Its production in 2008 reached 3152 hectolitres – 2200 hl of red; 1300 hl of *vin gris*; and 60 of white Vin de Pays from its single hectare of Sauvignon and Chardonnay. Machine harvested for the most part, wines ferment in a variety of tanks – cement, stainless steel and polyester. The Coop also invested in oak barrels for aging some of its reds.

These are easy-going wines – to discover while visiting the region or to knock back in a funky wine bar. The principle label " Prestige de Garennes", is made in red and *gris*. The 2006 red was almost too dry, with pleasant, light strawberry fruit; the 2006 *Gris*, clean, stony and tart, was a citric wake-up call. More biting still was the 2006 "Gris de Folie," with a lipstick pink cork, and a pungent nose of grapefruit and pineapple.

There are numerous cuvées of red, some under the label of the buyer – the Coop makes a pleasant quaffer for Henri Bourgeois – and there is usually a Vieilles Vignes from vines over fifty years old. The 2005 had a distinctly Pinot nose, a whiff of game, slightly bitter tannins and a dry finish. The 2005 "Sublinum," a deluxe red blend with a high percentage of Pinot Noir was similarly gamey but smoother and more concentrated than the Vieilles Vignes.

ໄ& Highly Recommended

ໄ& Domaine du Chaillot/ Pierre Picot
Place de la Tounoise 18130 Dun-sur-Arnon; 02 48 59 57 69;
pierre.picot@wanadoo.fr; www.domaine.du.chaillot.free.fr

Pierre Picot traveled the world before returning to the family farm in deepest Berry. The land was perfect for raising cattle and cereal crops but not for cultivating wine grapes. In the late 1980s/early '90s, Picot found a hectare of decent vineyard land at the eastern extremity of Châteaumeillant, bought a hectare of Le Chaillot (whence the domaine's name) and learned the basics of winemaking while working with a producer in Sancerre. His first vintage was in 1993 and he is currently the president of the growers' *syndicat*.

He has also expanded the Le Chaillot vineyard and added two additional sites, to make a total of 8.5 hectares of vines. There are basically two soil types: clayey sand and micaschist, and sandstone and gneiss.

With the exception of nine *ares* of Chardonnay and seven *ares* of Tressallier (a popular grape in nearby St. Pourçain) – with which Picot makes Vin de Pays – all the wines are pure Gamay, ranging in age from those recently planted to vines 60 years old. Picot prunes hard and thins clusters to keep yields moderate – around 50 to 55 hl/ha –, harvest is by hand. Grapes for the *gris* are pressed immediately; reds vat for 20 to 21 days. They are well made and, if you're like me, you'd be pleased to find them in a local bistro or in a casual wine bar anywhere in the world.

Floral, tart and clean, his 2006 *gris* was a pleasant, taut, rosé. My favorite among his basic cuvée of red was 2005 (no real surprise there). Fragrant and fresh, it had lively flavors of black cherry, black olive and a stony finish. A focused red for a wine bar. The 2006 was agreeable, too, but a bit tart and smaller in scale. Green pea aromas in the 2004 led me to think the grapes were somewhat under-ripe.

"Parenthèse, Une Cuvée a Devenir" is Picot's deluxe red whose grapes come from the Le Chaillot vineyard. The 2006 had more heft than the basic cuvée and was a step up in every sense, with pretty violet and red cherry fruit, more alcohol and a beefy note.

I've not tasted them but, as of 2008, Picot began making three Vins de Pays – a Chardonnay called "Nuit Blanche," a Tressallier called "Sainte-Agathe" and another red made from Gamay.

Domaine Geoffrenet-Morval

Office: 2, rue de la Fontaine,18190 Venesmes; 0248605015; 0607244494; fabien.geoffrenet@wanadoo.fr; www.geoffrenet-morval.com Cave: La Bidoire, 18370 Châteaumeillant

Excellent

A former dentist, Fabien Geoffrenet followed his bliss and, in the mid-'90s, made a mid-life career change to become a winemaker. In preparation, he studied for a year at the Lycée Viticole de Beaune and then worked in Menetou-Salon with Bernard Minchin at Domaine de La Tour St. Martin. In 2000 he bought a small, 46 *are* parcel of vines in the lieu-dit Les Combes in Châteaumeillant. His first vintage a success, he gradually added to his holdings. Today Geoffrenet has 10 hectares of vines.

Planted 70% to Gamay and 30% to Pinot Noir – with a bit of Pinot Gris, Sauvignon Blanc and Chardonnay – the vines grow on two types of soil; a mixture of sand and silt with a gradual degradation of silt, creating wines with greater finesse, and a small section with outcroppings of bedrock composed of gneiss, schist and micaschist.

Viticulture, if not entirely organic, is seriously eco-friendly. Geoffrenet keeps yields moderate to low by pruning hard in winter and, in summer, cluster thinning the exuberantly productive young vines. Harvest is by hand.

"Comte de Barcelone" is the name of the domaine's rosé/*gris*. Made from a direct press of 95% Gamay and 5% Pinot Noir, Geoffrenet considers this the wine that has given Châteaumeillant its reputation. The 2006, pale, taut and focused, drank like a brisk, feisty white with a stony, mineral finish. Very good indeed.

"V.O." or "Version Originale" is the domaine's basic red. Pure Gamay, it is made chiefly from vines under 30 years old with 30% older vines. The grapes are destemmed, put in stainless steel tanks where they cold soak for a brief period of time before Geoffrenet raises the temperature to set off fermentation. The 2006 was a pure charmer – smooth, nicely balanced, nicely fleshy, with ripe cherry flavors and an appetizing note of bitterness.

"Jeanne" is made from the domaine's oldest vines – over 50 years – and is a blend of 90% Gamay and 10% Pinot Noir grown on a complex mix of sand and silt on bedrock of gneiss, schist and micaschist. The grapes cold soak briefly and, while fermenting in stainless steel tanks, are punched down and pumped over. Most of the wine ages in oak, chiefly in large barrels. Smooth, spicy and fresh, the 2006 was somewhat more worldly than the "VO", with light tannins, a faint sense of barrel age, and toothsome sapidity. In all, a light red with real character.

The cuvée "Extra-Version" is something of a caprice. It is made from young vines, 80% Pinot Noir, 20% Gamay, fermented in a wood vat and aged in stainless steel. It represents only 10% of the domaine's production since, as Geoffrenet says, it does not square with his conception of the direction the wines from Châteaumeillant ought to take, to wit: pure Gamay with the possibility of adding up to 40% Pinot Noir.

The 2006 offered pleasant Pinot fruit as well as aromas and flavors of rose petals, melon, and griotte cherries. It was deliciously fresh, ripe and balanced and, as it opened up after a day or two, the griotte flavors became richer and blended with additional notes of raspberries and figs. It went very, very well with chicken in a white wine cream sauce. The domaine also produces a Vin du Pays du Cher, a Sauvignon-dominated white.

🐞 Domaine (Maurice & Patrick) Lanoix

Beaumerle 18370 Châteaumeillant; 02 48 61 39 59;
F: 02 48 61 42 19; www.domainelanoix.com

Talk about multi-tasking. Maurice and Patrick Lanoix cultivate fourteen hectares of vines as well as cereal crops, and also sell, rent and operate numeric musical equipment, video projectors and sound systems. The wines are essentially the same though Maurice's are bottled under Domaine du Feuillat and Patrick's under Cellier du Chêne Combeau. Their 2006 rosé was firm, dry, and fairly substantial, with flavors of ash and light strawberry. It turned out to be a fine match for a fish soup, a nice surprise as I'd opened it as a compromise for the dinner guest who doesn't drink white wine. Their 2006 red "Cuvée du Chêne Combeau", was a firm, easy-drinking Pinot Noir with flavors of strawberries and minerals. As charming as the rosé, it disappeared before you knew it. Perfect for a cozy late night supper by the hearth but not bad at any time. There's also a pungent Sauvignon blanc, sold as a Vin de Pays, and several special cuvées such as a bottling made from 80 to 100 year old vines aged in Tronçais oak barrels, and a minty, mineral Pinot Noir.

🐞 Domaine Lecomte

🐞 To Follow

(See Quincy)

In 2010 Lecomte *père et fils* acquired three hectares of vines in Châteaumeillant, not far from their vines in Quincy. The grapes are hand harvested and undergo a two to three day cold soaking before fermenting in tank. I tasted one red from the 2010 harvest. Smooth and strawberry-cherry scented, it was a seductive little quaffer and downright yummy. As the French would say, *on le boit sans soif*. Or, as I'd say, strictly PMG!

🐞 Vincent Siret-Courtaud

🐞 To Follow

(See Quincy)

Young Vincent Siret recently acquired three hectares in Châteaumeillant. His 2010 red nicely expresses its blend – warm, lightly jammy aromas of strawberry make one think 'Gamay,' and the cherry focus on the palate says, "there's some Pinot Noir here too." A charming wine bar red.

🐾 Domaine des Tanneries/ Raffinat

12 Rue des Tanneries, 18370 Châteaumeillant; 02 48 61 35 16;
f:02 48 61 44 27

Henri Raffinat and sons Jean-Luc (Lycée d'Amboise) and Eric cultivate 10.5
hectares of vines and raise Charolais beef. Unpretentious country wines,
the Raffinat's Châteaumeillants are a true taste of the country.

Their 2006 rosé was taut, fresh, dry, and so tart it could scrape the plaque
off your teeth. The Raffinats have planted six hectares of Pinot Noir and
the varietal flavors come through in their reds which are generally 80%
Pinot Noir. The slightly herbaceous 2004 red was light and fragrant and
drank like a dark rosé. It would work well with exotically spiced dishes. The
2005 red, from a much riper vintage, was meatier and richer. Any one of
them would be just fine with a platter of charcuterie in a wine bar. They
also have a small plot of Sauvignon Blanc from which they make a Vin du
Pays du Cher.

Chapter Nine
The Vins de Pays of the Nivernais: The Coteaux Charitois and the Coteaux de Tannay

A provincial town of slightly more than 5000 in inhabitants, La Charité-sur-Loire lies about 30 kilometers south of Pouilly and Sancerre. It was founded by a Benedictine abbot from Cluny and became an important stopover for pilgrims on their way to Santiago de Compostella who benefited from "*la charité des bons pères,*" whence the town's name.

A monastic city since the 11th century, it is hardly surprising that vines historically covered its best slopes – well exposed hillsides with poor, rocky, clay and limestone soils.

Cultivated by Benedictine and Cistercian monks of the Abbayes of Cluny – La Charité's Notre-Dame was called Cluny's eldest daughter — and Bouras, the region's wines were served by the Counts of Nevers and the Dukes of Burgundy.

After the revolution, local farmers and proprietors bought vineyard land once belonging to the Church. Seeking a rapid return on their investment, however, they moved the vineyards to the plains and replanted with more productive varieties. Quality declined but it is worth noting that in 1856 La Charité had more than 664 vignerons. The devastating effect of phylloxera, followed by two world wars, succeeded in annihilating the region's vineyards. Hillside vines, abandoned, returned to a state of nature; local farmers turned to more profitable crops like cereal.

In 1980 Fernand Pabion, whose descendants now run the Domaine de La Petite Forge, united a small group of growers to form a local *syndicat* and to restore the vineyards. In 1986 the appellation Vin de Pays des Coteaux Charitois was created and in 2001 was officially approved. (When the European laws are adopted, it will become IGP Côte de la Charité.)

The zone, which covers La Charité-sur-Lore and the communes of Arbourse, Châteauneuf-Val-de-Bargis, Dompierre-sur-Nièvre, Germigny-sur-Loire and Parigny-les-Vaux, all in the Nièvre département, covers

54 hectares. Principle white grapes are Chardonnay and Sauvignon Blanc, which may be augmented with limited quantities of Chasselas, Pinot Blanc and Aligote. Reds and rosés are chiefly based on Gamay, Pinot Noir and Pinot Gris (which also makes white wines). Gamay de Bouze and Gamay de Chaudenay, again in limited quantities, may be used for blending. As with other Vins de Pays, the minimum alcohol level is set at 10.5, with maximum yields set at 85 hl/ha for reds and rosés and 90 for whites.

For now, these are fruity wines to drink in their youth. Can this reborn wine region make wines to rival Sancerre and Pouilly? Time, and the ambitions of the pioneering vignerons, will tell.

Currently, fewer than ten growers produce Charitois wine. The two most prominent, described more fully in other appellations, follow:

❧ Serge Dagueneau & Ses Filles (See Pouilly)

Valérie Dagueneau, who lives in La Charité-sur-Loire, oversees a tiny, 1.8 hectare property in Les Montées de St. Lay in the Charitois, as well as a rather large domaine in Les Berthiers, part of the Pouilly-Fumé appellation. Her favorite wine from this region is her Pinot Gris (aka Pinot Beurot), the 2008 of which was vivacious and rather refined, a pleasure. The wine goes through malolactic fermentation, as does her Chardonnay which is made from relatively old vines (over 35 years) and ferments in an old demi-muid. The 2008 was a ringer for a simple Burgundy, highstrung, fresh and lightly mineral. Her Pinot Noir vines range from very young (just planted) to old-ish (20 and over). Harvested by hand, as are all the grapes here, the Pinot Noir ferments in one to ten year old barrels with regular pumping over and occasional punching down. Lightly oaky, the 2008 was very pure and truly charming.

❧ Domaine des Pénitents/Alphonse Mellot: $$
Bourg – 58350 Chasnay; 03 86 69 20 93 or 02 48 54 07 41;
www.mellot.com

Since 2003 Alphose Mellot *fils* has been developing the Domaine des Pénitents, an 18 hectare vineyard planted to Chardonnay and Pinot Noir. His partner in this venture is Vincent Geantet of Gevrey Chambertin's Domaine Geantet-Ponsiot. Viticulture is organic and biodynamic. Harvest is by hand. The Chardonnay, a small percentage of which ages in oak, is fresh, mineral, easy, and very pleasant. For his red wine, Mellot ages half of his Pinot Noir in new oak barrels and half in tank. It's a lightly oaky, pleasant, medium-bodied red with light cherry fruit.

❧ Other Growers Worth Trying:

Emmanuel Rouquette/ Domaine du Puits de Compostelle, 58700 La-Selle-sur-Nievre; 03 86 70 03 29; 06 18 06 14; www.puitsdecompostelle.fr: Rouqette is a young enologist who has been working in the appellation since 1997. In 1999 he was able to buy three hectares of vines and create his own domaine.

Daniel & Karine Pabion/ Domaine de la Petite Forge, 58400 Raveau; 03 86 70 30 80; www.lapetiteforge.fr. One of the handful of enthusiasts who began the renewal of the Charitois vineyard area.

❧ Vins De Pays Des Coteaux De Tannay

If you asked a Tannaysien, which is what the people of the Canton of Tannay call themselves, where, in the diverse regions of France, they would claim to live, my hunch is that they would say "Burgundy," and, more specifically, the subregion of the Morvan – at the eastern limits of the Nièvre département. Yet, in the logic of French wine bureaucracy, the wines of this microscopic region are affixed to those of the Loire.

At the time of this writing, the wines of the Coteaux du Tannay, which received "Vin de Pays" status in 2001, correspond to 40 hectares of vines planted in Tannay, Clamecy and Brinon-sur-Beuvron, in parcels both near the Loire as well as on the hillsides overlooking the villages of Saint-Lay, Chasnay and Nannay, due east of Cosnes-sur-Loire. Its whites are made from Chardonnay and Melon; its reds and rosés from Pinot Noir and Gamay, with the possible addition of up to 20% Gamay de Bouze or Gamay de Chaudenay (to beef up the color).

Like its close relative, the Coteaux du Charitois, the region does have a history of winemaking, in this case dating from the 13th century when the wines were called "Vins de Clamecy". It has been said that their quality rivaled that of the wines of Sancerre and, in the 19th century, before phylloxera struck, the region had 1087 hectares of vines which dwindled to 230 hectares by the time of the first World War. In 1995 a handful of enthusiasts decided to give the vineyards new life. They compare the renaissance of their wines and vines to those of nearby Vezelay.

❧ Les Caves Tannaysiennes
03 86 29 31 59 - 11 rue d'Enfer – 58190 Tannay
www.caves-tannay.com

A group of ten growers and a winemaker, the Caves Tannaysiennes makes one-dimensional, pleasant wines, including a Melon (which might benefit from sur lie aging), several Chardonnays and Pinot Noirs, including those labeled Maison Claude de la Porte.

Appendix 1
The Gastronomy of the Sancerrois

"One doesn't dine more luxuriously in Berry than one does in Paris but one dines better." So said Honoré de Balzac. Indeed, the hearty, frank, cooking, the long-simmered stews, the succulent game, the abundance of wild mushrooms, the stick-to-the-ribs potato pies and caramelized apple tarts make Berry and neighboring Sologne one of my favorite gastronomic regions in France for downright good eating.

The cooking is frank, full-flavored and hearty. The two most emblematic dishes — Sologne's *civet de lièvre*, a rich hare stew and Berry's *poulet en barbouille*, an equally rich chicken dish — resemble the blood-thickened stews of other French regions, for example, but are, for no readily apparent reason, more filling. The word *barbouille*, perhaps, reveals the Berrichon spirit: the word implies that the dish is so delicious that eaters make messes of themselves by going at it with all fingers — a distinctly un-French thing to do!

Other classic dishes are simply and clearly *heavy*. *Boulettes*, Berry's little dead weights for the stomach, are essentially well-seasoned meatballs of ground pork, veal and beef, potatoes and egg.

Local carp is traditionally stuffed with sausage, carp roe and bread crumbs which have been soaked in milk, hard boiled eggs, potatoes, shallots, mushrooms, onions and herbs. The fish is sewn up, placed on a bed of mushrooms (or carrots) and onions, doused with wine and butter, and cooked for an hour and a half. As chef Alain Nonnet of Restaurant La Cognette, said to me as he described this dish, "heavy." Finally, there's the ubiquitous potato pie called *pâté* (or *galette*) *de pommes de terre*.

The most popular of Berry's many potato dishes, the *pâté de pommes de terre* is usually a large disk-shaped, double-crusted pie made of puff pastry or short crust pastry encasing well seasoned potatoes, often blended with fromage blanc. When you take the pie from the oven you pour *crème fraiche* through the hole in the center of the crust. The recipe can be altered by kneading together the filling and the dough, and many cooks add ham or bacon, though purists claim that turns the dish into a *tourte*.

The potato pie touches on two other themes in local cooking. Cream is used with abandon and is liberally poured into most pies. Additionally, there is a large variety of *galettes, tourtes* and *tartes*, both savory and sweet. *Citrouillat*, or *pâté a la citrouille*, is a savory pumpkin pie made like the potato version. (Sologne is an important pumpkin-growing region.) The pumpkin meat is diced and left to macerate overnight with chopped onions, parsley and garlic. *Chaussons* or *galettes* filled with chevre are also popular.

Encasing terrines *en croûte* —particularly terrines made of game — is a specialty of the Orléanais which drifts into Berry as well. *Pâté dé Paques* is also called "*pâté à la oeu*" (with eggs). A lard-based pastry encloses a terrine of pork, veal, kid and hard boiled eggs. A lighter version uses a butter-based crust, or may omit the crust entirely. *Tourte Berrichonne* is made with potatoes, onions and eggs; another local tourte uses mushrooms, cream and ham. Sweet pies are made with pumpkin, pear, plum and apple. The most famous, *tarte Tatin*, specifies Orleans' reinette apples. Baked upside down and then served right-side up, this famous apple pie would seem a natural culinary consequence of an apple and grain-growing region.

Its creation, however, is traced to the turn of the century and is credited to Stéphanie and Caroline Tatin, the owners of Hotel Tatin across from the train station of Lamotte-Beuvron, a provincial town south of Orléans.

Some say that Caroline forgot to line her pan with dough before adding the apples and then improvised, laying the dough across the bed of fruit. The current owners of Hotel Tatin say that this was deliberate. The sisters were behind schedule and rather than lack dessert, Caroline placed sliced apples in a buttered *tourtière* over a bed of sugar, heated them until they were well caramelized, then laid on the dough, placed the pie in a hot oven for half an hour and unmolded it to the delectation of all present.

The ponds of Sologne and the streams of Berry teem with fresh water fish — carp, pike, eel, lamprey. Eel and lamprey often become the bases for winey *matelotes:* Cooked like a *civet*, the eel or lamprey marinates overnight in coarse red wine, onion and a *bouquet garni*. The marinade is reduced for several hours and the slices of eel are browned, then set to simmer over a low flame with the reduced marinade for four to five hours. Finally, the matelote is thickened with blood drained from the eel. Some regions add prunes or currants, some hard-boiled eggs and croutons fried in walnut oil.

It is carp, however, that seems to inspire more recipes than any other local fish. It is grilled; braised in red wine; sauced with cream and chives; encased in aspic; poached and served while still hot with mayonnaise; it's sliced, floured and fried, or it's cut into steaks and sauced with red wine. Often it is stuffed, its filling some variation on the recipe described above. But perhaps the most historic stuffed carp recipe is Carp *à la Chambord* which probably dates from the time of François 1er.

An avid hunter, François built the Château of Chambord in an isolated, marshy area typical of Sologne. Its only charm was its plentiful game. The dish — which called for stuffing the fish with sweetbreads and tiny game birds, cooking it for two hours in white wine, and serving it surrounded by woodcock, partridge and quail — celebrates a return from the hunt.

Sologne's game forests cover 40% of the region and are among the best in France. Road signs warn "Large Animal Crossing' and, in hunting season, you often have to brake for pheasants. And, indeed, its game terrines are as outstanding as its *civets*. In addition to terrines, wine-laced stews and *civets*, the catch may be baked, grilled or roasted. It may be stuffed with chestnuts or walnuts or garnished with cabbage. Small birds, like woodcocks, are larded, roasted, then stuffed with mashed livers, *crème fraiche* and eau de vie, and cooked again.

Berry also leads France's regions in the cultivation of lentils as well as seed-oil crops; Sologne, in asparagus production. It is also known for strawberries and cornichons. The latter are added to pork cutlets cooked with red wine and eau de vie, as well as to beef tongue cooked with tomato, red wine and cloves.

Berrichons once raised sheep for their wool. The meat seems to have been appreciated, too; no longer wool producers, Berrichons still enjoy *gigot à la sept heures* (lamb cooked slowly for seven hours), and lamb with white beans, as well as a variety of lamb stews. The pig is eaten with equal enthusiasm: *saupiquet* is braised ham, in a shallot, tarragon, white wine and cream sauce; *crépinettes* are cooked with wine, cream, onions, garlic and herbs; *sanguettes* resemble *boudins noirs*. *Andouillettes* are usually grilled but may also be served with a sauce of *crème fraiche*, mustard, shallots and local white wine or eau de vie.

Local fruit dominates the dessert repertory. *Cotignac* is a paste of quince made with or without apples; it is eaten on its own or with fresh cheese. *Poirat* is a covered pie filled with pears, seasoned with pear eau de vie, sugar, cinnamon and pepper, and doused with cream. Aside from tarte *Tatin*, Orléans' reinette apples are also made into cakes, beignets or *beugnons*, cooked in a thick crêpe batter. Berry borders on Limousin and desserts such as *gouère* (made with reinette apples) and *millat de Levroux* (with black cherries) are basically clafouti. *Sanciaux* are thick crepes served at Mardi Gras — or anytime, in my experience.

And there are several indigenous candies. A confectioner from Issoudun, frequented by Balzac, introduced local marzipan to Parisians in 1884. The town of Montargis, slightly off the wine route, is the birthplace of the prasline, or praline, an almond coated in caramelized sugar. The recipe, which dates from 1630, comes from the cook of the Duc de Plessis-Praslin. So successful were the candies that the cook left the duke's kitchens and opened a shop nearby, in the center of Montargis, called Maison de la Prasline which still exists today.

Cheese is generally featured in contemporary meals. Several interesting sheep and cows milk cheeses are made in the region but the Sancerrois is truly chèvre country. It gives the Loire its most famous goat cheese of all, the pungent small drum called Crottin de Chavignol.

According to producers, hot chèvre — with or without a salad – is not traditional; it was "invented" in Paris in the 1970s, but most Sancerrois restaurants now serve it. *Fromagée,* however, is traditional.

A popular appetizer or snack, it is fresh cheese (usually goat) mixed with chives and shallots or garlic. It goes very nicely with a glass of fresh Sancerre (in any color) or Chasselas. And every single one of the local wines — but particularly the region's best Sauvignons – goes sublimely well with a chunk of nicely aged farmhouse crottin.

Though Chavignol gave its name to the cheese, and though its slopes are within the appellation for Crottin de Chavignol, you will not seen any goats on them: this land is much too highly valued as vineyards to be given over to grazing ruminants.

Records show that goats have grazed the chalky hills and plains around Chavignol since the 16th century (though they are believed to have been present here much longer). Officials say the name "crottin" comes from a terra cotta oil lamp that had the same form as the mold used for making the cheese. A more popular theory says that it comes from the word for horse or mule dung, *crotte,* which corresponds to the way the cheese originally looked and tasted: the shape of a bullet, it was black, hard and barely edible.

Today's Crottin de Chavignol is a small, flat drum which weighs about 60 grams (2 ounces). The Appellation Contrôlée, which dates from 1976, extended the original cheesemaking area to include most of the Cher departement as well as parts of the Loiret and the Nièvre. Crottin de Chavignol must be made of whole goats milk (frozen curds are permitted but crottins made from them may not be labelled "fermier"). Some producers drain the curds on cloth before ladling it into molds, a practice unique to this region. By law, Crottin de Chavignol must age for at least ten days but is at its most classic at twenty to twenty-five days when its crust is nicely blueish. (Younger chevres used to go by the name Sancerrois but the INAO now forbids the use of other place names for chèvres made in the Crottin de Chavignol area.)

Another traditional way of serving crottin is *repassé*: Dry cheeses are piled one on top of another in an earthenware or glass jar for a month or longer until they look humid and squishy. Their flavor is almost too pungent for wine; a marc might be more appropriate.

Crottins originally were made by wives of farmers or vignerons, who kept small herds of three to twenty goats and used the cheese to help sell their wine. Today most is made by large dairies like Triballat or by *affineurs* such as Fromagerie Dubois-Boulay located in Chavignol who collect fresh cheese from producers, salt, mold and ripen them for at least a week. At any one of these stages, you can do no better than to pair them with a wine from Chavignol. Not luxurious but damned delicious.

Glossaries and conversion tables

I have tried to avoid technical words in this book where possible, and have substituted words from every day life, but some wine jargon is inescapable. Definitions for technical terms are given here. (In Chapter One, you'll find my own personal wine terminology (some of which has seeped into this book) as well as more common "winespeak.")

AC or AOC: An abbreviation for Appellation d'Origine Contrôlée, AC is a designation for wine that comes from a geographically limited zone and has been made according to legal specifications, including which grape varieties are used and the permitted yield, ripeness, and alcohol levels. With rare exceptions (for example, Muscadet), an AC is named after a place, like Sancerre. NB: When European Union laws take effect, AOC will be replaced with **AOP**, Appellation d'Origine Protegée.

Argilo-calcaire: a soil consisting of clay and limestone

Argilo-siliceux: flinty clay soils.

Assemblage: the blending of a number of wines (from the same or different grapes, depending upon the appellation) to produce a finished wine or wines.

Ban de vendange: The authorized date for the start of harvest.

Barrels: Wooden containers in which wines are fermented and/or aged. The best barrels are made of oak. Both the size of the barrel and the number of times it has been used influence the impact it will have on the wine. Large and/or old barrels will have little effect other than to provide a porous atmosphere that will soften the wine by facilitating limited oxidation. The smaller and newer the barrel, the greater its influence, not only because of the amount of contact with air the wine receives but also because the barrel contributes flavor (vanilla, toast, or oak, for example) and tannins. Barrel age is sometimes indicated on the label, often with the words *vieilli en fûts de chêne.* Some barrel terminology:

barrique: a Bordeaux barrel holding 225 liters.
demi-muid: a barrel of 300 to 600 liter capacity.
foudre: a large wood cask that can hold 200 to 300 hectoliters.
pièce: a Burgundy barrel with a 228 liter capacity.

Biodynamics: A philosophy of viticulture as set forth by Austrian philosopher Rudolph Steiner. Homeopathic vine treatments replace chemicals; planting, pruning and other vineyard operations are scheduled by the positions of the planets. As Noel Pinguet of Vouvray describes biodynamics, "It's a synthesis of agriculture over the course of history, the observations of farmers throughout civilization."

Blanc de blancs: A white wine made of white grapes.

Blanc de noirs: A white or a pale pink wine made from red grapes that have been immediately pressed off – or separated from — their skins and vinified like a white wine.

Bleeding: The drawing off of juice from a vat of fermenting red grapes. It is one method used to make rosé wines as well as a technique some vintners use to make their reds more concentrated.

Botrytis cinerea: The name of a mold that under certain conditions causes grapes to shrivel resulting in a concentration of sugar and acid. The wines made from these grapes, notably Sauternes, are characterized by aromas and flavors of honey and often, a dense, almost syrupy richenss. *Botrytis cinerea* is also called noble rot (*pourriture noble*).

Brassage: The stirring up of the lees of a white wine as it ages (presumably on its lees).

Brut: The term brut applies to dry sparkling wine that has a sugar content of .8 to 1.5 perecent, and to an unfinished wine that is taken from a tank or barrel for sampling, as in *brut de cuve,* a *cuve* being a tank.

Caillottes: pure limestone embedded with fossilized shells.

Carafe: (a) a beaker, with or without a stopper, into which a wine is poured; (b) a method of aerating wine by pouring it into a carafe. I have used the word "carafe" instead of the related term "decant." The latter is more closely associated with the serving of old wine in which the aim is to ensure that only clear wine enter the decanter, leaving the sediment behind in the bottle. When I speak of pouring a wine into a carafe, however, I am generally talking about young wines. Although there is no agreement on the subject, I think most young wines benefit from aeration. In other words: let it breathe, let it breathe.

Carbonic maceration: A method of fermentation in which bunches of whole grapes are put into a tank filled with CO_2. Fermentation starts within the individual berries. This method, which produces supple, early-drinking, very aromatic wines, is primarily used with Gamay, particularly in Beaujolais.

Cépage: Grape variety.

Chai: A winery building; an above ground cellar.

Chapitalization: The process of adding sugar to grape juice either before or during fermentation in order to raise the degree of alcohol of the finished wine.

Château: The translation is castle, and sometimes the winery does, indeed, have one. But this is not necessary.

Climat: Primarily associated with Burgundy, the term *climat* refers to a specific vineyard or part of that vineyard.

Clone: A plant reproduced asexually, retaining the genetic makeup of its ancestor. A number of clones may exist for a given grape variety; one may be a high-yielder, another may resist rot, a third ripen earlier, and so forth.

Clos: A walled (or otherwise enclosed) vineyard.

Cooperative: An association of wine growers in which the members bring either all or part of their production to a common cellar and share its winemaking facilities, winemakers, labs, and other costs. In most cases, the resulting wines are marketed by, and under the name of, the cooperative.

Cru: *Cru* translates as growth. The term is applied to a vineyard or a specific area of production, generally one of superior quality.

Cuvaison: Refers to the making of red wine—specifically, the practice of fermenting the grape juice with the grape solids (skins, pips, and so forth) in order to extract color, tannins, and aroma. Generally, the longer the *cuvaison* (or vatting) the deeper the color of the wine and the more tannic it will be.

Cuve: Tank.

Cuvée: Derived from the word *cuve, cuvée* usually applies to a specific blend or lot of wine, for example a reserve wine or a single vineyard or a young- or old-vines bottling.

Débourbage: In white wine production, *débourage* is the practise of allowing the *bourbes* (solid matter such as pits, stems, seeds, and bits of pulp and skin) to settle out of the grape juice before fermentation begins.

Département: One of ninety-five French administrative units, a department is smaller than a state but larger than a county. It has no precise equivalent in the United States.

Doux: A *vin doux* is an extremely sweet wine.

Fermentation: The process of transforming sugar into alcohol and turning grapes into wine.

Filtration: The process of clarifying a wine before bottling to remove yeast cells and other matter, usually by passing the wine through filter pads or diatomaceous earth (kieselguhr).

Fining: A method of clarifying wine by adding any of a number of coagulants or clays (egg whites, isinglass, gelatin, bentonite). As these substances settle to the bottom of the tank or barrel, they draw impurities with them, leaving the wine clear.

Finish: The flavors and sensations left in the mouth after the wine has been swallowed. Fine wines will have long, complex finishes (length is a closely related concept here). Simple wines may appear to have no finish whatsoever. It's "Hi. Good-bye."

Gris : A *vin gris* is a pale rosé; like a *blanc de noirs*, it is made by a direct pressing of red grapes.

Hectare: 2.47 acres.

Hectoliter: 100 liters or 26.4 gallons. One hectoliter produces eleven cases of wine.

INAO: The Institut National des Appellations d'Origine, frequently referred to as the INAO, is the government agency responsible for determining and regulating French appellations of origin.

Kimmeridgian Marl: clay-limestone soils specific to this section of the Paris Basin (see Chapter One), formed during the Jurassic period.

Lees: The deposit thrown off by a young wine, the lees, which are remnants of yeast cells, settle on the bottom of the tank or barrel.

Lieu-dit: Literally place name, *lieu-dit* is the time-honored way of referring to a particular parcel, which may or may not be a vineyard. It has no legal force.

Liquoreux: A very lush sweet wine

Lutte raisonnée: essentially means sustainable farming. There are no iron-clad laws governing who may use the term and/or under what conditions. It is safe to assume, however, that the use of weed killers, pesticides and fertilizers is kept to a bare minimum.

Maceration: See CUVAISON.

Malolactic fermentation: The transformation of sharp malic acid (think of apples) into creamier lactic acid (think milk), which normally occurs after alcoholic fermentation and which results in a less acid wine.

Millésime: Vintage.

Moelleux: A term referring to sweet wines, such as those from the Loire, *moelleux* literally means marrowy—a wine with marrow. It can, and often is, applied to dry wines, particularly those that have aged *sur lie*. In this sense – and in a broader, everyday sense – it may refer to texture. For example, what we might call a "thirsty" bath towel, in France, might be called "moelleux."

Mousseux: Sparkling wine.

Must: Unfermented grape juice.

Négociant: A wholesale wine merchant. The term generally refers to someone who buys grapes and/or finished wine, then ages or blends it before bottling the wine under his own label.

Noble rot: See BOTRYTIS CINEREA.

Passerillé: A term describing raisined or shrivelled grapes with sugars that have been concentrated as a result of the loss of water.

Perlant: Describes an ever-so-slightly sparkling wine.

Pétillant: A slightly sparkling wine.

Phenolic maturity: Also described as aromatic maturity. The stage at which the compounds in grape skins and seeds have reached peak ripeness.

Phylloxera: A vine louse transported from America that, between 1860 and 1890, ravaged the vineyards of France.

Pourriture noble: Noble rot. See BOTRYTIS CINEREA.

Presse: In the production of red wine the term *vin de presse,* or press wine, refers to the wine pressed from the grape solids after the major part of the wine has been drawn off (devatted). Usually quite tannic, press wine may be blended into an assemblage or kept apart.

Pumping over: the process of pumping the fermenting must from the bottom of the tank over the cap of grape skins during fermentation.

Punching down: think of it as grape stomping. Essentially, the cap formed by the grape skins is punched down – by feet or by mechanical means – so that it is moistened by the fermenting must underneath.

Racking: The siphoning of young wine from one tank (or barrel) to another in order to separate it from its lees.

Racy: A translation of the French *racé* which basically means pedigreed, aristocratic, blue-blooded. A wine that is racy shows its breeding.

Reduced, Reduction: See SULFUR.

Residual sugar: The sugar left in wine after fermentation has ended or been stopped.

Silex: flinty-clay soils.

Skin contact: A method of obtaining richer flavors and texture in white wines by leaving the grapes in contact with their skins for anywhere from several hours to several days before pressing them off their skins for fermentation. (Red wines are made by fermenting the grapes with their skins.)

Stage: A workshop, apprenticeship or clinical studies lasting from several hours to several months.

Sulfur: Sulfur is used in the vineyard to combat various fungi, pests, and maladies. In the cellar it cleans barrels, prevents oxidation, stuns indigenous yeasts, and arrests the fermentation of sweet wines. It is also added at bottling as a preservative. Wines with too much sulfur often smell and taste reduced—unexpressive except for a vaguely dirty aroma—until they are sufficiently aerated. Decanting is advised.

Sur lie: The practice of allowing a wine to rest on its lees, or dead yeast cells, as it ages. The lees sink to the bottom of the wine after alcoholic fermentation. They create amino acids that combine with polysaccharides and, despite the chemical sound, add flavor, fleshiness, and a wonderful, rich marrowy texture. By preventing oxidation, aging *sur lie* preserves a wine's breezy vitality and somehow seems to underscore the expression of *terroir*. While associated primarily with Muscadet, aging *sur lie* is a method increasingly used by vintners throughout France.

Tannin: A substance found in grape skins and stems, as well as in oak barrels, that imparts flavor and structure to a wine. It is also an antioxidant and helps the wine age. Tannic wines often taste astringent when young—think of strong tea or underripe walnuts-but become softer and rounder as the tannins precipitate as the wines age, forming part of a wine's sediment.

Terres blanches: the local term for soils composed of clay and limestone. (See Chapter One.) Kimmeridgian Marl is a type of *terre blanche*.

Terroir: The concept of *terroir* unites the specifics of a vineyard site, encompassing its soils, subsoils, exposition, and the opening of the countryside. When a wine expresses the specific aspects of its unique place of origin, it has a *goût de terroir*. This is a stamp of identity and an aspect of complexity. Depending upon its intensity, such a wine may be said to be *terroir*-driven.

Thermoregulated: Temperature controlled.

Tri (or trie): In winemaking *tri* has two uses. A *tri* is a labor-intensive method of harvesting by successive passes through the vineyard to pick selected bunches, or grapes, at each pass, rather than harvesting all the grapes at once. And it is also the sorting over of grapes once they have arrived at the winery, to discard those that have been affected by rot. The table on which this second *tri* occurs is a *table de tri,* or sorting table.

Vendange: A harvest; a *vendange tardive* is a late harvest.

Vieilles vignes: Literally old vines, the term *vieilles vignes* has no official definition. It is abbreviated as VV.

Vigneron: A wine grower or winemaker. When a woman, a *vigneronne*.

VDQS: An abbreviation for Vin Délimité de Qualité Supérieure, this is a rank for wines between that of AC and Vin de Pays. VDQS wine is produced within a designated zone according to laws regarding production that are similar to those governing an AC. Most VDQS wines have applied for promotion to AC. It is a category that will be eliminated under unified European regulations.

Vin d'honneur: The wine served to kick off a ceremony, for example a wedding or local fair.

Vin de méditation: A term used to describe a wine that is so fine and so complex, you don't want to pair it with food. You want to drink it all by itself and ruminate about it. It provokes thoughts that generally begin something like "to think that a cluster of grapes made this."

Vin de Pays: Loosely translated as country wine, Vin de Pays is a rank beneath VDQS, and generally covers broad regions such as Vin de Pays d'Oc or Jardin de la France. It's an increasingly important category, as the rules governing it are less strict than those for AC wines and, perhaps more important, the name of the grape can be featured on the label. Under European regulations, most Vins de Pays would be labeled **IGT (Indication Géographique Protegée).**

Vin de table: Literally, table wine, the term *vin de table* is generally used to describe wines not subject to any regulations.

Vinification: The process of turning grapes into wine.

Viticulture: The practice and methods of grape growing.

Yield: The amount of grapes harvested within a given vineyard area. .

Yeast: The agent that provokes fermentation, yeasts can either be indigenous (wild) or created in laboratories.

Conversion Tables

Hectares to Acres
- 1 hectare = 2.47 acres

Hectoliters to Gallons, Cases, and Tons
- 1 hectoliter (100 liters) equals roughly 26.4 gallons or 11 cases (of 12 bottles of 75 centilitre capacity) of wine
- 10 hectolitres a hectare (hl/ha) equals roughly 264 gallons a hectare (roughly 100 gallons an acre), about 40 cases an acre
- One ton of grapes an acre equals roughly 15 hl/ha

- One ton of grapes equals about 60 cases of wine
- 35 hl/ha equals a bit over 140 cases an acre
- 3 tons an acre equals 180 cases an acre

Temperatures

10ºC = 50ºF
15ºC = 59ºF
20ºC = 68ºF
25ºC = 77ºF
30ºC = 86ºF
35ºC = 95ºF

Wining, Dining and Touring

Where to eat

Prices are based on a meal for two, wine included. $ represents under $40; $$, under $90; $$$, up to $150; $$$$ above $150.

Auberge de la Pomme d'Or

$$($)

Pl de la Mairie, 18300 Sancerre 02. 48. 54. 13. 30

Homey setting, a brief, fresh-from-the-market menu highlighting French classics, a wine listed studded with regional gems, what more could you want? On my last visit I pigged out on dishes with girolle mushrooms – snails in a *girolle* cream sauce, *rognons de veau à la moutarde* with girolles and swiss chard. Simply delicious with a nuanced, lightly off-dry 2001 Sancerre "Cuvée Paul" from François Cotat.

L' Aubergéade

$$($)

321 Route d'Issoudun, 36260 Diou, 02.54.49.22.28.

You read it here first: l'Aubergéade has one of France's best and best-priced wine lists. You could spend two years here, drinking a different and differently great bottle every day, and still have money left in your bank account. Just focusing on France, the encyclopedic list includes Guy Bossard's Muscadet "Expression de Granite," Vernay's various Condrieus, Mas de Daumas Gassac, a range of Gauby and so forth. Of course there is an encyclopedic range of Reuillys, the fortunate appellation in which this restaurant sits.

But, to begin at the beginning: if you didn't know about this restaurant beforehand, you'd pass it by. A no-frills building on the side of a main local road not far from Issoudun, it looks like a truck stop. And the reasonably priced meals might, indeed, appeal to hungry truckers.

Jacky Patron, the chef-owner (yes, his name is really Patron), knows how to cook. He starts with top-notch ingredients and treats them with great intelligence. You could eat his food every night. (I could, anyway.) My last meal there: silky homemade ravioli filled with foie gras with girolle and *morille* mushrooms piled on top and infusing the light cream sauce with their woodsy flavor. Yum. Then there was a perfectly cooked, herb-encrusted saddle of lamb garnished with more mushrooms, buttery cabbage and polenta rounds that appeared to have been formed with a cookie cutter. The very good cheese tray included some lipsmaking Stilton; and, for dessert, an individual fig tart: a buttery, crunchy, CD-sized disk covered with flavorful fresh figs. Couldn't have been better. Even the coffee was delicious.

$$

Chapeau Melon
9, rue Bourbonnoux, 18000 Bourges, 02 48 24 03 78;
www.bistrochapeaumelon.fr;

A delightful English couple runs this excellent lunch and tea spot on a main street – something of a cobbled restaurant row — across from the historic Hotel Lallement and not far from D'Antan Sancerrois. Everything is home-made and delicious, even the Irish soda bread, the sensational ice cream and the sublime chocolates that come with coffee. On a hot summer's day, I started with a refreshing Pimm's Cup – lemonade, ginger, a slice of orange, mint and a strawberry. Two appetizers – green asparagus with hollandaise sauce and a poached egg, and a goat cheese and red onion tart served with a mesclun salad – made for a perfect lunch. The wine list is small and could use work. But the homemade chocolate ice cream is to die.

$$)

Le Chat
42 rue des Guérins-Villechaud, 58200 Cosne-Cours-sur-Loire 03. 86. 28. 49. 03

Laurent Chareau abandoned the bold-faced kitchens of Paris, where he worked with high-profile chefs such as Gilles Choukroun, to set up his own shop in a no-frills café on a side street in a whistle stop town north of Pouilly. Nathalie, his girlfriend, works the front room at meal times and the front office *chez* Didier Dagueneau at other times. (Yes, there's a broad selection of Dagueneau wines on the list, as well as cutting edge wines from every region in France such as a Benjamin Dagueneau favorite, the

Domaine de Mouscaillo Chardonnay from Limoux . (He claims it's the wine that made him like Chardonnay.)

But I digress. The eclecticism of the cuisine will come as no surprise to anyone familiar with Gilles Choukroun's *oeuvre*: for example, an amuse-bouche of cream of broccoli with San Daniele ham and parmesan, a "Mikad" of asparagus, which turned out to be thin white asparagus, served raw, cut into slivers and served with haddock tartare and eggplant caviar, followed by roast pork accompanied by curry-accented passion fruit and *al dente* fennel seasoned with coriander. A flawless strawberry tartlet with vanilla *crème patissière* caps off an extremely satisfying meal.

C'Heu l'Zib $$
Menetou-Salon, 02.48.64.81.20. (Call before going. The hours often change.)

I can't imagine going to the eastern Loire without stopping for a meal at this sentimental favorite with its warmhearted ambiance right out of Pagnol. (The name is the local dialect for Chez Zib — Zib being a nickname for the restaurant's founder.)

The restaurant is owned by Marie-Claude Fontaine, the cook, an outgoing woman who succeeded her parents. It occupies the corner of the main square of Menetou-Salon and seduces from the minute you open the door: Smells of winey stews, a room cluttered with faïence and dried flowers, crammed with copper pots, a sagging timbered ceiling, a bottle of cassis passed from table to table to make kirs with Menetou blanc. And no menu. A typical meal: terrine with home-pickled cornichons or fantastic home-smoked salmon or white asparagus served with a tangy mustard emulsion; then pike in a soothing shallot cream sauce followed by sensational roast boar, tasting like the free-range pig that it is, or a toothsome stew of guinea hen laced with whiskey. Roast potatoes and braised endives are served family style, as is salad and the plate of local chevres. The immutable house *charlotte au chocolat,* as delicious as ever, is accompanied summer's preserves — plums, pears and grapes in syrup or alcohol — just what was wanted with coffee and a shot of local eau de vie. Loire soul food. Get it while it lasts.

$$$

La Cognette

rue des Minimes/Blvd Stalingrad, 36100 Issoudun; 02.54.03.59.59;
www.la-cognette.com.

What's that line about all happy families being alike? Well, can this partic-
ular family – the Nonnets and the Daumy-Nonnets – adopt me? Please? (I
bet Tolstoy wouldn't have minded being a foster child here either.)

Alain Nonnet, the father of the clan, is as cheerful and as generous a chef
as you are ever likely to meet. His food is a fine reflection of his personality.
When I was researching the Loire book (first edition) in 1990 I interviewed
him about traditional Berry food. We were sitting in the overstuffed, period
armchairs of the front room while dinner was starting in the jewel-box of
a dining room beyond. "It's heavy," he said of Berrichon cooking. And he'd
punctuate his description of each specific dish, with a 'you see' nod, saying
"Heavy!"

So he's there in his chef's whites and his toque, as is his son-in-law Jean-
Jacques Daumy (who had just begun working with him in 1990), and the
women, mother Nicole and daughter Isabelle, as cheerful as Alain,

I had loved this restaurant in 1990 but hadn't been back since. I think it
has dropped from two Michelin stars to one. If that's in fact true, it's nuts.
What this recent meal showed me was that La Cognette is better than ever.
In fact, if you want really traditional (ever so slightly updated) Berrichon
food that will have you salivating in you memory of it, make a beeline for
this place. (The hotel is as heartily recommended.)

There have been a couple of changes – a PVC terrace added to the façade,
for example – but the soul of the place remains intact. This is Masterpiece
Theatre meets Balzac. In fact, Balzac wrote "La Rabouilleuse" while living
in Issoudun and frequented this restaurant/auberge when it was owned by
M. and Mme. Cognet. The décor seems properly vintage – thus, those over-
stuffed chairs, armoires, bibelots etc.

And the food! Dieters, search elsewhere. You will be miserable. Big
eaters, however, will want to move in.

After some perfectly lovely amuse-bouches – eg a "capuccino" of green
pea – we started in on the heavy Berrichon-alia with a Cognette classic,
cream of green lentils from Berry. The nod to modernism throughout was
that everything was served on a slate slab so that the soup came with side
dishes of sliced truffles and tiny, diced croutons. You added what you
wanted when you wanted it – which meant after you'd stopped sniffing the
truffles. The soup was heavenly – in the earthily soothing sense. Then came
a chausson filled with snails in a garlicky cream sauce. You know there can

be nothing bad about a well made garlicky cream sauce and this lipsmacker came with about as delectable and as buttery a turnover as I've ever eaten. Also large enough for a meal.

Next came individual souffled omelets with écrivisses. The crayfish were right out of Escoffier. The omelet – the size of a CD – was a minor miracle – light as air, a pillow of flavor. You couldn't stop eating it.

Then, a Nonnet signature dish and a Berrichon staple, filet of carp stuffed with bread crumbs, sausage and mushrooms. To die. Needless to say, I was so stuffed I couldn't touch the cheese. I did, however, eat the little salad made from wild purslane — which made me rethink ripping out the purslane that grows weedlike in my garden. Instead, I should harvest it when it just begins to sprout from the earth.

There were lots of very pretty little desserts but I couldn't eat the ones flavored with rosewater as that's one of the few flavors I really dislike. So my tablemates vacuumed them up. Then came platters of minuscule friandises – chocolate truffles, very creamy, very teeny financiers, and microscopic goblets filled with passion fruit cream or a mystery cream which turned out to be a mixture of beet and tomato flavored with pepper.

The vigneron Claude Lafond was with us so it's no surprise that the sommerlier selected a cuvée of Lafond's Reuilly blanc made for la Cognette. He also chose a wine new to me, a 2005 Valençay Cuvée des Griottes, 80% gamay/20% pinot noir from Francis Jourdin that was a succulent, nicely balanced, spicy, light red.

$$

Le Cosmopolitan
2, place des Quatre Piliers, 18000 Bourges, 02.48.66.42.20

Opened in 2008 by a young Berrichon couple – he worked for Bistro Bocuse and D'Antan Sancerrois – this is an address to treasure. Ideally located – not far from the Cathedral, across the street from Jacques Coeur's palace, is this delightful restaurant, serving tantalizing, fresh, contemporary dishes at prices that can't be beat. (The generous 8,50 plat du jour at lunch may be one of the best deals in town.) Among other gems, a *millefeuille* of mozzarella, pesto and thin layers of peeled, lightly cooked tomato which may have been the best take on salad Caprese I've ever had; sensational langoustines and scallops served with toothsome white asparagus risotto garnished with a lacy parmesan *tuile*, and fresh spinach – all of which went brilliantly with a 2007 Châteaumeillant rosé from Geoffrenet-Morval – and then a *millefeuille* layered with caramel *au beurre salé* pastry cream and topped with a scoop of caramel *au beurre salé* ice cream.

$$ (for the bistro)
$$$ (for the resaurant)

La Côte des Monts Damnés

Chavignol 18300 Sancerre, Tel. : 02 48 54 01 72;
contact@montsdamnés.com

Jean-Marc Bourgeois, son of wine impresario Jean-Marie Bourgeois, is an experienced chef who has done stints at Taillevent, Apicius and at La Côte St. Jacques. On the ground floor of his handsome and oh-so-comfortable hotel, he has installed an inviting bar – where, after a hard day of tasting wines, you can drink a characterful local microbrew called La Sancerroise – as well as a bistro and a more formal restaurant (what we used to call a 'white table cloth' restaurant).

On a recent trip I started with a delectable appetizer of asparagus and roasted langoustines (two of my favorite things, and the dish went beautifully with one of my favorite Sancerres, Bourgeois' cuvée Jadis), followed by excellent *ris de veau*. If I hadn't eaten a dessert soufflé at lunch, I surely would have ordered a house specialty, *Soufflé à la mandarine*. Instead, a selection of homemade ice cream provided a tasty sweet finish to a fine meal.

I'd have to agree with the local vintner who commented that La Côte Monts Damnés and La Tour in Sancerre are the two best restaurants in the region. But the bistro is equally attractive, particularly its faithful renditions of classic French soul food such as pig's trotters and *petit salé*, as well as more delicate fare like chicken breast in a light tarragon sauce. I think you'll find this is an address you'll use often.

$$$

D'Antan Sancerrois

50 Rue Bourbonnoux 18000 Bourges; 02 48 65 96 26

Back in the last century, D'Antan Sancerrois was a popular winebar. Now, under the direction of Stéphane and David Retif, it's a sleek, urbane restaurant with imaginative, tasty, sushi-sized dishes, a stunning wine list, and what may be the most enlightened wine policy on the planet: innumerable temptations offered by-the-glass; and wines not on the official by-the-glass list will probably be uncorked for you, if you express an interest. It was thus that I started a meal with a 2005 Vouvray "Le Mont" demi-sec from Domaine Huet to accompany an amuse bouche of crab tartare delicately seasoned with chives and mixed with diced cucumber, as well as an assortment of asparagus-themed dainties followed by buttery foie gras lacquered with *pain d'épice* and served with slices of warm brioche. A 2006 Sancerre rouge from Lucien Crochet – a cuvée made only for restaurants – smoothly accompanied two seared chunks of John Dory on a bed of carrot cream and "fish sticks" of langoustines.

Grand Hotel du Lion d'Or,

$$$ to $$$$

69, rue Clemenceau, Romorantin-Lanthenay, 41200 Romorantin-Lanthenay, 02.54.94.15.15.

This is the best restaurant in the Loire Valley. Exemplary in every sense of the word. Service is perfect, under the direction of Marie-Christine Clément, who runs the restaurant that her parents founded. The setting is luxurious, a 17th-century carriage house updated with plush carpets and smoked mirrors and the occasional magnificent flourish, like a stupendous chandelier with real candles and a luxuriant bouquet of fresh flowers. And the food, prepared by Didier Clément, the chef, is exquisite. Clément's menu is exciting. Everything is finely conceived, finely tuned, masterly, starting with a profusion of amuse-bouches: a slice of excellent hare terrine, for example, a saucer of fricasseed girolles and a tray of canapés.

Mrs. Clément, who has written several cookbooks featuring her husband's recipes, obviously enjoys explaining the history of a sauce or a particular preparation. She cautioned us that her husband's risotto was not classic. In fact, it was mostly wild rice - wild rice from heaven. Brightened with zests of orange and lemon, it showcased fat, perfectly cooked langoustines. The whole sat on a sauce of langoustine stock surrounded by a drizzle of excellent vinaigrette. It was endlessly appetizing, a succession of brilliant, clear flavors.

I can't think of the last time I've seen a vol-au-vent (a puff pastry shell) on an up-to-the-minute French menu. So it was with pleasure mixed with curiosity that I ordered Mr. Clément's version. What a treat! The puff pastry was light as air and encased a heap of girolles seasoned with chives and bathed in a deep, woodsy sauce. On top was a slice of juicy foie gras.

Mr. Clément has a way with game. One example: saddle of hare in a sweet-sour sauce, garnished with root chervil and figs, was the finest game dish I've ever eaten. The flavor was haunting; Tuscan in balance, finesse and modernity. With a bite of ripe fig, it was voluptuous and decadent, evoking ancient hunt scenes in châteaus. On another visit, the saddle of hare was again stellar. A portion for two, it was tender as butter and complemented by a tasty sauce smitane, a blend of hare stock and creme fraiche. Excellent peppery noisettes of venison came on a lightly sweet-tart sauce made from unsugared grape jam and were accompanied by beets, pearl onions and the unusual, sweet-tart physalis peruviana, also known as cape gooseberry. In addition to their individual garnishes, main courses came with souffled potatoes as delectable as Joel Robuchon's mashed potatoes.

You can order a single dessert, but Mr. Clément prefers to concoct an assortment of three. Ours consisted of individual chocolate soufflés served with praline ice cream, an intriguing gingerbread soup garnished with cardamom and date ice cream and a wedge of gingerbread, and a wonderful combination of fig ice cream, cream of date sauce, toasted almonds and pistachios.

The wine list at Lion d'Or is superb – offering the very best of the Loire and elsewhere.

$$$

La Tour
31 Nouvelle Place 18300 Sancerre; 02 48 54 00 81

For those who decry molecular cooking, be forewarned : thirtysomething Baptiste Fournier does *foams*. But if you stay away you'll be the loser. When it comes to cooking, this thirtysomething chef who breathed new life into the venerable La Tour after having worked with Guy Savoy and Alain Passard in Paris, has perfect pitch. I don't think he could cook something less-than-delicious if his life depended on it. Among the many lipsmacking options, a velouté of Jerusalem artichoke on a foam of smoked ham, with shrimp, lime juice and parmesan; then, langoustines on a bed of lentils which sat atop a foam of *marc*. Diced apples in the mix gave the whole a light Granny Smith lift. Don't miss the individual lime soufflé served with yogurt sorbet and a small lemon cake. Know, too, that the wine list is fully equal to the quality of the kitchen.

Where to stay

Prices are based on a double room: up to $120, $; up to $200, $$; above $200, $$$.

$ to $$

Hotel D'Angleterre
1, Place des Quatres Piliers, Bourges; 02.48.24.68.51; www.best-western-angleterre-bourges.com

Centrally located – across the street from the Palais Jacques Coeur – this moderately priced hotel has 30 comfortable, if small, rooms with all the amenities you want as well as an accommodating staff.

La Cognette $$ to $$$
(See restaurants)

The hotel rooms (in an annex) and the breakfasts are among the nicest in the region — as nice as the family and their restaurant.

La Côte des Monts Damnés $ to $$$
See Restaurants) $ to $$$

If memory serves, it used to be impossible to find a really nice, inviting hotel in the middle of Sancerre's vineyards. Simple B&Bs, sure; mini-palaces an hour away, no problem. But a well-equipped bona fide hotel in one of the most charming wine villages in one of France's most charming wine regions? Nada. Take heart all you Sancerre lovers who like your mattresses large and firm, your bathrooms modern and filled with little shampoos and moisturizers, your showers capacious – not to mention working air conditioning and free WiFi. La Côte des Monts Damnés has all that and more in its 12 charmingly decorated, comfortably outfitted rooms.

Ermitage $
18500 Berry-Bouy; 02.48.26.87.46; hotes-ermitage.com

Géraud and Laurence de la Farge, in addition to making Menetou-Salon and cultivating cereal crops, run this bucolic B&B in the heart of the vineyards and five kilometers from Bourges.

Hotel Château de La Verrerie $$$
18700 Oizon; 02 48 81 51 60

Owned by Comte Beraud de Voguë, this magical private château, now a Classified Historic Monument, was built in the 15th and 16th century by the Stuarts and is set in a magnificent park with a tree-lined lake fed by the river Nère. Most of the guest rooms are on the second floor of the château and they are all beautifully decorated with antiques and rich fabrics. You may also dine in the château or at a restaurant on the property.

$$$$

Lion d'Or
(See restaurants)

The hotel has all the comforts of home, if home happens to be Trump Tower.

$ to $$

Le Panoramic
Rempart-des-Augustins 18300 Sancerre; 02 48 54 22 44; panoramicôtel.com

Now owned by the Guy Saget family, this conveniently located hotel offers the basics as well as a sweeping view of Sancerre's vineyards and a heated swimming pool.

$ to $$

Le Relais de Pouilly
Quai de Loire 58150 Pouilly-sur-loire; 03 86 39 03 00; relaisde-pouilly.com

Off the main highway south of Pouilly, this pleasant hotel isn't luxurious but the rooms have everything I need and the staff couldn't be nicer. There's an enormous lawn out back, ending at the Loire. A restaurant, too, but I never had the chance to try it.

Fairs

- Easter: Wine fairs in Reuilly and Châteaumeillant.
- April: What may be the largest rock festival in France is held in Bourges every April – Le Printemps de Bourges;
- Pentecost: Sancerre, Foire aux Vins;
- First Sunday in August, Bué, Foire aux Sorciers;
- Last week-end of August, Quincy, Journées de l'Ocean; and Sancerre, Foire aux Vins
- First week-end of September, Foué Avaloue wine fair in St.Père (Coteaux du Giennois)
- Last week-end of October, Romorantin-Lanthenay, Journées Gas-tronomiques de Sologne.

Other things to see and do

Bourges

A delightful provincial city with cobbled streets, good galleries and several important sights. The Gothic Cathedral St. Etienne, a Unesco World Heritage site, is a must for its richly sculpted exterior and its soaring interior with magnificent stained glass windows dating from the 13th to the 17th centuries. Jacques Coeur's palace is a 15th century mansion built by the merchant who, among other things, financed the campaigns of Jean d'Arc. Bourges is a year-round festival city, starting with its celebrated rock festival, Le Printemps de Bourges which is held in April. Herewith, a sampling of Festivals Mid-July-Mid-September:

- Nuits Lumière: nightly in July and August; Thurs – Sat in May, June and Sept.
- Un Eté a Bourges: nightly from June 21 to Sept. 21. Free. www.ville-bourges.fr
- Les Très Riches Heures de l'Orgue en Berry, Tues and Sun from July 12 to August 14. 02.48.20.57.66; www.grandorguebourges.com
- La Fête des Marais: Sept. 5 and 6, 02.48.65.25.57.

Châteaux: Chambord

The largest and most flamboyant of the Loire Valley châteaux, Chambord was built in the 16th century as a hunting lodge for François 1er. It has 440 rooms, 13 major staircases (including the famous double-spiralled staircase) and 70 minor staircases. Its towers, turrets and chimneys give it a skyline all its own. During Louis XIV's stay in Chambord, Molière staged Le Bourgeois Gentilhomme. (Smaller châteaux in the region include: Meillant, Menetou-Salon and la Verrerie.)

Chavignol

This picture postcard village gave its name to the region's goat cheese, Crottin de Chavignol. You probably won't see any goats grazing the hillsides: they're completely covered with vines. A good number of Sancerre's best slopes are located here, eg les Monts Damnés, as well as some of its best wine makers and cheese affineurs.

Nohant

Georges Sand spent her childhood in this picturesque village with the tiny church Ste Anne set on a lovely square. Sand returned often during her adult life, and died here in 1876. Sand evoked the Berrichon countryside in works such as Petite Fadette. Her home – including parks she designed— has been turned into an enchanting museum.

Pottery

In addition to having exception soils for wine, the Sancerrois has excellent soils for pottery. The zone extends in an arc from Gien to la Borne to Nevers.

Gien

The premier attraction is the Faiencerie de Gien, a pottery factory which has a museum and a "seconds" shop where the selection is broad and the prices, half what you'll find in town.

La Borne

A community of potters who have settled here from all over the world. There is a permanent exhibition of the works of fifty local potters in what was formerly the village school.

Nevers

Nevers is known for its pale blue pottery. A leading manufacturer is Montagnon, a small, artisanal firm. Its beautiful faience is always impeccable: the owner smashes anything that doesn't pass muster. The Municipal Museum, several blocks away, has an excellent collection of Nevers pottery. Also of interest are the Ducal Palace, the cathedral and the Porte du Croux.

Sancerre

There are only a few (worthwhile) wineries left in its center, but the hilltop town of Sancerre remains the heart of this micro-region. It's charming, too, despite a Les Halles-type excrescence where a fine town square ought to be. (Pouilly-sur-Loire is an anti-climax.)

Vic (Indre département)

The Eglise St Martin has one of the largest ensembles of frescoes from

12 to 19th century. The choir is completely covered with frescoes depicting the *Cycle de la Passion*, beginning with the entry of Christ into Jerusalem to the Last Supper and the kiss of Judas.

Suggested two-day wine-itinerary

- Day One: Morning: Domaine Vacheron and Pascal Cotat;
- Lunch: La Tour
- Afternoon: Domaine Claude & Stéphane Riffault; Domaine Thomas-Labaille and Domaine Henri Bourgeois
- Dinner & Hotel: La Côte des Monts Damnés
- Day Two: Morning: Domaine Didier Dagueneau, Jonathan Pabiot and Domaine Henri Pellé
- Lunch: Cheu l'Zib
- Afternoon: Domaine Tatin-Wilk and Domaine de Reuilly
- Dinner & Hotel: la Cognette

Bibliography

In addition to the works listed below, I relied on reports by the Bureau Interprofessionel des Vins du Centre as well as on specific statutes promulgated by the INAO governing each appellation of origin or Vin de Pays. From time to time I consulted the *Guide Hachette Vins* as well as Gault-Millau. I have also cannibalized my own books, *A Wine & Food Guide to the Loire,* and *The Wines of France: the Essential Guide for Savvy Shoppers.*

Bisson, Jean. *Les Origines du Sauvignon.* Montpellier. December 2010.

Bréjoux, Pierre. *Les Vins de Loire.* Paris: Compagnie Parisienne d'Editions Techniques et Commerciales, 1956.

Dion, Roger. *Histoire de la Vigne et du Vin en France, des Origines aux XIXeme Siècle.* Paris. Flammarion, 1959, 1977.

Galet, Pierre. *Cépages et Vignobles de France.* Vol. 3. Montpellier: Galet, 1958 and 1962.

Lachiver, Marcel. *Vins, Vignes, et Vignerons.* Paris: Fayard, 1988.

Lavignac, Guy, *Les cépages du Sud ouest, 2000 ans d'histoire.* Editions du Rouergue, 2001.

Rance, Patrick. *French Cheese.* London: Macmillan, 1989.

Le Rouge et Le Blanc. *Le Chemin des Vignes, Vallee de la Loire.* Paris. Sang de la Terre, 2010.

Tardif, Vernard and Nina, and Jean-Louis Boncoeur. *Cuisine et Vins en Berry.* Editions Horvath.

Wade, Nicholas. *Lack of Sex among Grapes Tangles a Family Vine.* New York Times, January 24, 2011.

Wilson, James E. *Terroir: The Role of Geology, Climate, and Culture in the Making of French Wines.* Mitchell Beazley, 1998.

Index of producers

Classified index of producers

Note: An explanation of the classifications is given on pages 12–14. Page numbers in **bold** indicate main descriptions.

Outstanding

Excellent

To Follow

General index

Made in the USA
Lexington, KY
07 April 2012